Communist Czech

1945–89

CW00833181

European History in Perspective
General Editor: Jeremy Black

European History in Perspective
Series Standing Order ISBN 978–0–333–71694–6 hardcover
Series Standign Order ISBN 978–0–333–69336–0 paperback
(outside North America only)

You can receive future titles in this series as they are published by placing a standing order. Please contact your bookseller or, in the case of difficulty, write to us at the address below with your name and address, the title of the series and one of the ISBNs quoted above.

Customer Services Department, Macmillan Distribution Ltd,
Houndmills, Basingstoke, Hampshire, RG21 6XS, UK

Communist Czechoslovakia, 1945–89

A Political and Social History

Kevin McDermott

First published 2015 by
PALGRAVE

Palgrave in the UK is an imprint of Macmillan Publishers Limited, registered in England, company number 785998, of 4 Crinan Street, London, N1 9XW.

Palgrave Macmillan in the US is a division of St Martin's Press LLC, 175 Fifth Avenue, New York, NY 10010.

Palgrave is a global imprint of the above companies and is represented throughout the world.

Palgrave® and Macmillan® are registered trademarks in the United States, the United Kingdom, Europe and other countries.

ISBN 978–0–230–21714–0 hardback
ISBN 978–0–230–21715–7 paperback

This book is printed on paper suitable for recycling and made from fully managed and sustained forest sources. Logging, pulping and manufacturing processes are expected to conform to the environmental regulations of the country of origin.

A catalogue record for this book is available from the British Library.

A catalog record for this book is available from the Library of Congress.

Printed in China

To Professor R. Leslie Reid,
March 1924–September 2014

Contents

Acknowledgements

Greatest appreciation goes to my good friend, Vítězslav Sommer, whose intellectual stimulation and practical support have proved vital to this project. He diligently read, and in many ways improved, the whole manuscript and as co-author of a piece on Czechoslovakia in 1956 helped to sharpen my understanding of state–society relations. I have learnt much in the last ten years or so from another great friend and colleague, Matthew Stibbe, who continues to inspire me with his fresh ideas on communism in Eastern Europe.

Huge thanks to those colleagues and friends who read, and made invaluable comments on, the entire text: Jeremy Agnew, Jarmila Looks and John Morison. I am really grateful for all their efforts.

Thanks, too, to those who read individual chapters: Christiane Brenner, Miroslav Klučka (who also generously gave me his large book of newspaper cuttings for 1968–69), Alan MacDougall, Jan Mervart, Miroslav Pospíšil, Alfred Rieber, who also kindly provided me with notes on Russian archival sources, and Kieran Williams. They will surely recognise their inputs. A special acknowledgement to Radka Šustrová, who carried out important work in the Public Opinion Research Centre in Prague, and to David Green, who kindly sent, and permitted me to cite from, his doctoral thesis on the Czechoslovak Communist Party and the 1989 Revolution.

Other colleagues, friends and archivists assisted in numerous ways: Jitka Bílková, Jonathan Bolton, Wendy Bracewell, Paulina Bren, Tom Dickins, Miriam Dobson, Jakub Doležal, Eva Hahn, Peter Heumos, Igor Jílek, Jeremy King, Anna Kladnik, James Krapfl, Stefan Lehr, Jiří Nedvěd, Hana Němcová, Slavomír Ondica, Klára Pinerová, Jiří Pokorný, Tomáš Pospíšil, Michal Pullmann, Pavel Rampula, Eva Šafránková, Jan Šindelář, Adam Skála, Ondřej Vojtěchovský and Volker Zimmermann.

My sister Daryl deserves a very special mention for all her affection and generosity over the years. The same goes for Ivan Vomáčka and Eloïse Adde-Vomáčka, my gracious hosts in Prague.

Not least, a huge 'thank you' to Susie Reid, our son Alex and especially our daughter, Frankie, who after reading parts of the book pointed out in her polite way my convoluted and pompous writing style! As the saying goes, any errors and oversights remain my own.

Finally, my editors at Palgrave Macmillan, Sonya Barker, Felicity Noble and latterly Jenna Steventon and Rachel Bridgewater, have been remarkably patient and supportive for which I am most grateful.

KEVIN MCDERMOTT

Abbreviations and Glossary of Terms

ABS	Security Services Archive
Action Committees	Grassroots communist purging bodies
aktiv	Body of full-time party officials and engaged voluntary workers
apparatchik	Party-state official
archivní jednotka (a.j.)	Archival unit
cadre	Communist party activist
CCW	Council of Czechoslovak Women
Central Committee	Leading body of communist parties below the Politburo level
chata	Country cottage
Comecon	Soviet-led economic organisation of socialist states
Cominform	Communist Information Bureau
Comintern	Communist International
CPSU	Communist Party of the Soviet Union
ČSM	Czechoslovak Union of Youth
ČSR	Czechoslovak Republic
ČSSR	Czechoslovak Socialist Republic
ČSSŽ	Czechoslovak Socialist Union of Women
CVVM	Public Opinion Research Centre
fond (f.)	Archival Fund
FRG	Federal Republic of Germany (West Germany)
GDR	German Democratic Republic (East Germany)

glasnost	Gorbachev's policy of 'openness'
inventární číslo (inv. č.)	Inventory number
K-231	Club of Ex-Political Prisoners
KAN	Club of Committed Non-Party Members
kartón (k.)	Box
KSČ	Communist Party of Czechoslovakia
KSS	Communist Party of Slovakia
kulak	Better-off peasant
list (l.)	Folio, page
majorizace/ majorizácia	'Majority-domination', or out-voting of Slovaks by Czechs
MOL	Hungarian National Archive
NA	National Archive of the Czech Republic
National Committees	Organs of local and regional administration
nomenklatura	List of key administrative appointments approved by the party
NWF	National Women's Front
OF	Civic Forum
OSA	Open Society Archive
Ostpolitik	West German policy of improving relations with the GDR and Soviet bloc
People's Militia	Armed wing of the Communist Party
perestroika	'Reconstruction' of Soviet economy under Gorbachev
Politburo (or Presidium)	Main executive organ of communist parties
přestavba/ prestavba	Czech/Slovak equivalent of *perestroika*
ROH	Revolutionary Trade Union Movement
Rudé právo	'Red Right': KSČ daily newspaper
ŠA	Škoda Archives (Plzeň)
samizdat	Self-publishing
SDP	Social Democratic Party
SNA	Slovak National Archive
SNR	Slovak National Council

SOAP	State Regional Archive in Plzeň
SSM	Socialist Union of Youth
StB	State Security (secret police)
STR	Scientific and technological revolution
STUHA	Independent student movement
svazek (sv.)	Volume
TNA	The National Archive
ÚRO	Central Trade Union Council
USSR	Union of Soviet Socialist Republics
VOA ČMKOS	All-Trade Union Archive, Czech and Moravian Chamber of Trade Unions
VPN	Public Against Violence
Warsaw Pact	Soviet-led military alliance

Glossary of Leading Figures

Beneš, Edvard	President of the Czechoslovak Republic, 1935–38 and 1945–48
Bil'ak, Vasil	A leading hard-line 'normaliser', 1969–89
Brezhnev, Leonid I.	General Secretary of the Soviet Communist Party, 1964–82
Černík, Oldřich	Prime Minister, 1968–70
Dubček, Alexander	First Secretary of KSČ, January 1968 to April 1969
Ďuriš, Július	Communist Minister of Agriculture, 1945–51
Fierlinger, Zdeněk	Leading pro-communist Social Democrat; Prime Minister, 1945–46 and Deputy Prime Minister, 1946–53
Gorbachev, Mikhail S.	General Secretary of Soviet Communist Party, 1985–91
Gottwald, Klement	General Secretary of KSČ, 1929–45; Chairman of KSČ, 1945–53; Prime Minister, 1946–48; President of Czechoslovakia, 1948–53
Havel, Václav	Playwright; founder-member of Charter 77; leader of 'Velvet Revolution'; President of Czechoslovakia, 1989–92
Husák, Gustáv	Chairman of Slovak Board of Commissioners, 1946–48; imprisoned from 1951–60; First Secretary of KSČ, 1969–87; President of Czechoslovakia, 1975–89
Jakeš, Miloš	First Secretary of KSČ, 1987–89
Khrushchev, Nikita S.	First Secretary of Soviet Communist Party, 1953–64

Kopecký, Václav	Communist Minister of Information, 1945–53; Deputy Prime Minister, 1954–61
Masaryk, Jan	Non-party Minister of Foreign Affairs, 1945–48
Masaryk, Tomáš G.	President of the First Republic, 1918–35
Mlynář, Zdeněk	A leading communist reformer in 1968
Novotný, Antonín	First Secretary of KSČ, 1953–68; President of Czechoslovakia, 1957–68
Palach, Jan	Student whose self-immolation in January 1969 shocked the nation
Šik, Ota	Prominent economic reformer, 1962–68
Slánský, Rudolf	General Secretary of KSČ, 1945–51; tried and executed in 1952
Smrkovský, Josef	A leading communist reformer in 1968
Stalin, Josef V.	General Secretary of Soviet Communist Party, 1922–53
Štrougal, Lubomír	Prime Minister, 1970–88
Svoboda, Ludvík	President of Czechoslovakia, 1968–75
Tiso, Jozef	President of the war-time Slovak Republic
Vaculík, Ludvík	Writer and author of the '2,000 Words Manifesto', June 1968
Zápotocký, Antonín	Communist Chairman of Revolutionary Trade Union Movement, 1945–50; Prime Minister, 1948–53; President of Czechoslovakia, 1953–57

Presidents of the Czechoslovak Republic, 1945–92

1945–48	Edvard Beneš
1948–53	Klement Gottwald
1953–57	Antonín Zápotocký
1957–68	Antonín Novotný
1968–75	Ludvík Svoboda
1975–89	Gustáv Husák
1989–92	Václav Havel

Leaders of the Communist Party of Czechoslovakia, 1929–89

1929–53	Klement Gottwald
1953–68	Antonín Novotný
1968–69	Alexander Dubček
1969–87	Gustáv Husák
1987–89	Miloš Jakeš
1989 (November–December)	Karel Urbánek

Timeline, 1918–93

October 1918– October 1938	Democratic First Republic
September 1938	Munich Agreement dismembers First Republic
October 1938– March 1939	Authoritarian Second Republic
March 1939	Nazi invasion of Czechoslovakia
March 1939–May 1945	Protectorate of Bohemia and Moravia under Nazi tutelage
March 1939–April 1945	Nominally independent pro-German clerical Slovak Republic
December 1943	Soviet–Czechoslovak Friendship Treaty signed in Moscow
August–October 1944	Slovak National Uprising
March 1945	Agreement of National Front coalition government
April 1945	Košice Programme
5–9 May 1945	Prague uprising and final liberation of Czechoslovakia from Nazi rule
May 1945–February 1948	National Front coalition governments run Czechoslovakia
June 1945–October 1946	Expulsion of Sudeten Germans and exchange of Slovak Magyars
25 February 1948	Formation of Communist dominated government

1948–54	Years of Stalinist repression, show trials and mass arrests
November 1952	Slánský trial
5 March 1953	Death of Stalin
March 1953	Novotný appointed party leader
June 1953	Plzeň workers' uprising
February 1956	Khrushchev's 'secret speech'
October–November 1956	Hungarian Revolution
April–November 1958	Brussels World Fair Expo 58
May 1960	Main amnesty of political prisoners
July 1960	New Constitution: Czechoslovak Socialist Republic declared
1962–63	Zero growth in economy
1964–68	'New Wave' in Czechoslovak culture, especially film
June 1967	Fourth Union of Writers' Congress
January 1968	Dubček appointed party leader
January–August 1968	'Prague Spring' reforms
June 1968	'2,000 Words Manifesto'
20–21 August 1968	Soviet-led Warsaw Pact invasion
1969–1989	Era of 'normalisation'
January 1969	Federalisation of the country; self-immolation of Jan Palach
April 1969	Husák replaces Dubček as party leader
January–December 1970	Purge of party members
May 1975	Husák replaces Svoboda as President
January 1977	Foundation of Charter 77
March 1985	Gorbachev appointed Soviet party leader
December 1987	Miloš Jakeš appointed party leader
November–December 1989	'Velvet Revolution' and resignation of communist government
December 1989	Havel replaces Husák as first post-communist President
January 1993	Creation of Czech Republic and Slovak Republic

A Note on Czech Pronunciation

á	long a
c	ts as in bits
č	ch as in church
ch	ch as in loch
ě	ye as in year
j	always soft y sound
ř	unique sound, equivalent to 'rzh'
š	sh as in shoe
ů	oo as in doom
ý	long ee sound
ž	zh as in pleasure

Chapter 1: Introduction – Communist Czechoslovakia in Historical Perspective

In the summer of 1958 a young working-class lad from Liverpool went with his communist parents to visit the World Fair in Brussels. There, they were captivated by the award-winning Czechoslovak pavilion with its vibrant displays of glass, china, textiles and furniture designed in a remarkably contemporary avant-garde style, while 'retaining a subtle socialist sensibility'. It seemed to them that Czechoslovakia must be a country that 'combined the humane rationalism of the Soviet system with a lyrical, magical spirit all its own'. Only years later did the boy, Alexei Sayle, who was to become a famous comedian, realise that 'most of the items in the Czech pavilion...were only prototypes that were never actually produced'.[1] When I read Sayle's funny, yet poignant, memoirs, it struck me that this vignette serves as an apt metaphor for the dashed hopes, dreams and illusions of a new 'socialist modernity' and 'socialist person', which in many ways encapsulate the essence of communist Czechoslovakia. His reminiscences also hint at an enduring dilemma for the historian: how to tame the mixed blessing of historical hindsight by at least attempting to capture the 'spirit of the times'. That is, how to strive towards an 'objective' account of post-war Czechoslovakia without succumbing entirely to the teleology that the communist experiment in Eastern Europe stagnated and irrevocably collapsed with startling rapidity in the autumn of 1989. As such, I do not wish to write yet another 'communism was awful' book. We all know that, or think we do. I lived in 'normalised' Czechoslovakia for over two years in the 1980s as a postgraduate student and saw with my own eyes the depredations of that regime, and its negative features should never be ignored or attenuated.

I am just as interested, however, in what motivated a young Czech worker-believer to join the Communist Party in the early 1950s, later enrol in the People's Militia and in this capacity defend his local radio station against the Soviet occupiers in August 1968, to remain in the party during the dark years of 'normalisation', though becoming increasingly disillusioned, and end up more or less welcoming the tearing down of the Berlin Wall in November 1989.[2] This is, I suspect, the life cycle of numerous working-class Czechs and Slovaks in the second half of the twentieth century and it needs to be explained. Hence, this book is not only about the murky high politics of the 'system' and its undoubted malign attributes, but also about why communism in Czechoslovakia attracted at times substantial levels of support, lasted with relatively scant overt opposition for over 40 years, and how Czech and Slovak citizens adapted to the regime and lived their everyday lives under 'state socialism'.[3] I will start by way of historical context with a survey of Czechoslovakia in the first half of the twentieth century and of the early years of the Communist Party of Czechoslovakia. The main goal here is to familiarise readers with the often turbulent events – underlying themes, issues and interpretations will be discussed later in the chapter.

Historical Background: Czechoslovakia, 1918–45

In the twentieth century, Czechs and Slovaks were subject to repeated buffetings by foreign powers, ideologically driven transformations and internal upheaval: from semi-constitutional Austrian and Hungarian monarchical rule as part of the vast Habsburg Empire from 1867 to 1918 to the democratic independent First Republic of the interwar period; from the humiliation of the Munich agreement, the dismemberment of the state and a short-lived authoritarian Second Republic to the horrors of the subsequent Nazi Protectorate and collaborationist Slovak state during World War II; and finally from the 'totalitarian' communist dictatorship of 1948–89, via the brief regeneration of the Prague Spring crushed in August 1968 by Soviet tanks, to the anti-communist 'Velvet Revolution' of late 1989 and the subsequent transition to capitalist democracies in the Czech and Slovak republics from 1993 to the present. It is clear from this briefest of overviews that the Czechs and Slovaks have rarely been masters in their own house. Indeed, they have rarely been assured of their existence as a 'nation' and of their geopolitical space, as evidenced in the opening line of the Czech national anthem: 'Where is my homeland?' (*Kde domov můj?*) At many conjunctures in their modern history Czech and Slovaks have had to live with the palpable knowledge that their precarious national identity and state were under existential threat, or at least might be subjugated by foreign aggressors. In these circumstances it is not surprising that a powerful and enduring national, or more accurately Czech, myth evolved, embraced not only by the majority of Czechs and some Slovaks, but also by many sympathetic outsiders. The essence of the myth is best summarised by Andrea Orzoff:

> Under Habsburg rule, the innately democratic, peace-loving, tolerant Czechs were viciously repressed by bellicose, authoritarian, reactionary Austrians, under whose regime the Czech language and national consciousness almost died out...After 1918... Czechoslovakia made itself an island of democratic values, rationalism, and fair mindedness amid a Europe falling quickly into the thrall of authoritarianism and fascism...After 1938, the myth shifted to depict Czechs...as victims – of geography, the perfidy of the West, and internal fifth columns. The first betrayal, at Munich in 1938, was by Czechoslovakia's Western allies and creators France and Great Britain, who essentially handed the country to the Nazis...The second betrayal followed in 1948 at the hands of the Soviet Union...and a handful of ruthless, Stalinized Czechoslovak Communists and their fellow travelers. Czechoslovakia then disappeared behind the Iron Curtain, forgotten by the West, save when Czechoslovak attempts to reform Communism failed in 1968 and Soviet-bloc tanks rolled into Prague.[4]

The cornerstone of this myth is the interwar First Republic (1918–38) with its multi-party democracy, vibrant civil society and pluralist cultural forms overseen by the great humanitarian 'President-Liberator', Tomáš Garrigue Masaryk, a figure still today revered by most Czechs.

The First Republic was declared by euphoric politicians in Prague on 28 October 1918, just two weeks before the end of World War I. It was created out of the ruins of the defeated Habsburg Empire partly because of the nationalist strivings of the Czechs and Slovaks themselves and partly because the victorious Western powers, Britain, France and the USA, wished to establish a physical buffer zone in Central and Eastern Europe between the Bolshevik 'devil' in the east and the democratic 'free world', as it became known in the West. Hence, the Allied governments extended official international recognition to the new country at the Paris Peace Conference in the summer of 1919. A Czechoslovak state, as an independent and unified entity, had never previously existed. Ever since 1526 the Czech lands (Bohemia, Moravia and Silesia) had been part of the Austrian Habsburg Empire which dominated huge swathes of central and south-eastern Europe. This subjugation was confirmed by the Czechs' humiliating defeat at the Battle of the White Mountain in 1620. The Slovak lands to the east had been under Hungarian suzerainty for almost a millennium and had suffered a strict campaign of 'Magyarisation' in the late nineteenth and early twentieth centuries. Despite these geopolitical differences, the Czechs and Slovaks spoke related Slavic languages, their elites generally regarded themselves to be closer to 'European' culture than their more easterly Russian and Ukrainian Slavic neighbours, and their Christianity was Catholic (like the Poles) or Protestant rather than Orthodox.

In the last decades of Habsburg rule, Bohemia, Moravia and Silesia were among the most industrialised and urbanised regions of the monarchy and a modern differentiated class system was in the making. A strong Czech national identity was gradually constructed in the course of the nineteenth century and a powerful nationalist movement with distinct anti-German overtones emerged led by intellectual elites – writers, journalists, academics, ethnographers – who were widely regarded as the 'conscience of the nation', a label that accompanied them throughout the twentieth century.[5] Socialist political, trade union and cooperative organisations, often heavily influenced by Marxist theory, were also created and it is fair to say that a pronounced strand of egalitarianism ran through Czech society, in part as a result of the destruction of the indigenous aristocracy by the Austrian authorities. The Habsburgs also bequeathed a certain bureaucratic mentality in state and local administration. By contrast, Slovakia remained socially and economically more agrarian, the Catholic Church was more influential and popular nationalism was relatively under-developed, although anti-Magyar sentiment was widespread. From the 1870s onwards, the Czechs created an embryonic multi-party and ideologically broad-ranging political framework and by the 1900s all parties participated in Austrian elections and virtually all Czech politicians were committed to constitutional forms of government. One of these leaders, Masaryk, was to play a singular role in twentieth-century Czechoslovak history. A respected professor of philosophy at Prague's acclaimed Charles University, Masaryk came to embody Czech, but less so Slovak, aspirations for national independence, pluralist democracy and social justice. He became President of the First Republic in November 1918 and remained in this post until 1935 when he was replaced by his protégé, Edvard Beneš, who, it is argued, carried on Masaryk's pioneering work into the tempestuous late 1930s and 1940s. In the opinion of many scholars writing in the Cold War era, this consensual and tolerant Czech political culture espoused by progressive elites, when combined with economic and social modernisation, laid the foundations for the efficient functioning of a liberal democratic system after 1918.

The First Republic, therefore, was conventionally regarded as a haven of national progress, a veritable 'island of democracy' in the middle of an angry totalitarian sea. Although this interpretation has been challenged by many scholars in recent decades and is now widely disputed, plenty of persuasive evidence was garnered in support of the 'traditional' view. While the other interwar successor states in Central and Eastern Europe moved increasingly towards right-wing authoritarianism, Masaryk oversaw a democratically constituted state. That is, the Constitution, modelled on the French and American presidential systems and ratified in February 1920, formally provided for a bicameral parliament (Senate and Chamber of Deputies) based on multi-party elections with universal male and female suffrage. The mainstream governing parties were the Czechoslovak Social Democrats, a non-revolutionary formally Marxist working-class party; the Agrarians, a centre-right party which drew most support from small and medium farmers; the National Socialist Party, definitely not to be confused with its German namesake as it was a moderate leftist, but also Czech nationalist, party; the National Democrats, a right-wing grouping of industrialists and entrepreneurs; and the People's Party, which represented largely the Catholic population of the country. On the political margins, there was the Communist Party on the far left and by the mid-1920s neo-fascist groupings on the far right, and only in extreme circumstances was the legality of these organisations threatened. Parliamentary elections were held regularly and because none of the many parties could command an overall majority, all interwar Czechoslovak governments were broad coalitions, occasionally spanning the left–right ideological divide, although increasingly dominated by the Agrarians who, not alone in the troubled 1930s, moved increasingly to the right.

The First Republic also met democratic criteria in terms of civil rights, freedom of the press, association and assembly and, crucially, in terms of an independent judiciary. Women's equality, a problematic and contested issue, was legally enshrined, though rarely implemented in practice. Cultural life was pluralistic and diverse with a flourishing modernist avant-garde community: Prague was the city of Kafka, Čapek, Mucha and Teige. Leftist and even communist trends contributed to this vibrant atmosphere in the arts, architecture and design. Czechoslovakia became the political refuge of anti-Nazi German leftists in the 1930s, notably the outlawed Social Democrats. At many levels, then, the First Republic was a functioning civil society based on the notions of consensus, compromise, tolerance and 'progressive' thinking. And these noble attitudes extended to the social sphere. A far-reaching land reform was undertaken which expropriated the aristocratic estates, most of which were in non-Czech hands, and redistributed them to a large number of Czech and Slovak smallholders. Labour legislation was among the most progressive in the world. The early Social Democratic led coalition governments legalised the eight-hour working day, provided unemployment, sickness, invalidity and pension benefits for employees, and, most controversially, introduced laws recognising the existence of powerful works councils in the mining industry and works committees in all other factories and enterprises employing over 30 people. These innovations went some way in assuaging worker demands and in easing the undoubted class tensions, epitomised by the General Strike of December 1920, that threatened the stability of the new republic in the years 1918–21. Despite initial difficulties, the predominantly capitalist economy was one of the most developed and successful in the region, products such as armaments, glass and shoes enjoying a healthy international reputation.

As for the thorniest issue in interwar Czechoslovak politics and society – the nationalities question – here again it was often maintained that the First Republic adopted liberal attitudes and policies and in comparison to neighbouring states treated its ethnic minorities with more than a modicum of respect and understanding. The republic was a multi-national entity ruled as a nation-state. According to the 1921 census, out of a total population of approximately 13.4 million, there were over 8.7 million Czechs and Slovaks, 3.1 million Germans, around 750,000 Hungarians, 460,000 Ruthenes and Ukrainians, 180,000 Jews, 76,000 Poles and 26,000 'others'.[6] Given the historical enmities and mutual suspicions, this ethnic patchwork made it difficult to govern the country, to say the least. Nevertheless, in an atmosphere of inflamed passions, the provisional parliament ratified the Language Law of February 1920, which permitted national minorities to use their own language in civic communication in districts where they comprised 20 per cent or more of the population. Ethnic Germans, for example, had their own schools, universities, press, theatres and other institutions and moderate German political parties had ministers in several interwar Czechoslovak cabinets beginning in 1926. Even in the crisis years of the 1930s, the Czechoslovak state was prepared to make concessions to German sensibilities. As for the Slovaks, they were officially regarded as part of the single 'Czechoslovak' nation that comprised the 'state-forming' element of the new state. Because Slovakia was less economically and socially developed than the Czech lands, many Czech administrators, teachers and doctors went to work in Slovakia, and defenders of the republic argue that economic, social, cultural and educational levels were raised in Slovakia in the 1920s and 1930s and that the centralised government in Prague helped to modernise the eastern half of the country. If we scratch a bit deeper below the surface, however, this rosy picture becomes more contradictory. We could indeed construct a radically different interpretation of the First Republic, noting that several of its imperfections were to have long-lasting repercussions. In the political sphere, parliamentary democracy was undermined by two extra-constitutional institutions – the *Pětka* (the 'Five') and the *Hrad* (the 'Castle'). The former was in effect an unaccountable oligarchy of the leaders of the five main political parties, who hammered out policy, set an agreed common agenda for parliament, ensuring passage of key legislation, and protected each party's control over 'their' ministries and resources. It was, then, a kind of behind-the-scenes unofficial cabinet, which certainly found no provision in the Czechoslovak Constitution. The *Hrad*, created by Masaryk and Beneš and often in conflict with the *Pětka*, was an 'informal but extremely powerful nexus of institutions and allies', notably 'a coterie of literary intellectuals' and propagandists, who enabled the two leaders to 'affect the political process from outside the halls of Parliament'.[7] Other somewhat dubious bodies were Masaryk's Chancellery of the President of the Republic, from whose ranks he regularly appointed ministers, and his 'extensive intelligence services' which kept the President and Castle 'well informed about all activities in the political parties' and as such 'had to have a corrupting impact on the political culture of the country' while also indicating the President-Liberator's 'low interest in or respect for the formal and legal aspects of democracy'. Similarly, Masaryk's very philosophy of democracy has been criticised as paternalistic and suspicious not just of elected parliamentarians, of whom he had a rather negative opinion, but of the pivotal notion of popular participation and involvement.[8] He was, for some non-Czechs, not far removed from an enlightened despot surrounded by a potentially damaging cult-like aura.

It would also be premature to assume that gender and class tensions were spirited away in the progressive social and labour legislation of the early 1920s. Women may have officially gained citizenship and equal rights, but their active role in society and in the workplace appeared to imperil traditional values, the stability of the family and the 'national home'. As such 'politicians and the public eventually moved to curtail [women's rights], not caring that doing so might go against both the laws and ideals of their democratic movement'.[9] Similarly, the threat of political extremism, on both the far left and far right, stretched the democratic credentials of the new state. Communism established firm indigenous roots in many parts of the country, including poor rural Sub-Carpathian Ruthenia. There were violent clashes between police and strikers in the early post-war years, and the Great Depression hit German industries and Slovak and Ruthenian agriculture particularly hard from 1930 onwards, resulting in very high levels of unemployment, poverty and subsequent intense social conflict. The Prague authorities were not above a repressive response. In 1923, after the assassination of the Minister of Finance, the Law for the Protection of the Republic was introduced and broadly applied restricting inter alia the democratic freedoms of association and of the press. It was bitterly opposed by the Slovak nationalists, communists and all minority parties, but became a relatively common feature of everyday political struggle, used against fascist insurgents, German 'nationalists' and in the frequent censorship of communist newspapers. Other anti-extremist legislation followed in the 1930s.[10] Neither did the land reform prevent fierce accusations from ethnic Germans and Magyars that it was designed to weaken the socio-economic position of the national minorities and strengthen that of the hegemonic Czechs and Slovaks.

Indeed, it was the nationalities issue that really ate away at the legitimacy of the Czechoslovak state. Above all, the First Republic has been castigated as a virtually exclusive Czech nationalist undertaking, a nation-state rather than a state of nationalities.[11] Tensions between Czechs and Slovaks, at both an elite and popular level, were evident from the start as Masaryk's concept of a unitary, but non-existent, Czechoslovak nation and language ('Czechoslovakism') alienated national-minded Slovaks. Many resented Czech centralism, apparent condescension and even economic 'colonisation' and thus demanded a greater degree of autonomy from Prague, as had been agreed by Czech representatives in the Pittsburgh declaration of May 1918. To be sure, not all Slovaks favoured self-government, a minority accepting the centralist state, and the Czechs were not

solely motivated by national ideology and paternalism – many feared
a resurgent Germany and insisted on a strong united centralist state
as the first line of defence. But conflicts grew far more pronounced in
the crisis-ridden 1930s with the rise of the nationalist Slovak People's
Party, and these antagonisms were to have far-reaching ramifications
during and after World War II. The situation in Slovakia was further
complicated by the presence of a large Magyar community, which
was regarded by Czech and Slovak nationalists alike as a revanchist
force seeking reunification with Hungary. Relations between Prague
and Budapest were continually strained by this unresolved problem.
Furthermore, territorial and other tensions among Czechs and ethnic
Poles in northern Silesia culminated in a military confrontation in
1919 between the Czech and Polish armies.

The Czech–Jewish relationship was also highly problematic, epitomised by Masaryk who harboured an ambivalent, at times openly
negative, attitude towards Czech Jewry and on his own admis-
sion was never able emotionally to 'overcome...the antisemitism
of the common people'. These ambiguities were reflected in the
nationality policies of the First Republic and in the contradictory thinking of Czech political and intellectual elites. On the one
hand, 'Czechoslovakia's concessions to Jewish nationalism were...
unprecedented' in European history. The state 'recognized the
claim to Jewish national distinctiveness' and 'made room for Jewish
cultural and national self-expression without diminishing the value
of emancipation or intending to reduce Jewish social and political
integration'. On the other hand, 'Czech leaders [adopted] a general
stance of distance and suspicion towards the Jews', often lumping
them together with the 'alien' German community. 'Rarely...did they
entertain the conviction that the Jews were, or could become, fully
Czech.'[12] It was a sentiment that retained its relevance even after the
virtual decimation of Czechoslovak Jewry during the Holocaust and
the end of the prolonged era of Czech–Jewish cultural coexistence.

The most deep-rooted and fateful disputes, however, were between
the Czechs and the so-called Sudeten Germans, concentrated in the
northern and western borderlands of the republic, but geographi-
cally far-flung throughout the country. This was, and remains, a
hugely controversial issue. Some scholars insist, as we have seen,
that comparatively speaking official Czechoslovak policy towards the
German 'minority' – in reality Germans outnumbered Slovaks by
some margin – was more equitable and less oppressive than other
central and east European countries at the time.[13] Others emphasise
the fact that the vast majority of Germans at the end of World War I

did not wish to reside in a Czechoslovak state which they feared would persecute them. This meant that the Sudeten Germans were incorporated into post-1918 Czechoslovakia essentially by military force, accompanied by ethnic demonstrations and counter-demonstrations which cost scores of lives. Moreover, the 'Sudeten Germans' right to self-determination was not even acknowledged in terms of their autonomy' and the Prague government's grave concern that nationally inclined Germans represented an irredentist threat to the integrity of the new state ensured that no reconciliation was possible regardless of the limited political cooperation of the mid-to-late 1920s.[14] Indeed, this Czech–German rapprochement was terminated by the Great Depression, which severely damaged the Sudeten Germans' export-led light and tourist industries. Consequently, bolstered by the rise of a belligerent Third Reich after 1933, many Germans turned to the local radical right-wing party and its chief Konrad Henlein to save them from economic turmoil and fulfil their frustrated national demands. Nazi propaganda stoked this campaign and in the May 1935 parliamentary elections Henlein's Sudeten German Party polled almost 1.2 million ballots, the overwhelming majority of German voters.

By this time Czechoslovakia was spiralling into crisis. The republic was undoubtedly trapped geopolitically between aggressive expansionist regimes, notably Nazi Germany, and its leaders' room for manoeuvre was massively curtailed by the late 1930s, but flawed domestic policies and ethnic and social tensions certainly helped to undermine the state's cohesion and legitimacy. The outcome, tragic for the vast majority of Czechs, was the Munich agreement of 29 September 1938 signed, without any Czechoslovak government involvement, by Nazi Germany, Fascist Italy, Britain and France. Under its terms, the First Republic was dismembered: the 'Sudetenland', its German population, industry, agriculture and military fortifications, was ceded to the Third Reich. In addition, Hungary and Poland took advantage of the crisis to demand, and eventually receive, large areas of disputed territories in southern Slovakia, Ruthenia and northern Silesia (Těšín/Cieszyn). In total, over one-fifth of Czechoslovak land area and almost a quarter of the population were lost. The national security and territorial integrity of the state were seriously undermined overnight. Among the Czechs, a caustic sense of victimisation, resentment and bewilderment prevailed, fostering critiques of the politically fragmented nature of a republic which had seemingly failed abysmally to defend the nation in its hour of need.[15] Anguished soul-searching raged (and continued to rage) about whether to resist militarily the Nazi occupation of 'Czech' land, but President Beneš, his domestic and pro-Western foreign strategies in tatters, decided grimly in consultation with his government and generals to accept the draconian agreement.[16] Within three weeks a dejected Beneš, having resigned on 5 October, fled abroad to become head of a Czechoslovak government-in-exile ending up, somewhat paradoxically, in London, where he remained for the duration of the war.

At home, crucial developments followed in the wake of Munich. The First Republic was rapidly replaced by a short-lived but increasingly right-wing Second Republic (October 1938–March 1939), which, in the controversial words of one expert, turned 'Czechoslovakia from an imperfectly democratic to a frankly authoritarian state, one whose central and autonomous governments ruled by decree, promoted racism, neutralized political opponents, rigged elections, set up forced-labour camps and persecuted Jews and Gypsies, all before any of this could plausibly be blamed on Nazi Germany'.[17] No doubt under pressure from Berlin, post-Munich Czech leaders began to 'regenerate' and 'simplify' the political system, meaning that the multi-party system was transformed effectively into a one-party state led by the newly created National Unity Party. The Communist Party was soon outlawed and the other leftist parties amalgamated into a legal, though spineless, National Labour Party. Fascist and extreme right-wing groups became more visible and influential, though never achieving mass popularity. Slovak nationalists immediately pushed for and gained virtual self-government from Prague and the federated state was renamed Czecho-Slovakia. Repressive measures were also undertaken in the newly autonomous Slovakia. Here, all Slovak-speaking parties were united into a single Party of Slovak National Unity protected by a paramilitary organisation, the Hlinka Guard. Political Catholicism grew in importance and anti-communism and anti-Semitism were more pronounced than in the Czech lands. These political and territorial results of Munich left several unresolved legacies, not least heightened Czech–Slovak discord and the propensity to seek authoritarian solutions at times of crisis.

The *coup de grâce* came in mid-March 1939 when the *Wehrmacht* invaded what remained of an independent Czecho-Slovakia wiping the country, temporarily as it turned out, from the face of the map. A 'Protectorate of Bohemia and Moravia' was created in Prague more or less under the direct control of Berlin and a nominally independent, though pro-German, state was proclaimed in Bratislava thereby fulfilling the claims of the Slovak nationalists. Czechs and Slovaks experienced the traumatic wartime events in different ways.[18] In the

Protectorate, Nazi military priorities, racial policies and violent oppression brutalised and divided society, promoted a 'statisation' of the economy and labour relations and encouraged a moral devastation in social and ethnic relations. This was most evident in a marked radicalisation of Czech animosity towards the 'traitorous' Sudeten Germans, but also conspicuous in regard to Slovaks who were widely accused of stabbing the Czechs in the back after the Munich crisis. Active organised resistance to the Nazi overlords was relatively meagre – indeed, many industrial workers and other employees were well compensated for their labour – and most Czechs kept their heads down and did their best to survive the occupation, while engaging in myriad forms of passive dissent with the aim of keeping the nation alive. The Slovak Republic (1939–45) stands accused of introducing 'clerical fascism' and participating in the deportation of around 70,000 Jews to the Third Reich, but for many Slovaks the very existence of the republic proved that they could govern themselves without Czech patronage. Slovak communists and democrats also undertook the only large-scale act of domestic armed resistance against German hegemony – the Slovak National Uprising from August to October 1944.

In sum, the harsh socio-economic experiences of the depressed 1930s, the 'betrayal' by the Western powers at Munich, the failure of Beneš's government to resist the Nazi dismemberment of the state and the subsequent aspirations for national and social justice born out of six years of German tutelage did much to discredit the First Republic and dampen Czech enthusiasm for liberal democracy, capitalist economics and ethnic tolerance.

The Communist Party of Czechoslovakia, 1921–45

The Communist Party of Czechoslovakia (*Komunistická strana Československa* – KSČ) was formed in 1921 and remained for most of the decade essentially a product of its origins in the left wing of the Social Democratic movement. Although it was affiliated to the revolutionary Communist International (Comintern) based in Moscow and thus subject to gradual 'Bolshevisation' and 'Russification', the party operated legally, sought and achieved a mass membership, endeavoured to maintain organic links with the Czech and Slovak labour movements, was led by figures, such as Bohumír Šmeral, who could not easily be described as militant Bolsheviks and competed, rather successfully, in parliamentary and municipal elections. Indeed, in the polls in 1925 the party received almost one million votes making it the second largest in the republic after the Agrarians. Hence, in terms of membership and electoral support the KSČ was one of the strongest communist parties in Europe, sharing to a certain extent a pluralist conception of politics and influenced by the dominant democratic political culture which characterised the First Republic. However, this ideological moderation had its limits. The KSČ adopted the radical Leninist concept of national self-determination for the country's 'oppressed' ethnic minorities, which in its maximalist form advocated secession from the state. If applied, this would have meant the destruction of the territorial integrity of Czechoslovakia. Also, though electorally robust, the communists consistently refused to participate in coalition government, seeing Czechoslovakia as a product of the imperialist 'Versailles system', a 'bourgeois' preserve that did little or nothing for the 'exploited proletariat'.

Like all communist parties, the Czechoslovak was internally riven among 'rightist', 'centrist' and 'leftist' factions and, with the advent of the Stalinists in the Soviet Union and Comintern, the last came to the fore. In 1928–29, a new leftist leadership was acrimoniously installed under Klement Gottwald, who was to head the KSČ until his death in March 1953. Most of the older 'right-wing' luminaries were expelled and replaced by younger 'proletarian' elements, steadfastly loyal to the USSR and its Stalinist bosses. The process of 'Stalinisation', duplicated throughout the international communist movement, was reaching fruition. Gottwald himself gave a clear inkling of what this meant in his inaugural address to the Czechoslovak National Assembly in December 1929. Responding to accusations from non-communist deputies that the KSČ was under the command of a foreign state, Gottwald boasted: 'we are the party of the Czechoslovak proletariat and our highest revolutionary headquarters are in Moscow...We go to Moscow to learn from the Russian Bolsheviks how to wring your necks. (*Outcry*) And you know that the Russian Bolsheviks are masters at that! (*Uproar*).'[19] This was largely rabble-rousing bravado, but the party did lose much of its support in the early 1930s as the Comintern's ruinous ultra-leftist 'class against class' policies and 'social fascist' terminology isolated the communists from their working-class constituencies. The KSČ only began to recover its positions after 1934–35 with the advent of the 'Popular Front' strategy, a nationally inclined policy which sought broad cross-class alliances against the spread of fascism and which in many ways foreshadowed its successful tactics in the years 1945–47.

The Munich agreement proved a double-edged sword for the KSČ. As noted above, already in December 1938, three months before the

Nazi occupation, the party had been declared illegal and forced into an underground existence, its leaders dispersed. Gottwald, his deputy Rudolf Slánský and a few other top functionaries spent the war in Moscow, many others went into exile to Paris and London, while those who remained precariously at home formed a series of illegal Central Committees, constantly at risk of arrest and suppression, even death.

In May 1939 more nationalistically inclined Slovak communists took advantage of the lack of centralised control from Prague to found a separate Communist Party of Slovakia (*Komunistická strana Slovenska–*KSS), which was a portent of future Czech–Slovak tensions. The communists were able, however, to profit from their self-proclaimed patriotic anti-fascist stance at a time of mortal danger to the nation and state. As news of the Munich diktat came through, Gottwald urged Beneš to fight, saying reportedly that even 'barefooted Ethiopians found courage to resist the armed might of Italy'.[20] The KSČ also massively benefited from the 'legend', as some scholars have termed it, of the 'offer' of Soviet military aid to Czechoslovakia in accordance with the Soviet–Czechoslovak Treaty of May 1935.[21] Although the affair was shrouded in mystery and almost certainly Stalin had no intention of providing unilateral armed support, Gottwald and the Czechoslovak communists thereafter consistently hammered home the message that the USSR was the *only* reliable friend of the country. This interpretation was to pay big dividends in the post-war years.

Communist strategy during the war was tortuous, often confused and at times viewed as deeply anti-national by many Czech and Slovak patriots, especially following the Nazi–Soviet Pact of August 1939 and the outbreak of hostilities. This shocking deal between the two dictatorships was highly disorienting, but was eventually accepted by most party functionaries and members both at home and abroad.[22] However, it signified that the KSČ leaders shunned 'anything that could give preference to one side or the other in the war: they therefore isolated themselves from Beneš and the West which remained the nation's main hope of liberation'.[23] One might add that the party also distanced itself from the mass of Czech citizens suffering under the Nazi yoke, a sectarian line which was maintained more or less unchanged until the turning point of 'Operation Barbarossa' on 22 June 1941. Overnight, the Nazis became the overarching enemy and all communists were commanded to resist the Germans. In the Protectorate, KSČ militants engaged in individual acts of sabotage and later in the war formed partisan groups. This resistance, never exclusively the preserve of the communists, was most striking in Slovakia during the National Uprising. In addition, the party leaders in Moscow now sought cooperation with Beneš's government-in-exile in London and gradually developed a strategy for a liberated post-war Czechoslovakia that was largely, though not fully, compatible with Beneš's. The broad policies were elaborated in consultation with the Stalinist bosses in Moscow and reflected the evolving interests of Soviet foreign policy in the region, but the detailed proposals, to be examined in the next chapter, were generally the outcome of discussions and disagreements among the exiled Czechoslovak communist leaders themselves based on their understanding of conditions at home. A degree of limited autonomy was thus granted to national communists by their Soviet patrons.

Indeed, it would be wrong to imply that in the 1930s and 1940s the KSČ (or any other communist party) was a totally monolithic Stalinist body completely divorced from national political currents by its utter devotion to the USSR and an 'alien' ideology, or that its entire membership fully embraced Stalinist values. Throughout its existence, the Czechoslovak party experienced a constant tension between 'its insertion in the national community and in the international communist movement'.[24] The boundary lines between these so-called 'national communist' and 'Muscovite' tendencies may have often been blurred, running even through individual leaders and functionaries, but the two mentalities were nonetheless palpable. At the risk of over-simplification, the 'national communist' inclination came to the fore during the 'Popular Front' period, the 'people's democratic' phase of 1945–47 with its defining slogan of a 'Czechoslovak road to socialism', and most conspicuously during the reformist Prague Spring of 1968, while the 'Muscovite' tendency predominated in the Stalinist 'era of socialist construction' in 1948–54 and in the 'normalisation' process after 1969.[25] That said, an important conclusion to be drawn, and one that is often overlooked, is that there existed among many communist officials and militants a tenacious predilection for Stalinist conventions and practices, and these 'Stalinist' modes of thinking and action were evident throughout the 1930s, 1940s and 1950s, and even beyond.

Main Themes, Issues and Interpretations

My overall methodology seeks to integrate conventional political and 'new' social history by prioritising the fluidity and interplay of state–society relations in communist Czechoslovakia and the lack of fixed and exact boundaries between party and citizen. My focus is thus on both the impersonal power structures of the party-state Moloch and on society (or societies) and its dynamic interactions with the political project of the regime. There are five main overlapping themes that run throughout the volume, some of which we have touched on above: first, the 'rootedness' of the Czechoslovak party and the necessity of viewing the communist period as an integral component of the two nations' modern experience; second, the influence of external forces and outside pressures on the communist regime; third, popular opinion and the contentious issue of resistance versus consent; fourth, the moot 'totalitarian' model of the Czechoslovak party and state; and finally the burning fuse of the 'nationality question', and in particular Czech–Slovak relations. I will elaborate on each in turn, but first a few words about what this book is *not* concerned with. The major omission is that the details of economic performance and foreign policy fall outside the remit of my interests, although the economy and inter-state diplomacy can hardly be ignored, most obviously with regard to the USSR. The economic crises of the early 1950s, early 1960s and late 1980s and the concomitant pressures on living standards had profound socio-political ramifications, and intra-Soviet bloc relations often impacted heavily on domestic affairs, particularly during the Prague Spring. Neither do I examine the intricacies of the party's cultural decrees and campaigns, with the partial exception of developments in the early 1950s and mid-1960s. I understand 'culture' more broadly as everyday lifestyles and modes of thinking and behaviour. Finally, space constraints preclude a sustained transnational approach. Where necessary, I do make limited comparisons with other East European socialist states, but the focus remains squarely on Czechoslovakia.

My first argument is that the 40-year communist experience in Czechoslovakia should not be seen as a foreign imposed aberration, dislocating an otherwise unsullied democratic history. It is not good enough in my opinion to view the communist regime as an alien implant with few, if any, domestic affiliations. Regardless of its allegiance to Moscow, the Communist Party was able to strike deep roots in Czech society, though to a lesser degree in Slovak, and to associate itself with certain prevailing national traditions, identities and myths (while undoubtedly rejecting others).[26] This was partly because, unlike in Poland and Hungary, there was very little Russophobia among Czechoslovaks, at least before 1968. After the war, the KSČ became a socially diverse mass party, appealing not just to its 'natural' working-class constituency, but also to the intelligentsia, some clerical and administrative staff, even farmers, men and women, young and old. Crucially, it appeared to offer persuasive solutions to the multiple problems facing the country in the post-war era of reconstruction. What is more, many of these problems were 'hangovers' from the First and Second Republics. While it is true that Czechoslovak political culture showed strong democratic and pluralistic trends, there were noteworthy contradictions: the relative weakness of parliamentary rule and participatory democracy, the tendency to oligarchic government, centralism and the concentration of executive power, the cult-like aura of the presidency, the unresolved ethnic tensions between Czechs, Slovaks, Germans and Magyars, the disillusionment with the 'bourgeois' capitalist economy and the authoritarian impulses of many mainstream politicians and elites, not just of the far right and left. Communist rule emerged, in part, as a response to these integral dilemmas of modern Czechoslovak history. It was not, to paraphrase Padraic Kenney, 'a detour from [Czechoslovakia's] true path'.[27] In this sense, the communist seizure of power in February 1948 did not represent a total break with past practices and mentalities.

We have established that foreign powers have played an inordinately prominent role in Czechoslovak history, and this often determining external presence – in our case post-war Soviet hegemony over Central and Eastern Europe – means that the complex interplay of indigenous and exogenous factors and the troubled international context of the Cold War will form an important framework of this book. A classic, and controversial, example of this dichotomy is the extent of internal and external inputs in the communist takeover of power in February 1948. Was it essentially Soviet inspired and directed from without, as many anti-communist contemporaries and historians have insisted?[28] Or should we prioritise the national circumstances and experiences which facilitated the communist triumph, as many reformist Czechoslovak historians writing in the 1960s and several Western scholars have tended to do?[29] Or again, was the so-called 'Velvet Revolution' of November–December 1989, which overthrew the despised communist 'dinosaurs', largely a product of Gorbachev's liberalising *glasnost* (openness) and *perestroika* (reconstruction) in the USSR, or did the dictatorship implode from within, the victim of disastrous economic and political policies and an emerging Czech and Slovak civil society which had lost its fear? Clearly, both internal and external factors are present at all times, but the relative weight of each needs careful examination.

Another central concern is the highly problematic question of popular opinion and changing public attitudes towards the communist state; or to put it in stark terms: 'resistance' versus 'consent'. It is extremely difficult to gauge with any certainty the nature of popular opinion, especially in dictatorships that seek to suppress open debate, curtail heterodoxy and mould social discourse in line with ideological preferences. However, that said, should we unthinkingly accept the stereotypical Western notion, originally conditioned by the binary divisions of the Cold War and now widely accepted in the Czech and Slovak Republics, that the majority of citizens consistently opposed the regime and desired a speedy return to capitalism and liberal democracy? Or is it more applicable to conceive the socialist dictatorship not as a static 'totalitarian' monolith or field of unambiguous conflict between 'regime' and 'society', but as a living dynamic organism in which individuals struggled to empower themselves and thereby shape and make sense of the world around them?[30] And how did public moods alter over time in response to changing domestic and foreign realities? To what extent was it possible, in conditions of fierce one-party authoritarianism, for 'ordinary' Czechs and Slovaks to devise various forms of interaction, negotiation and bargaining with party-state organs and create limited spaces in which to 'work the system' to their advantage? Did some people even welcome aspects of the system and benefit from its policies? Or did most simply get on with their lives as best they could with little or no overt political engagement whatever? In this scheme, 'conformist' tendencies are more relevant than 'resistant' activities, as are intermediate attitudes like adaptation, apathy and what might be called 'muddling through'.[31] In short, a critical element of social history needs to be injected into the political history of communism.

Closely related to this is my interpretation of the nature of the Communist Party and state. It has been standard to depict communist regimes as totalitarian entities in which the party's political, economic and socio-cultural goals were overtly articulated and universally understood – the 'plan' was self-evident and could not be questioned, and pre-existing policies, almost always of Soviet origin, merely needed to be implemented by finding the correct organisational mechanisms and mass propaganda techniques.[32] Those who did not accept the 'progressive' vision of the party were coerced into submission. This conception of communist systems is not inherently 'wrong'. Their Marxist–Leninist masters did have long-standing macro-level goals and the regimes they created were without doubt miserably oppressive, increasingly morally corrupt and guided by an ideological transformatory mission that was frequently at odds with popular values and aims. Nevertheless, to my mind totalitarian theories are one dimensional and unnecessarily restrictive. By focusing on high politics, the state and its repressive apparatus, adherents of totalitarianism are prone to exaggerate the level of sustained control exerted by the central authorities, are inattentive to micro-level functioning and to the discrepancies between highly personalised decision-*making* and widely dispersed decision-*implementation*, and fail to appreciate the contingent nature of policy formation. Above all, they have great difficulty in explaining the sources of systemic change and development over time – once a totalitarian regime, always a totalitarian regime. For these reasons, I seek to challenge the paradigm and its static conception of communist politics, power relations and state–society interconnections. There is, of course, nothing new about this critique in Western scholarship, but a similar reappraisal has only relatively recently appeared in Czech historiography.[33]

My fifth theme is the explosive issue of the treatment of national 'minorities'. This is not merely a matter of describing the post-war 'transfer', often violent, of nigh on three million Czechoslovak Germans (and the exchange of several tens of thousands of Magyars) from their homelands, as is often the case in existing historiography. It is also vital to assess the longer-term impact of this historic cleansing of the Czech borderlands. If we are to believe recent research, this forced resettlement of populations was inextricably linked to the consolidation of communist rule and may offer us new perspectives on the sources of the relative popular appeal of the regime. Just as pivotal are mutual Czech–Slovak relations and the assumptions and (mis)perceptions that underlay their competing nationalisms. What was the communist leadership's understanding of the sources of these tensions and how did the authorities attempt to 'solve' the so-called 'Slovak question' after 1948? Why did the post-war notion of separate and equal nations based on a real degree of Slovak autonomy soon relapse into Prague centralism and renewed Czech hegemony? Why were leading Slovak communists imprisoned for 'bourgeois nationalism' in the 1950s and what influence did their rehabilitation have in the early and mid-1960s? What were the consequences of the resurgence of 'Slovak nationalism' and the aim of federalisation during and after the Prague Spring? What role, if any, did Slovak grievances play in the 'Velvet Revolution'?

Finally, as an important sub-theme, I would argue that there were several communist Czechoslovakias in our period: Stalinist (1948 to the mid-1950s), post-Stalinist (1956 to the mid-1960s), reformist (1968–69), 'normalised' (1969 to the mid-1980s) and 'pre-terminal' (mid-1980s to 1989). The boundaries between these phases are often blurred and a central core of the system can be detected – the one-party political structure dominated by the executive, state control of the economy and the virtual elimination of private enterprise, the reliance on coercion and the secret police, and the seemingly all-pervasive existence of censorship and state propaganda. But these phenomena subtly altered over time in response to changing international, intra-bloc and domestic priorities. Communist leaders, theoreticians and propagandists were perpetually searching for new mechanisms and policies to mobilise the population and achieve the elusive Holy Grail of political legitimacy. On occasion they introduced reforms in order to divert pressures from below. Moreover, Czechoslovak communism may have shared many key features with, say, its Polish or Hungarian counterparts, but they were not identical creations. Heterogeneous national political cultures, social and economic structures, cultural values and religious beliefs affected the regimes in myriad ways. To this extent, there was no single 'communist system'.

These are all intractable themes to which I don't pretend to have 'definitive' answers. But my basic premise is this: contrary to the post-1989 master paradigm which emphasises the fundamentally alien essence of the Czechoslovak communist experience and the inherent and diffuse social resistance to the regime, I contend that popular attitudes to the socialist aims and visions of the Communist Party modulated from broadly 'supportive' in the late 1940s to 'critical loyalty' in the 1950s and 1960s to 'disengaged collusion' by the 1970s and 1980s. It is certainly the case that fierce Stalinist (and post-Stalinist) repression and, notably, ongoing socio-economic hardship engendered real dissentient public moods, and the dismantling of the Prague Spring reforms after August 1968 and subsequent 'normalisation' undoubtedly dealt a fatal blow to popular 'faith' in the renewal of socialism, but oppositional currents were never sufficiently strong or widespread to threaten seriously the regime until the international 'crisis of communism' in the late 1980s. My overall goal, then, is to provide a challenging and controversial, but I hope accessible and convincing, interpretation of these issues based on the most recent Western, Czech and Slovak historiography, incorporating where appropriate archival sources and published documentary editions. In this way, I seek to contribute to our knowledge of a country which stood at the centre of cataclysmic European events many times in the twentieth century.

Chapter 2: Communism on the Road to Power, 1945–48

In the years 1945–48 the fate of Czechoslovakia hung in the balance. Would the country maintain its pre-war democratic pluralist and pro-Western orientation? Or would it shift towards socialism under the pressures of the USSR and the bi-polarisation of the emerging Cold War? Or would it be able to build some new status acting as a 'bridge' between East and West? The eventual outcome was a semi-constitutional seizure of power by the Czechoslovak communists and their supporters in late February 1948. This denouement was not entirely pre-determined, though the correlation of external and internal forces undoubtedly favoured a communist victory. Stalin's insistence on Soviet national security, the resultant wider historic changes in the region, normally referred to as the 'Sovietisation' of Central and Eastern Europe in the years 1944–48, and the West's indecisive, almost resigned, response proved pivotal in the communists' success. But so did propitious domestic contexts: the 'regulated' or 'limited democracy' of the post-war Czechoslovak governmental structure, the relative weight of the competing parties and their visions of the two nations' past as much as their future, the forced expulsion of the vast majority of the country's ethnic Germans, popular leftist aspirations and the imperative of state-led socio-economic reconstruction after the war.

Hence, this chapter will examine in some detail both endogenous and indigenous developments in this period of transition. The underlying task is to answer the question which has exercised scholars ever since: why was the KSČ able to gain mastery of a country that prided itself on its democratic and humanistic heritage? The first essential step in addressing this conundrum is to assess the consequences of the war on Czech and Slovak politics and society by showing how the traumatic events of 1938–45 transformed elite and popular understandings

21

of democracy, socialism and political power in general. Thereafter, I will discuss Soviet diplomatic goals and political strategies in post-war East Central Europe and conclude with an analysis of communist tactics in the broader context of Czechoslovak party politics, contested cultural discourses and power struggles. Rather than follow established practice by concentrating solely on high politics and the 'personalisation of blame', I will incorporate the view 'from below' by outlining relevant developments in the labour and women's movements.

The Impact of War

A comprehensive account of the communist takeover must take on board the underlying continuities, as well as the sharp discontinuities, that span the tumultuous decade 1938–48 when the world was torn apart. It is imperative to begin with World War II and its impact on East European societies, and not with the conventional 'zero hour' of 1945, as if the rise of communism was purely a product of the Cold War power struggles between the USA and the USSR, an 'imposition from the east'. The scholarly consensus today accepts that the truly profound transformations wrought by the 'Munich complex', the Second Republic and in particular six years of total war, brutal occupation and the Holocaust are key factors in helping to explain the communists' ascendancy. As Bradley Abrams has boldly asserted: 'no Second World War, no Soviet-style communist Eastern Europe'.[1] The equation is, perhaps, too neat, but there is a good deal of mileage in it. The most important wartime phenomena which created favourable environments for future communist success, not just in Czechoslovakia but throughout the region, were the decimation of entire social and ethnic groups and the sheer scale of material destruction; the concentration of industry and the state regimentaion of economic structures and labour relations by the Nazi overlords; popular disillusionment with the 'West' and 'bourgeois' politics, signifying an ideological shift to the left; and, linked to this, the buoyant reputation of the Red Army as 'liberators' from Nazi dominion combined with local communist partisan struggles against extreme right-wing authoritarianism. These radicalising shocks to the established status quo can be described as 'revolutionary' in their own right with far-reaching implications.

It is common knowledge that the human losses in Eastern Europe during the war beggar belief. Poland, for example, lost approximately 20 per cent of its pre-war population. Yugoslavia lost 10 per cent and

Hungary 4.4 per cent. The figure in Czechoslovakia was lower at 3.7 per cent, but still almost four times as high as Great Britain. The vast majority of East European Jewry was destroyed in the Holocaust, including the virtual annihilation of Poland's Jews. It is estimated that of Czechoslovakia's pre-war total of 255,000 Jews a mere 40,000–45,000 survived.[2] In addition to deaths, several tens of millions were wounded, uprooted, forcibly resettled or displaced, or experienced slave labour in the Third Reich, 37,000 workers from Slovakia alone. Eastern Europe was quite simply 'on the move'. Those who remained behind were exhausted, under-nourished and bewildered, many seeking revenge for their own plight and that of their nation. Physical and material destruction was also on a colossal scale. Countless towns, villages, mines, factories, bridges, transport facilities and livestock lay ruined. Czechoslovakia was not the worst affected, but even here total losses were calculated at over four billion dollars. Parts of central Slovakia, scene of the National Uprising, were devastated and in 1942 two Czech villages, Lidice and Ležáky, were reduced to rubble by the Nazis, all male and some female inhabitants murdered in retaliation for the assassination of Reinhard Heydrich, the *Reichsprotektor*, in Prague by London-trained Czech and Slovak resistance fighters.

But where, we might ask, is the equal sign between this purgatory and the subsequent rise of communism? Part of the answer becomes clear when we look at the specific strata of the population that were victims of the Nazis. The elimination of around 3.75 million Jews in Eastern Europe signified inter alia a gross depletion of the ranks of the entrepreneurial bourgeoisie, merchants and intellectuals. Very large numbers of urban elites and intelligentsia – doctors, lawyers, teachers, journalists, academics, students, army officers, bureaucrats and managers, not to mention leading politicians – were wiped out by the Nazis as bearers of dangerous alternative ideas and anti-German patriotisms. In short, the middle classes suffered terribly and, in the words of Abrams, 'the physical weakening of the class with both the ability and inclination to oppose radical social change is certainly a factor that must be constantly borne in mind'.[3] What is more, these people needed to be replaced, allowing for the upward social mobility of hundreds of thousands of skilled workers, artisans and peasants, men and women. It was nothing less than a 'social revolution', a grand equalisation process endorsed and fostered by local communist parties. It is true that the destruction of 'national elites' and the bourgeoisie was far more devastating in Poland than in Czechoslovakia, but even in the latter its effects were certainly felt in the post-war political and economic reconstruction.

In addition, the unprecedented savagery of the war and the Nazis' exterminatory racial policies brutalised societies and individual psyches. The result was a moral crisis and desensitisation, a belief that might was right. Acts of collaboration with the occupying regime bitterly divided communities, inflamed class animosities and engendered denunciations and demands for judicial, and extra-judicial, retribution. Participation in the expropriation and looting of Jewish (and, post-war, German) property represented a breakdown of 'normal' values. As Jan Gross argues, 'the old operative definitions of legality, justice, legitimacy, common purpose, national interest, or *raison d'état* were put in doubt, shattered', leaving space for 'new regulatory ideas to set up proper foundations for life in common'.[4] This is not to say that we can detect some direct line of causality between wartime brutalisation and post-war popular susceptibility to communist militancy, as if the Nazi dictatorship 'led to' the communist dictatorship. But there does appear to be a certain logic at play, whereby Czechs' and Slovaks' commitment to humanistic values, democratic procedures and legal norms were to a considerable degree undermined by the barbarities and moral turpitude – some of it, to be sure, self-inflicted – of the years 1938–45.

Longer-term structural economic processes and Nazi statist policies dictated by wartime exigencies also impacted on later developments. The effects are most succinctly put by Robin Okey: 'industrial concentration, trade union regimentation and the transfer of vast assets into German hands which now [in 1945] defaulted to the state all made an *étatiste* approach to economic management more plausible.'[5] The Nazi authorities' intervention in the economy, social welfare and food provisioning boosted notions of state coordination and 'care' for citizens. Economically, this was most evident in the Czech coal and steel industries, and this experience, it can plausibly be argued, 'laid important...groundwork for the postwar practice of central planning'. What is more, the autarchic tendencies of the Nazi-dominated local economies decoupled them from international trade with the West in favour of the needs of the German economy.[6] Other important corollaries were the growth of Czech and notably Slovak industrial production, though this was uneven and tempered by wartime destruction, and the expansion of the industrial workforce in larger enterprises with very high numbers of peasants and women entering the factories. By the end of the war, Czechoslovakia 'would have a larger share of its population in the industrial working class than ever before'.[7] These transformations resulted in increased worker confidence and sense of class identity, particularly as the huge task of post-war reconstruction relied primarily on the efforts of industrial labour. In terms of organisations, the Nazis enforced a 'levelisation' programme eliminating the intermediary system of parties, social associations and interest groups.[8] Overall, in Nazi controlled East Central Europe 'comprehensive processes of social [and economic] change...were set in motion' that were to be '*implemented a few years later according to the principles of scientific socialism*'.[9]

Politically and ideologically, the events of 1938–45 engendered a sea-change in popular attitudes. In this regard, it is hard to overestimate the historic import of the perceived Munich 'betrayal', burnt into the Czech and Slovak collective memory and national consciousness. As a result of this humiliation, liberal democracy itself, the basis of the delegitimised First Republic, was dealt a heavy blow. Pro-British and French sentiment was seriously eroded overnight and profound doubts persisted about the future reliability of the 'cowardly appeasers'. Indeed, they 'looked, at best, weak and fearful in the face of the Nazi threat or, at worst, like imperfectly self-interested collaborators with Hitler...the international order created by the Western democracies was...failing, and that failure could be seen as part and parcel of Western-style democracy'.[10] Taken together with the horrendous hardships of the Great Depression, it is understandable that for many Czechs and Slovaks the appeals of liberal democracy and market economics had been gravely undermined, if not thoroughly discredited. Furthermore, there was a widespread belief that right-wing parties and their 'bourgeois' leaders had collaborated with the Germans under the occupation. In these circumstances, the 'right' in general was irredeemably tarnished.

This estrangement from erstwhile foreign allies and the derailment of the established pre-war system encouraged the search for new international partners and political and institutional safeguards. In many ways it was logical that the USSR should step into the breach. The Soviet Union's seemingly supportive stance at the time of Munich, its heroic battle to the death against Hitlerism and the Red Army's liberation of the vast majority of Czechoslovakia, including Prague on 8–9 May 1945, raised the stock of socialism and the USSR in a country which was traditionally Russophile.[11] Similarly, the communists' partisan struggles at home against the Nazi occupiers after 1943 enhanced the reputation of the KSČ, as did the emerging propaganda cults of communist national 'heroes', such as Julius Fučík, who was beheaded by the Nazis in September 1943.[12] To be sure, the underground anti-German resistance was far from the preserve of the communists – many patriotic democrats fought bravely in the Slovak

National Uprising and elsewhere – and compared to countries like Poland and France was less than impressive. However, the communists were disproportionately represented in the resistance movements that did exist and it is estimated that as many as 25,000 of their number perished under the Nazis, over 1,500 Slovak communists were imprisoned, and the KSČ and Communist Party of Slovakia each lost four illegal Central Committees and many committed cadres.[13] This wartime persecution and sacrifice of the communists, ably embellished by post-war propagandists, gained them more than a measure of popular sympathy and respect.

Pro-Soviet sentiments even affected many non-communist politicians, including Beneš. Disillusioned with the lack of sustained Western support during the war and, as a realist, recognising that the Red Army would surely liberate his homeland, Beneš came to regard the USSR as a firm ally of a reconstituted post-war Czechoslovakia, which he believed could act as a geopolitical 'bridge' between East and West. He even envisioned the possibility of a democratisation process in the Soviet system, which would further strengthen the relationship between the Allies. Crucially, Beneš was convinced that Stalin would support his plan to expel the country's German inhabitants and, linked to this, viewed the Soviet Union as the main protector of the Czechs against a potentially resurgent German revanchism. To this end he signed the highly significant Soviet–Czechoslovak Friendship and Mutual Aid Treaty with Stalin in December 1943, shifting the centre of gravity of Czechoslovak foreign policy towards the East. Although Beneš was a sufficiently astute politician not to put all his eggs in the Soviet basket and never fully overcame his fears about communist intentions, archival transcripts of his discussions in Moscow reveal the extent of his placatory attitudes to Stalin and his wish that 'in regard to issues of major importance, [we] would always speak and act in a fashion agreeable to the representatives of the Soviet government'.[14] The domestic corollary of Beneš's international visions was an analogous conciliatory stance to the Czechoslovak communists and an ideological reorientation towards a 'new democracy' embracing an expanded role for the state, social justice, economic reform and even restricted party representation in any future cabinet. In public discourse, these important geopolitical and theoretical shifts to the left were often couched in a rather nebulous, but influential and historically rooted, pan-Slavism which identified the 'brother' Russians as natural defenders and leaders of the Slavic peoples, of whom the Czechs were the most westerly branch.

By emphasising the positive perception of the Red Army and the USSR in general, I do not wish to underestimate the negative backlash that accompanied the wholesale looting and deplorable raping indulged in by Soviet soldiers during the 'liberation' of Central and Eastern Europe. Although the Czech lands, but less so Slovakia, escaped the worst excesses, in some quarters such actions severely tainted the reputation of the Red Army. Nor do I want to suggest crassly that all Czechs and Slovaks became solidly pro-Soviet or pro-communist in outlook. Catholicism remained strong in Slovakia and southern Moravia (but weaker in Bohemia), key strata in the lower-middle classes were essentially immune to the communist appeal, and many non-communist politicians became increasingly wary of the 'totalitarian' dangers of Marxism–Leninism. Nevertheless, it is widely recognised that a significant turn to the left occurred at the popular level as in many other war-torn countries, including in Western Europe. This ideological mutation was felt particularly among large sections of the industrial working class, youth and professional intelligentsia and was reinforced by longer-term structural changes. For instance, the 1947 census revealed that approximately 25 per cent of the Czechoslovak population was aged between 15 and 30,[15] and many young people, revolutionised by their formative encounters with the crisis of capitalism, the collapse of the state in 1938 and subsequent extreme right-wing authoritarianism, coupled with growing exposure to Soviet military prowess and the 'economic miracle' of planning and 'socialist modernity', queued up after 1945 to enter the radiant socialist future. A prominent representative of this impatient generation, Antonín Liehm, later graphically depicted the utopian ideals and revolutionary élan of the post-war radical Czech youth. Desiring to make a clean sweep, Liehm and his enthusiastic colleagues were convinced that 'with banners flying and bands playing [we] would march into the wide-open gates of the millennium'. He recalls how:

> we ran through those gates of paradise in 1945 and once again in 1948…We felt that we knew how to solve human problems. We stepped from the darkness of Nazism straight into the sunny realm of freedom, friendship, happiness – in short, socialism. We considered anyone who failed to understand this as a reactionary bourgeois; people were neatly divided into good and bad; everything was clear and simple.[16]

It is easy now to adopt a cynical patronising attitude to such naïve and ultimately harmful views. But in the conditions of a war-ravaged and brutalised country in 1945 they encapsulated the hopes, visions and dreams of millions of citizens, and not just young people. The attractiveness of 'socialism', even in its Stalinist guise, should never be ignored.

Let me conclude this section with another quotation from Abrams, which admirably summarises my main points:

> The experiences of 1938 to 1945 ripped the fabric of the interwar societies, reconfigured social hierarchies, reorganized economies, reshuffled political allegiances, caused a reevaluation of both foreign and domestic political priorities, triggered a rethinking of the meaning of the nations involved, and catalyzed forces aiming at the fundamental restructuring of the states of the region…Taken as a whole, the war and its effects created conditions propitious for radical reform, redounding to the benefit of the Communist parties.[17]

This crucial restoration of the indigenous wartime context to the rise of communism is, however, incomplete without an examination of the role of Soviet foreign policy and the origins of the Cold War in Eastern Europe. Without Stalin, there would be no KSČ in power?

Stalin, the Cold War and Czechoslovakia's 'Limited Autonomy'

With the opening of relevant archives in the former Soviet Union since 1991, there is a measure of historical consensus emerging on Stalin's aims in Central and Eastern Europe in the years 1943–48. Whereas for many Western scholars writing in the early decades of the Cold War it was axiomatic that the Soviet dictator possessed an expansionist master plan to rapidly 'Sovietise' those areas liberated by the Red Army in 1944–45, recent archival discoveries strongly suggest that his strategies, dependent on constantly evolving national and international conditions, were more cautious and differentiated, revealing the existence of alternative paths, even a measure of uncertainty, in the Kremlin. There is no doubt that Stalin kept a very tight rein on foreign policy decision-making throughout this crucial period and hence determined the main thrust and overall conception of Soviet diplomatic, military and ideological goals in Eastern Europe; but we now know that he was not the sole initiator of policy and that Soviet ambitions and methods were constantly subject to revision and fine-tuning. Competing strategies and tactics were thrashed out in specialist commissions and in the Foreign Ministry, and these strategies varied from country to country and were modified over time. Although Stalin could, and did, reject expert proposals and insisted on the final say, there was no one single Soviet 'line', applicable to all circumstances and situations. What was considered operative for Romania was not necessarily so in the different environment of Czechoslovakia. Indeed, according to Alfred Rieber, between 1943 and 1947 'Stalin's orders to his army commanders and his advice to local communists do not add up to a clear and consistent policy. The picture is one of trial and error informed by a Marxist perception of the world'.[18]

However, in the swirling vortex of ever-changing international, national and military conjunctures, one imperative remained constant for Stalin: the all-consuming quest for national security. Russia/ the USSR had been attacked through its Western borders three times in the twentieth century – 1914, 1919–20 (the little-known Russo-Polish War) and 1941 – and Stalin was utterly determined that no such disaster would again befall his creation. The preferred mechanism for achieving this elusive aim of 'total' security was traditional *Realpolitik* by consolidating a Soviet sphere of influence in Central and Eastern Europe. But, as Rieber rightly suggests, ideology played an important role for Stalin. He retained an unmistakable commitment to Marxist revolutionary goals and a firm faith in the final triumph of international socialism over capitalist imperialism. Stalin's dilemma as the war was coming to an end in 1944–45, and thereafter, was how to establish a Soviet geopolitical sphere of influence in his western borderlands without unduly antagonising his Grand Alliance partners and risking a breakdown in relations among the Big Three. Such a prospect was definitely not in the USSR's best interests if only because Moscow needed US loans to reconstruct its shattered economy and infrastructure. It was a conundrum that ultimately proved insoluble. But between 1943 and mid-1947 Stalin generally adhered to an interrelated strategy of seeking to preserve amicable relations with the USA, Britain and pro-Soviet East European democrats, like Beneš, while elaborating for national communist parties an intermediate non-revolutionary political formation – 'people's democracy' – that was predicated on the assumption that radical socialist transformations were not on the immediate agenda. For Stalin, such transitional measures also had the important advantage of minimising the risk of both civil wars in the region and the prospect of foreign interventions, outcomes which had seriously jeopardised the success of the Bolshevik Revolution after 1918.[19] In the event, these moderate perspectives were abandoned in the second half of 1947 as Cold War tensions became increasingly acute and Stalin responded by rapidly cementing his foothold in Eastern Europe.

Soviet policy towards Czechoslovakia in the latter stages of the war was broadly in line with these conceptions, adopting a dual-pronged approach. On the one hand, the USSR established cordial diplomatic relations with Beneš's government-in-exile in London, having officially recognised it in 1941, with a view to influencing future developments in the country. On the other, Stalin and his ideological chiefs sought to inform and direct the overall strategies of the KSČ leaders domiciled in Moscow, while permitting them, and perforce their beleaguered comrades in the Protectorate and Slovak Republic, a fair degree of tactical flexibility on the ground. At the diplomatic level, the Kremlin pledged support for the territorial recreation of Czechoslovakia after the war, one of Beneš's sacrosanct goals, and was prepared to promote Beneš himself as president-in-waiting of a renewed post-war democratic and anti-Nazi Czechoslovakia. Furthermore, although Moscow refused to acknowledge the return of the London government as the sole legitimate authority in this restored Czechoslovakia, it backed the idea of a negotiated, but restricted, coalition in which communists and non-communists would be represented. The Polish 'solution' of an imposed pro-Soviet government was thus avoided in Czechoslovakia. This line of thinking culminated in December 1943 with the signing of a bilateral Soviet–Czechoslovak Treaty of Friendship, by which Moscow appeared to guarantee the future independence of its smaller Slavic neighbour. At that time, and on later occasions, Stalin professed his intention not to interfere in domestic Czechoslovak affairs, reportedly stating: 'there can be no talk of Soviet hegemony.'[20] Simultaneously, he insisted that the Czechoslovaks should maintain 'friendly' relations with the USSR and support its foreign policy. In this sense, the treaty marked an important step in the emergence of a Soviet sphere in Eastern Europe. Indeed, soon after the December 1943 agreement high-ranking Soviet advisers began to emphasise the need for a strong post-war Czechoslovakia in order to make the country 'the foremost bastion of our influence in central and south-eastern Europe'.[21] In short, the Stalin–Beneš relationship offered distinct geopolitical advantages to both sides.

At the ideological level, the underlying theoretical principle, tortuously evolved in Soviet 'think tanks' in the shifting conditions of 1943–45, was termed the 'people's democracy' and was to be adopted in varying forms by all communist parties.[22] This concept, emanating from the Comintern's pre-war anti-fascist policy of the 'popular front', was never systematically elaborated, but represented in essence a two-stage transition to socialism that eschewed both Western 'bourgeois capitalist' models and the Bolshevik 'dictatorship of the proletariat'. The first stage would be a 'national democratic revolution', which through its progressive socialising measures would lay the foundations for a second socialist stage, though no time frame was placed on this eventuality and 'socialism' itself remained vaguely defined. Czechoslovakia was deemed an ideal location for the 'people's democratic' experiment in that political cooperation between communists and non-communists, epitomised by the hopeful relationship between Beneš and Gottwald, opened the possibility of a parliamentary, or at least non-violent, road to socialism. Soviet and KSČ theorists envisaged a 'National Front' government in post-war Czechoslovakia as the structural basis of this 'people's democracy'. It was to be a left-leaning coalition in which the communists and their allies would ensure the legal enactment of a range of broadly popular political and socio-economic reforms. However, it was left unclear whether the 'people's democracy' should be considered an end in itself as a longer-term evolutionary strategy for the forging of socialism, or if it was merely a tactical interlude before the ultimate revolutionary seizure of one-party communist power. If it was the latter, the Czechoslovak communist leaders were faced with the acute problem of establishing the precise methods of, and timing for, the conquest of sole power. And Moscow rarely delivered definitive answers. I shall return to these debates in the next section.

Stalin's repeated protestations of non-intervention in Czechoslovak internal affairs were not completely disingenuous and formed part of his strategy of maintaining reasonable relations with his Western allies while asserting non-negotiable Soviet security needs in Eastern Europe, particularly in Poland. Hence, he was prepared to make not inconsiderable concessions. The first of these was the dissolution of the Comintern in June 1943, partly as a sop to Churchill and Roosevelt, but primarily because he believed the organisation was largely redundant and hindered the independent development of national communist parties. After the war, Stalin refused to accept Yugoslav claims to portions of Italy and Austria; he counselled caution to the French, Italian and Belgian communists, who before spring 1947 were members of their respective governments; he refrained from direct interference in the Greek Civil War which raged from 1946–49 pitting British, and later US, backed nationalist monarchist forces against local communists; and after 1946 he rather reluctantly conceded his designs on Turkey and northern Iran. All this does not mean that Soviet actions in Europe and beyond were not perceived as aggressive in Western government circles, but it does signify that Stalin wished to maintain maximum tactical flexibility and had no wish to plunge the world into a precipitous 'Cold War'.

As far as Czechoslovakia is concerned, Stalin appears to have followed a similar model of insisting on strict compliance in matters considered vital to Soviet security interests, but in most circumstances he contented himself with indirect influence through party subordinates and official diplomatic channels. Although Soviet influence was pervasive, it is difficult to discern any sustained 'control' in the country in the years 1945–48. Czechoslovakia was, after all, an independent state and not the sixteenth republic of the USSR. Before 1949 there was no coherent or permanent network of Soviet political, military or security advisers in Czechoslovakia, the KSČ retained its commitment to the National Front coalition until the crises of mid-to-late 1947 and, most important, the Red Army was removed from Czechoslovak territory in November 1945, together with US troops. However, it would be naïve to assume that the Soviet leadership did not seek to sway the Prague government in both its internal and external policies, and as such Stalin and Foreign Minister Molotov were kept closely informed of developments via an elaborate communications nexus. This included comprehensive reports from several sources: the Soviet ambassador, Valerian Zorin, envoys despatched from Moscow to Czechoslovakia on specialist missions, KSČ dignitaries summarising recent events, and face-to-face meetings with Czechoslovak communist and non-communist ministers. On the basis of this information, Soviet East European experts periodically drew up 'analytical memoranda' on the state of affairs in Czechoslovakia, some of which were highly critical of communist tactics.[23] The general pattern appears to be that the dictator insisted on being kept abreast of events and would on occasion meet personally with Czechoslovak representatives, but delegated everyday oversight to underlings in the Soviet Central Committee apparatus and Foreign Ministry.

There were, though, exceptions to this rule when Stalin deemed it necessary to intervene decisively in internal Czechoslovak affairs, limiting the autonomy of the government and severely testing its loyalty to the mutual friendship treaty. The first concerned the fate of Sub-Carpathian Ruthenia, the easternmost outpost of interwar Czechoslovakia bordering the Ukrainian Soviet Republic. Here, following the entry of the Red Army in autumn 1944, the Soviet authorities refused to hand over the territory to the Czechoslovak plenipotentiary and fostered a 'popular' campaign among the inhabitants for incorporation into the USSR. Beneš at first demurred, but eventually agreed to the de facto annexation in a separate bilateral Soviet–Czechoslovak treaty signed in June 1945. Other complications arose towards the end of the war over the hierarchy of the Czechoslovak armed forces and the Soviets' exhortation that Beneš should recognise the pro-Soviet Polish Lublin government. In both cases, Beneš again complied after initial misgivings. Later, in February 1947 Stalin insisted in no uncertain manner that the Prague government should ratify a treaty of alliance with Poland after the Czechoslovaks had dragged their feet for many months. Within ten days the agreement was signed in Warsaw. The eminent Czech historian Karel Kaplan has concluded that these 'bitter experiences indicated that the Soviets had sufficient means at their disposal to enforce their interests'.[24]

Nowhere was this compulsion more evident than in the intense controversy over the Marshall Plan. On 5 June 1947 US Secretary of State, George Marshall, announced a European Recovery Programme to stabilise the continent's economic, and by implication political and social, order by the injection of large quantities of dollars. Coming only three months after the Truman Doctrine, which had pledged the USA to a worldwide crusade against communist expansionism, the plan's main strategic aim was to ensure that the return of economic prosperity to Western Europe would marginalise the appeal of communism. Although the USSR and its allies in the emerging Soviet bloc were invited to participate in the plan, the offer was, according to the British and French Foreign Ministers, 'little more than window dressing'.[25] The standard story is that the Czechoslovak coalition government at first eagerly accepted the American proposal, but was then forced by Stalin to repudiate it. In reality, it wasn't quite that simple. Stalin himself was not consistent in his attitudes to Marshall Aid and the Czechoslovaks were also ambivalent to a certain extent.[26] Initially, it appeared the Soviet response was entirely negative and Jan Masaryk, Czechoslovak Foreign Minister and respected son of the pre-war President, was concerned, at least publicly, that the plan might divide Europe rather than unify it. However, when the Czechoslovak government met on 24 June to discuss the American idea, Vladimír Clementis, communist State Secretary for Foreign Affairs, surprised his audience by stating that the Soviet authorities believed 'it was suitable for Czechoslovakia to prepare itself and come up with an initial concept of the aid'. Steps were taken to this effect and on 1 July Masaryk said that his government 'with one voice welcomes' the

US offer and on 7 July the enlarged cabinet Presidium unanimously agreed, communists included, that Czechoslovakia should participate in the preparatory conference for the Marshall Plan scheduled for 12 July in Paris.

Before this, on 5 July, Stalin had hardened his position deciding that the plan represented a danger of Western economic interference in the states of Eastern Europe and hence seriously threatened Soviet regional interests. Nevertheless, Moscow's communications intimated that the Czechoslovaks, like other East Europeans, should attend the Paris conference, but once there reject the US and Anglo-French proposals and leave the meeting. By 8 July, crucially, 'new circumstances' had convinced Stalin that the plan's real aim was to 'establish a Western bloc in which West Germany would be included'. In other words, ultimately it had anti-Soviet political, not economic, goals and therefore the Czechoslovaks should 'refuse participation'. It is not the case that Stalin peremptorily summoned a Czechoslovak government delegation to Moscow to hear the Soviet veto directly from the 'boss': the Prague cabinet had already decided on 4 July that Masaryk and Gottwald should have talks with Stalin and Molotov in the Kremlin. The fateful meeting took place on 9 July. Almost immediately Stalin made it abundantly clear that if the Czechoslovaks participated in the Paris meeting they would be 'objectively...helping to isolate the Soviet Union', which meant breaking the terms of the Soviet–Czechoslovak friendship treaty. In his Manichean world view, it was clearly a test of the Czechoslovaks' fealty to the USSR: were they friend or foe? In order to assuage Masaryk's polite remonstrations, Stalin promised economic aid, industrial equipment and immediate grain supplies.[27] Back in Prague, on 10 July the government decided after fraught discussions to accept the Soviet 'recommendation'. Masaryk summed up the stark reality of the situation, commenting bleakly: 'I left for Moscow as Minister of Foreign Affairs of a sovereign state. I am returning as Stalin's stooge.'[28]

The Czech chronicler of these events, Karel Krátký, has judged that 'not only the economic, but also the political independence of Eastern Europe ended in Stalin's office in the Kremlin on the night of 9 July...From this moment on, Czechoslovakia...stage by stage, shifted toward the Soviet bloc'.[29] It might be objected, however, that well before the Marshall Plan Prague had been drawn into the Soviet orbit, not least because after 1943 *all* Czechoslovak politicians, not just the communists, had avidly defended the mutual friendship treaty and viewed the USSR as the ultimate source of support against the greater evil: the threat of renewed German revanchism. Masaryk and other non-communist ministers may well have been sceptical about Soviet intentions and keen to maintain close economic relations with the West, but in the final analysis they all chose to adhere to the Soviet line. To this extent, Stalin's veto represented the logical culmination, not the unanticipated start, of Czechoslovakia's dependency on Soviet foreign policy.

Arguably, the most important outcome of the Marshall Plan was the Soviet determination to consolidate their grip on Eastern Europe. The Kremlin interpreted the plan, together with the Truman Doctrine and other 'anti-communist' measures in the first half of 1947, as clear evidence of an emergent aggressive 'Anglo-American' bloc, which aimed to divide the world into two antagonistic camps even at the risk of a new war. This hardening of the Soviet outlook took two forms: first, the formation of the Communist Information Bureau (Cominform) in September 1947 and, second, renewed pressure on local communist parties to adopt more systematic offensive tactics. The Cominform was a coordinating centre for the main European communist parties designed to unify their political and ideological strategies in line with Soviet practices and theories. It undoubtedly acted to tighten Moscow's control over those parties and by extension push them towards more militant policies both at home and abroad. Even before its creation, however, and as the ferment over the Marshall Plan was brewing in late June 1947, a top Soviet analyst had despatched a detailed report to Stalin and other key leaders lambasting the KSČ for its complacent emphasis on achieving a parliamentary majority, its lack of Marxist–Leninist organisational structures and its 'limited' propaganda against 'reactionary elements', who, backed by the 'Anglo-Saxons', were becoming increasingly assertive.[30] Such alarmist assessments, replicated by other stinging memoranda in September, can only have strengthened Moscow's resolve to clamp down on its sphere of influence in Eastern Europe, including Czechoslovakia, turning the region into a unified Soviet-led bloc of communist satellites.[31] We must now turn our attention to internal developments in this battle for power.

The Communists' Tortuous Road to Power

In this section I will discuss several interlocking controversial themes all of which are highly relevant for the eventual KSČ takeover: the post-war National Front government and the communists' emphasis on a 'national democratic revolution' and a 'Czechoslovak road to socialism'; the transformation in the understanding of Czech national culture and history and the resultant 'struggle for the soul of the nation'; the political dilemmas and relative weaknesses of the non-communist parties; the forcible expulsion of the Sudeten Germans and its socio-political consequences; Czech–Slovak relations and political affairs and intrigues in Slovakia; the view 'from below' in the trade union, factory council and women's movements; and the political crises of autumn 1947 to February 1948, culminating in the formation of a communist-dominated cabinet.

A 'Czechoslovak Road to Socialism'?

At crucial talks in Moscow in late March 1945, leading delegates from four Czech and two Slovak parties resolved to implement sweeping institutional changes which fundamentally transformed the country's political landscape, prevented any return to the pre-war status quo and hence served as key factors in the rise of communism. All this was achieved behind closed doors and only many months later were the electorate permitted to have their say. Above all, the parties approved the composition of a new National Front government, a grand coalition of the KSČ, the National Socialist Party, the Social Democratic Party, the People's Party, the Slovak Communist Party (KSS) and the Slovak Democratic Party. The agreement emerged out of a strong consensual desire prevailing among both exiled politicians in London and Moscow and in Czechoslovak society at home for national unity and reconstruction and the need for a 'new order', following the traumas of Munich, anti-Nazi resistance, wartime occupation and the geopolitical and psychological rifts between Czechs and Slovaks. For the first time communists entered the Czechoslovak government and they were doubly represented in that the KSS was permitted equal status to the other parties, even though it was effectively, and increasingly, subordinate to the central KSČ leadership in Prague. This was to be a multi-party system, but on the insistence of the communists the 'collaborationist' conservative right, notably the Agrarians and the Slovak People's Party together with neo-fascist groups, were debarred and declared illegal. At a stroke, 'bourgeois' influence had been severely curtailed, shifting the spectrum of Czechoslovak politics definitively to the left. More than this, the National Front concept left no room for a legal opposition as all coalition partners were collectively responsible for government policy.

The composition of the new cabinet was confirmed relatively painlessly. Beneš was reinstalled as President of a newly proclaimed Third

Republic. A Social Democrat, Zdeněk Fierlinger, who was widely regarded as a communist sympathiser, was appointed Prime Minister and Gottwald became one of five Deputy Prime Ministers shared among the coalition parties. In an echo of the pre-war *Pětka*, these six men collectively formed the government Presidium which was to act as the supreme executive organ of the state. Absolutely crucial for future developments, the communists demanded and received five highly influential ministerial portfolios: Interior, Agriculture, Information, Labour and Social Security, and Education and Culture. A communist, Clementis, was also named State Secretary for Foreign Affairs under Masaryk, and in addition the Minister of National Defence, Ludvík Svoboda, though officially non-party, was, like Fierlinger, close to the communists. The other eight ministries were divided equally between the four non-communist parties. Thus, the KSČ may not have been totally dominant, but it was in a very power-ful position and in the months after the war the party experienced a rapid increase in membership from around 25,000 to a staggering one million by March 1946. This spectacular growth was demon-strated most dramatically in the free elections in May of that year in which the communists won 40 per cent of the votes in Bohemia and Moravia, but only 30 per cent in Slovakia, to become the single larg-est party in parliament. It was a historic achievement – the highest percentage ever gained by a communist party anywhere in the world in unrigged elections. As a consequence, Gottwald was declared Prime Minister.

It was also agreed in Moscow that the new government would pursue policies that were in line with the Soviet-inspired 'people's democracy' strategy. For several months before the end of the war, Czechoslovak communists had been insisting on the need for a 'national democratic revolution' and this concept formed the basis of the Košice Programme of the National Front, announced on 5 April 1945 in the recently liberated eastern Slovak city of Košice. The 'national' aspects of this revolution were to be the creation of a Czech and Slovak nation-state through the expulsion and expro-priation of the 'traitorous' Sudeten Germans and Magyars, the rec-ognition of Czech–Slovak equality and of a separate Slovak nation, and a strict orientation towards the USSR in foreign policy. The 'democratic' features were the banning of right-wing 'collaboration-ist' parties and state-sponsored retribution against Czech 'collabora-tors' with the Nazi authorities, the purging of 'reactionary' officials in public administration, the armed forces and security services, a thoroughgoing land reform, and the endorsement of elected local and district National Committees as the foundation of a new state administrative apparatus. These radical proposals were agreed by the non-communist parties, and some, above all the removal of the Germans, gained unanimous and enthusiastic support. As ever, unity was the watchword of the day. Overtly socialist socio-economic goals, such as large-scale nationalisation of industry or collectivisation of agriculture, were left off the agenda as, most definitely, was any talk of Soviets, socialisation and the seizure of power. The ratification of the Košice Programme represented a great triumph for the communists, particularly as it proved genuinely popular among wide strata of Czech and Slovak society. Independent public opinion surveys carried out in 1946 revealed that over 90 per cent of Czechs entirely agreed, or agreed with reservations, to the programme.[32]

What was the prime goal of the KSČ in the National Front government? For historians such as Kaplan the answer is unequivocal: 'the aim was the monopoly of power…the Communists entered the coalition with the clear intention of monopolizing power by liquidating all democratic principles and in the process, the people's democratic coalition itself.'[33] Indeed, this was the overarching interpretation of many Western and émigré Czech scholars writing during the Cold War: between 1945 and 1948 the communists implemented a carefully wrought master plan, 'operation grand deceit', to seize total power with the support of Moscow.[34] Did not Gottwald himself say in February 1946 that the party possessed 'sufficient means', including 'arms', to 'correct simple mechanical voting'?[35] While there is no doubt that the communists sought to construct a socialist Czechoslovakia closely aligned with the USSR and never lost sight of politics as a locus of power struggle (which political party ever does?), the teleological thesis outlined above is problematic for two reasons. First, it tends to demonise the 'omniscient' party leaders and fails to acknowledge the heterogeneity of the KSČ and the flexible nature of communist policies, which had to adapt to rapidly changing political and international events. It also presupposes that Gottwald and his colleagues had a moderate public programme of winning over the masses, while adhering to a 'secret' plan to enforce one-party rule. No conclusive evidence exists for the latter. An alternative view is that communist oligarchs and intellectuals possessed 'neither a preconceived, preformulated strategy designed to carry them to power nor a complete conception of how the state would look at various stages along the way'.[36] What is more, the entire National Front structure, its principle of cross-party cooperation and the intermediate goals of the 'national democratic revolution' were predicated on the main tenets of Soviet foreign policy at the time, which aimed as far as possible to preserve the Grand Alliance and maintain amicable East–West relations. Why would Gottwald have the temerity to undermine Stalin's strategy by planning a risky coup? It seems more feasible that the party leaders, though undoubtedly having political power in their sights, were uncertain of the path to achieve it and tortuously groped their way towards a mechanism for seizing power as Cold War tensions grew in 1947.

The second problem with 'operation grand deceit' is that it dismisses as a mere ruse the theory of a 'Czechoslovak road to socialism', which from autumn 1946 to summer 1947 lay at the heart of KSČ policy. The idea was inherent in the 'people's democracy' and 'national democratic revolution' strategies of 1943–45, but the immediate catalyst for it was Stalin's recognition in August 1946 of a peaceful 'parliamentary road' to socialism avoiding the bloodshed of the Bolshevik experience. It was then applied to several East European countries, Gottwald first outlining it publicly in a speech in October 1946, in which he talked of a 'new type of democracy' in Czechoslovakia distinct from Russian conditions in 1917.[37] A month earlier at a KSČ Central Committee plenum he had gone further, asserting that 'this path, our path, is our own – special, longer…more roundabout'.[38] This cautious emphasis on a specific, gradual and by implication democratic transition to socialism more attuned to indigenous Czechoslovak political culture and levels of socio-economic development and eschewing overt forms of political repression struck deep chords among the party intelligentsia and many rank-and-file members, even perhaps among some non-communist workers and intellectuals. It was also sufficiently ambiguous to offer hope to the more radical elements in the party who found it difficult to renounce the Comintern heritage of revolutionary activism and devotion to the Soviet prototype. However, the concept of 'national roads' remained fatally ill-defined: what exactly was this 'new type' of democracy in terms of institutions and mentalities? Did the 'Czechoslovak road' simply envisage a different *way* to power or a different *model* of power? Was it merely a parliamentary route to a one-party state?[39] These crucial questions were never adequately explored or resolved, and it appears that ultimately the Stalinised hierarchy of the KSČ was not equipped, theoretically or practically, to articulate a concrete vision of a socialist state that diverged significantly from their preferred option of a 'dictatorship of the proletariat'. And nor after mid-1947 were they permitted to do so by their Soviet overlords.[40]

'The Struggle for the Soul of the Nation'

Bradley Abrams has persuasively argued that a cardinal precondition of the communists' victory in February 1948 was their ability to win the battle over a new conception of the nation, its history and future; or, to be more precise, the Czech nation and its past.[41] In this important insight, communist success was as much cultural as strictly political: they 'won' the hearts and minds of large numbers of people in the towns and villages across the country as much as in the rarefied corridors of power in Prague. Immediately after the war communist intellectuals began to focus on the need for a profound 'revision of the national character' as a means of restoring certainty, belief and a sense of unified purpose to an exhausted, disoriented and radicalised population. In doing so, they strongly implied the communists' commitment to patriotism, the 'nation' and their association with the innate 'progressive' proclivities of the 'people'. Often explicit in this was a pronounced anti-German rhetoric as the Czechoslovak communists, regardless of their Marxist internationalist pretensions, were not averse to exploiting nationalist sentiments and popular animosities harboured over many centuries and massively exacerbated by wartime experiences. The obverse of this approach was an insistence on redemption 'from the East', identifying Slavic brotherhood, the Soviet Union and the 'glorious' Red Army as the guarantors not just of Czechoslovak sovereignty, but of all the smaller Slavic peoples in their historic contest with Germandom and other national oppressors. The future, so it seemed, lay in the East, not least because of the perceived superiority of the Soviet system which had crushed Nazism.

This cultural offensive was an integral component of the party's vision of the 'national democratic revolution', and was summed up by the new Minister of Information, Václav Kopecký, thus: 'our new culture...should be national in form, and in content democratic, from the people, and progressive'.[42] Time and again, the theorists portrayed the communists as the vanguard of the nation, of freedom, democracy, peace and progress. Time and again, they hammered away at the historical links between the present-day communists and the age-old democratic traditions of the Czech people. In this important sense, the communists were able to redefine the national myth of 'inherent' Czech democracy and humanism by charting a direct line of continuity between themselves and the historic symbols and representatives of this 'progressive' political culture: Jan Hus, the White Mountain, the national awakeners of the nineteenth century, even Masaryk. As Zdeněk Nejedlý, the influential communist Minister of Education, put it: 'we truly are the continuers and inheritors of the best and most national strivings and yearnings of the popular layers...of our nation'. In short, the popular understanding of history was partially distorted and made into a 'usable past' for contemporary ideological goals and in the process the picture was convincingly portrayed of the KSČ as a patriotic, even nationalist, party rooted in, and successfully reappropriating, the democratic and radical traditions of the Czech people and remoulding them in a socialist direction. Indeed, this patriotic, and by extension anti-German, essence of the communists, so it was claimed, had been abundantly proven by their sacrifices in the resistance movement which had demonstrated their 'deep love for the nation in the most critical times, at Munich and in the Second World War'.[43]

A remarkable aspect of the communists' cultural onslaught was the virtual hegemonic position that they were able to achieve. None of their erstwhile opponents, with the exception of tenacious Catholic intellectuals in, or close to, the People's Party, successfully articulated an alternative independent vision of the Czech past, present and future. Even renowned democratic literati, such as Ferdinand Peroutka and Václav Černý, were reluctant to dismiss the communist message. This was largely because public discourse on democracy, socialism, national identity and politics in general had experienced an almost seismic shift since Munich.[44] 'Democracy' in post-war Czechoslovakia, as elsewhere, was not an uncontested static concept. It was subject to redefinition and re-elaboration and had different meanings in different contexts. So, in the Czechoslovak conditions of 1938–48, democracy had been partially unchained from its 'old world' liberal parliamentary free market connotations and came to signify a 'socialising democracy' or 'new order', embracing social and welfare reform, economic justice, state intervention for national reconstruction, a prominent role for the working people, and a debourgeoisified and de-Germanised 'national culture', or what the communists called 'people's democracy'. Similarly 'socialism', which was just one, albeit influential, current in pre-war Czechoslovak politics, became the basic framework of post-war political and social activity, creating the moral conditions for a 'harmonious national community' and an 'authentic' way of life, although the concrete meaning of 'socialism' was rarely spelt out.[45] These attitudes, to a greater or lesser extent, prevailed among all Czech and Slovak political parties after 1945, but were most persuasively propagandised by the KSČ which was able to project its vision of a progressive industrial modernity in a nation-state of Czechs and Slovaks. The communist triumph in the May 1946 elections appeared to vindicate this strategy. But why were the non-communists comparatively so weak?

The Non-Communist Dilemma

Ever since the communist takeover, Czechoslovak politics in the period 1945–48 have been conceptualised by the losers as an uneven battle between the adherents of 'democracy' and 'totalitarianism'. Was it not clear that the former – the National Socialists, the People's Party, Social Democrats and the Slovak Democratic Party – were fighting the latter in the name of freedom, parliamentarianism and respect for human and civil rights? Was it not the case that the communists, conspicuously backed by Moscow, consciously deceived the population about their intentions, grossly abused their ministerial portfolios and engaged in the 'politics of the street' while the democrats, left high and dry by a supine West, were meticulously honest and played by the constitutional rules of the game? Were not the communists, regardless of their impressive showing in the 1946 elections, in the minority with their popularity falling even further in 1947–48? In light of the subsequent Stalinisation of the country and the Cold War ruptures of the 1950s and beyond, this rendition appeared palpably obvious, and still today it holds a strong fascination for many Czech and Slovak historians. Indeed, it is not altogether misleading, and two key aspects of it in particular cannot be dismissed: the communists' abuse of power in the ministries under their control, notably the interior (police and security services), and, as we have seen, the party leaders' deliberate ambiguity on whether the 'dictatorship of the proletariat' was their ultimate goal. On neither issue was the KSČ prepared to compromise.

However, the 'democracy versus totalitarianism' dichotomy tends to obscure the complex interrelationships between the parties and oversimplifies the battle lines. For a start, *all* parties essentially concurred over the central components of the Košice Programme and the broad direction of post-war domestic and foreign policy: all agreed on the banning and punishment of 'collaborators', on the violent expulsion and expropriation of the Germans and Magyars, on radical social and land reforms, on the introduction of state planning and the nationalisation of large enterprises, on the 'regulated democracy' of the National Front, and, as we shall see, on the need to limit Slovak autonomy. On the crucial issue of pro-Sovietism as a vital counter-weight to perceived German revanchism there was absolute unanimity.[46] Neither was there anything 'liberal' about much of the rhetoric and actions of the non-communists, including Beneš, when it came to anti-German 'cleansing'. More than this, there was a measure of political trust between the coalition partners, at least until the imminent crises of 1947, and this blurring of the boundary lines tended to disarm citizens in the showdown of February 1948. Rather than the image of endless principled disputes between uncompromising antagonists, as portrayed in the 'democracy against communism' argument, the reality was consensual politics and mutual concessions tempered by intermittent confrontation over specific policies and proposals. Disputes there certainly were, but, outside of the 1946 electoral campaign which was quite bitter, any clashes were generally confined behind closed doors or to the party press. That said, the non-communists were caught in an unenviable dilemma which exposed their comparative weakness: no opposition to the communist-inspired National Front programme could be publicly expressed without undermining the veil of unanimity and collective responsibility. Hence, any criticism that was aired could be convincingly construed as 'oppositional' activity threatening 'national unity' and breaking the political consensus. No party wished to be tarred with this brush.

The limitations on democratic practices and the effective ban on overt clashes of opinion hamstrung the non-communists, especially the National Socialists who were the communists' main rivals and who often criticised specific KSČ policies in the coalition government. However, the National Socialists had very few convincing alternative proposals and their electoral manifesto relied on broad slogans and a Czech nationalist appeal, largely to the urban middle strata. They appear not to have adequately perceived the depth of political and social rethinking in much of society, which meant that their noble conceptions of defending parliamentary democracy failed to rally mass support during the crisis of February 1948. Moreover, the party, while numbering over 600,000 members in early 1948, was sporadically organised and in many communities and factories it had no representation at all.[47] The Catholic People's Party was the only explicitly non-socialist party, but it was badly divided, especially after the May 1946 elections in which it gained less than 16 per cent of the nationwide vote. Thereafter a right-wing rebellion was launched ending in the expulsion of its leader and interminable internal wrangling. Perhaps precisely because the party strongly defended conservative social and religious values and the need for private enterprise and ownership, it was regarded by many as behind the times, even 'reactionary'.

The major difficulty for the Social Democrats was how to carve out a clear separate identity from the communists, not least because as self-proclaimed Marxists they fully endorsed the radical post-war changes and shared a deep commitment to a planned economy and nationalised industry. Like the other non-communist parties, the Social Democrats were devastated by their poor showing in the elections (12 per cent), which was partly the result of the physical loss, and legal disenfranchisement, of very large numbers of Sudeten German workers and activists who had formed an important back-bone of the party in the interwar period. Following the elections, the right and centre demanded that the party leadership under the communist sympathiser, Fierlinger, adopt more independent poli-cies and distance itself from the KSČ. The rifts over this issue were so profound that the party almost split at its congress in November 1947 and in this weakened divided state the Social Democrats proved highly susceptible to communist infiltration.

The pivotal outcome of these inner and intra-party schisms was that, despite the grave doubts that many non-communist politicians privately harboured about communist intentions and the direction of the National Front, they were unable to forge any real sense of cross-party unity until it was too late in 1948, and even then no firm anti-communist united front could be formed. Political, ideological and personal rivalries precluded such solidarity. What is more, this lack of internal cohesion among the three non-communist parties facilitated the communists' 'fellow traveller' campaign which aimed, quite suc-cessfully, to subvert the parties from within by wooing, encouraging and ultimately intimidating pro-KSČ 'leftists', of whom Fierlinger was just one example. Finally, the great hopes that the National Socialists in particular placed on Western intervention and help never materi-alised. Beyond verbal support and somewhat reluctant and belated promises of economic aid, Western officials such as US ambassador to Prague, Laurence Steinhardt, could offer no succour to the non-communists. The West had in reality given up on Czechoslovakia by 1947, perceiving it to be de facto part of the Soviet sphere.[48]

The Consequences of the German Expulsion

At first glance, it is not immediately apparent how the forced resettle-ment and expropriation of almost three million Germans in 1945–46 affected the communist rise to power. Euphemistically referred to by Czechs as a 'transfer', the vast ethnic expulsion was carried out in two stages: the first wave, known as the 'wild transfer' (*divoký odsun*), occurred between May and August 1945 and was accompanied by widespread 'revolutionary' vigilante violence and brutality born of six years of daily humiliation and repression under the Protectorate. In this rampage, 650,000 to 800,000 Sudeten Germans fled or were ejected to what was left of war ruined Germany and Austria. Although the conventional wisdom is that these horrific events were largely spontaneous explosions of pogrom-like fury 'from below', R. M. Douglas in his recent detailed assessment maintains that generally 'the worst atrocities...were perpetrated not by mobs but by troops, police, and others acting under color of authority'.[49] In short, it suited the central and local governments' agenda to remove as many Germans as rapidly as possible. The second phase, ratified by the Big Three at the Potsdam Conference in August 1945, was more organised and better supervised, but nevertheless entailed much unnecessary compulsion, hardship and arbitrariness. Ministry of Interior orders from October 1945 give a flavour of the indiscriminate nature of the early 'organised' expulsions. Local abuses were commonplace, including the banishment of Social Democrats and other 'anti-fascist' Germans and 'harsh actions' even against those who had suffered in Nazi concentration camps.[50] These expulsions to the American zone of occupied Germany lasted until October 1946 and affected approximately 2.2 million people, whose land, property and businesses were confiscated and gradually redistributed.

It is estimated that 19,000 to 30,000 Germans were murdered, mainly in the 'wild transfer', and many more thousands died from disease, exhaustion, hunger and maltreatment in labour camps and on 'death marches', even in 'massacres' such as the one at Ústí nad Labem on 31 July 1945 in which up to 100–150 Germans were killed. By 1947, a mere 170,000 Germans remained in Czechoslovakia, deprived of their rights and doing their best to eke out a meagre existence.[51] The overall result was that the Czech lands became essentially nationally homogeneous and in the country as a whole the proportion of Czechs and Slovaks grew from 64 per cent in 1921 to 94 per cent in 1950.[52] In Slovakia, the planned removal of the substantial Magyar minority was blocked by the Allies, but the Prague and Budapest governments eventually agreed that some 74,000 Hungarians should be exchanged for a roughly equal number of Slovaks resident in Hungary. This left over half a million ethnic Magyars in southern and eastern parts of Slovakia.

The German expulsion was rooted in the highly dubious assumption of 'collective guilt' – 'all Germans are Nazis' – and based on a Czech national consensus that 'only the removal of ethnic minorities could ensure the long-term security of the state'.[53] Only those individuals who could prove their active 'anti-fascist' credentials, were deemed experts or irreplaceable skilled workers or were in mixed marriages could be reprieved, and even these caveats were often ignored. The President himself led the way, issuing a series of so-called 'Beneš Decrees' in the summer of 1945, which legalised the expulsions and deprived Germans of their citizenship and properties. In one speech he insisted: 'we must de-Germanize our republic... names, regions, towns, customs – everything that can possibly be de-Germanized must go'.[54] It was a veritable 'national cleansing' of 'unreliable aliens' couched in the phraseology of 'historic justice' and the need for a 'united national state of Czechs and Slovaks' based on the notion of national-ethnic purity. As such it is difficult to overestimate the political, socio-economic, cultural and psychological effects of these actions, which totally ruptured centuries of Czech–German cohabitation in all their manifold dimensions, or what one senior Czech historian called a 'partnership of conflict'.[55] At a minimum it must be concluded that the violent expulsions, combined with the retribution trials also implemented under the 'Beneš Decrees', which were directed against ex-Nazi officials and their Czech collaborators and enforced with ferocious zeal, contributed to a partial moral breakdown and were used by the communists to eradicate class and ideological 'enemies'. Indeed, in the years 1945–48 in the Czech provinces alone 723 death sentences were pronounced, of which 686 were actually carried out, by some way the highest ratio (95 per cent) in the whole of Europe and, it should be noted, far exceeding the number of judicial executions during the Stalinist terror of 1949–54.[56]

In the short term, the forced deportations opened up vast scope for patronage in that the properties and land of the expelled were redistributed to over 1.5 million mainly Czech, but also some Slovak and Magyar, 'new settlers', most of whom were from deprived backgrounds and therefore perhaps disproportionately susceptible to the communists' egalitarian and nationalist rhetoric. Initially, these opportunities for loot, housing stock and land were bagged by thousands of 'gold diggers' and profiteers, but they were soon brought under the administration of the communist-run Ministries of Agriculture and Interior and the Settlement Office, and it is here that we can detect a clear correlation between the expulsions and growing communist popularity. It is well known that the percentage of votes cast for the KSČ in the resettled borderlands in the May 1946 parliamentary elections was substantially higher than the national average. In the north Bohemian electoral districts of Ústí nad Labem, Karlovy Vary and Liberec the party gained 56.4, 53.6 and 48.3 per cent respectively while nationally it won 38 per cent.[57] In some towns and localities the proportion was higher still. Communist leverage and largesse, resulting in upward social mobility and economic advancement for very large numbers of under-privileged Czechs, had evidently worked.

But the forced deportations meant far more than this tangible, even cynical, causal interrelationship. They left a demographic vacuum of huge proportions, a highly industrialised and fertile region denuded of skilled labour, 'bourgeois' entrepreneurs, traders, merchants and expert farmers, all of whom had to be replaced. In sum, they changed the social, ethnic and class composition of the country and in the process created the perfect laboratory, a virtual *tabula rasa*, for a major state-planned social transformatory experiment: the construction of a new 'socialist modernity'. As Eagle Glassheim has brilliantly argued, 'the general thrust of Communist policy for the region, above all the promotion of a rationalized, modern, labor-friendly industrial and agricultural identity', struck deep chords among the new incomers many of whom enthusiastically embraced the communists' manufacture of a strong productivist regional character and pride, while materially benefiting from local communist patronage and pro-labour policies. Among the latter were organisational measures 'offering the disoriented settlers the solidarity of unions, political clubs, and agricultural societies' and pithy class-based gestures such as 'opening the great spas of [the region]...to workers...with the once-animated elite social scene yielding to a populist and utilitarian focus on the health of laborers'.[58] It appeared that the endlessly repeated communist mantra of 'we are building a new democratic order' in the interests of the common people was actually grounded in reality. At least it seemed so in parts of Bohemia and Moravia. But what was happening in Slovakia in these critical years?

The Slovak Question

Conditions in post-war Slovakia stood in marked contrast to the Czech lands in important ways. The Slovak Communist Party was weaker, the Democratic Party, an ill-assorted amalgam of Protestant and Catholic politicians and resistance fighters, was stronger. Religion, in the form of political Catholicism, was popularly embedded and influential. The economy was less industrialised, the working class less numerous and the Magyar minority, not the German, was the prime internal 'enemy'. Slovak politics was also overshadowed by two massively complex interlinked phenomena: on the one hand, the legacy of the wartime authoritarian collaborationist Slovak clerical state and the domestic resistance movement, and on the other, the convoluted post-war constitutional arrangements and tensions between the authorities in Bratislava, the Slovak capital, and the centralised government in Prague. An intractable question haunted Czech–Slovak relations at all levels: how much autonomy, if any, should the Slovaks be granted while maintaining a functional, united and defensible state? This fundamental issue, which divided Czech and Slovak communists as much as non-communists and sundered the two communities in general, was never satisfactorily mediated throughout the transition years 1945–48, continued to rumble just below the surface for the entire period of communist rule and was only 'solved' on 1 January 1993 with the creation of two separate entities, the Czech and Slovak Republics.

In December 1943, an underground Slovak National Council (*Slovenská národná rada* – SNR) was jointly established by communist and non-communist political leaders as the organisational focal point of the resistance movement against the nominally independent, but pro-German, Slovak clerical regime led by Father Jozef Tiso. The climax of the SNR's resistance was the mass National Uprising of August–October 1944, which, although brutally crushed by superior Nazi forces, was a hugely significant moral and political statement strengthening elite and popular demands for post-war Slovak autonomy within a reconstituted Czechoslovak state, and also acting as a symbol of Czech–Slovak rehabilitation and reunification. The heightened sense of national self-affirmation even affected the formally 'internationalist' home-based Slovak communists such as Gustáv Husák. In its maximal guise, it was a federalist desire that clashed unequivocally with the centralist beliefs of Beneš's government-in-exile. Therefore, after tough negotiations between communist and non-communist Czech and Slovak political representatives a compromise was worked out as part of the Košice Programme, whereby the new republic 'officially recognised the existence of separate Czech and Slovak nations, each with its own separate language, and promised sweeping autonomy to Slovakia'. From now on, Czech–Slovak relations would be 'equal with equal'. Gottwald called it, with a fair degree of exaggeration, the Slovak 'Magna Carta'. The SNR and its executive branch, the Board of Commissioners, both of which had equal Communist and Democratic Party representation, were to form the basis of post-war Slovak government and self-administration.[59] The agreement was essentially a victory for the Slovak autonomists, but it was successively whittled down in the face of harsh political realities.

The most important of these was the election triumph of the Democratic Party in May 1946. It gained a huge 62 per cent of the vote to the communists' 30 per cent, a result which assured the Democrats a dominant position in the SNR and which was to have long-lasting repercussions. Whereas before the election, Slovak communists and Democrats had collaborated relatively well in government, thereafter the KSS decided, in concord with the Czech communists, that as power in Slovakia had shifted into the hands of the 'reactionaries' it was necessary to launch a campaign to undermine the Democratic Party and its Catholic affiliates, some of whom were former adherents of the wartime Slovak clerical state. In light of the growing cooperation between the Democrats and political Catholicism, the non-communist Czech parties also wished to see the authority of the Slovak national organs reduced, fearing potential 'dualism' as a threat to state unity and an indication of a maturing 'Slovak problem'. This tentative cross-party alliance culminated in the so-called Third Prague Agreement signed on 28 June 1946 by all six Czech and Slovak parties, including, reluctantly, the Democrats. Under its terms, the jurisdiction of the SNR was severely restricted and the Board of Commissioners was effectively subordinated to the central government. The KSS leaders in Bratislava, who had not entirely renounced their zeal for self-rule, apparently believed this was a temporary arrangement that would be annulled after the installation of a future communist government. It turned out to be permanent. A key reason for this was that the Slovak communists were split between 'centralists', such as Viliam Široký and Július Ďuriš, who were closer to Gottwald and other Czech party leaders in Prague, and more nationally inclined figures like Husák, Ladislav Novomeský and Karol Šmidke, who remained in Bratislava and, while loyal communists, were better attuned to the intricacies of Slovak politics and popular sentiment. Relations between the two factions were poor and it is fair to say that the eventual rise to pre-eminence of the former spelt the death-knell for the communist proponents of Slovak autonomy.

Regardless of these internal disputes, in the course of 1947 the communists intensified their campaign against the Democratic Party and by autumn there was a full-scale crisis in Slovakia, a component of the bitter political power struggles that preceded the KSČ triumph. The crux of the KSS attack was that the Democratic Party, so it was alleged by the communist-controlled security services, had ties to organisations led by supporters of the war-time Slovak 'clerico-fascist' state who, by definition, represented a threat to the integrity of the republic. Hence, there should be a purge of Slovak public administration, including several top Democratic Party functionaries. The trial of the Slovak state's President, Father Tiso, which galvanised the whole country from December 1946 to April 1947, afforded a prime opportunity to strike at the unity of the Democrats. By insisting on the death penalty and Tiso's execution on two counts of treason, the communists believed they could engineer a split in the Democratic Party, whose leaders had agreed with Catholic politicians that Tiso would be given a light sentence. The failure to achieve this would, it was believed, force the Catholics to create their own party, one that was possibly more amenable to communist pressure and solicitation than the intransigent Democrats. In the event, Tiso's controversial execution on 18 April 1947 did not compel a rupture in the Democratic Party, whereupon Slovakia drifted into a series of political intrigues, accusations and counter-accusations. These culminated in the 'Slovak conspiracy' of autumn 1947 in which the security services essentially fabricated an anti-republic underground plot involving leading Democratic Party politicians, one of whom, though innocent, was forced to resign. The intermediate result was a reconfiguring of the composition of the Slovak governing bodies so that no one party had a majority. The definitive outcome was Husák's dismissal of all non-communist ministers on 21 February 1948.

The View 'From Below': The Labour and Women's Movements

One of the great under-explored mysteries of the communists' road to power is that while successive generations of historians have noted the mass nature of the KSČ – over 1.2 million members by spring 1947 – they have written very little about the activity, views and motivations of these 'ordinary' people. It is as if they were mere automata manipulated by the party executive in Prague without any real human agency to shape their own destinies. Indeed, till today this crucial micro-history is largely terra incognita and several fundamental questions remain unanswered. What did it mean to be a 'mass party' and what did the influx of new KSČ members in 1945–46 signify for party policies, ideology and discipline? Were the recruits more 'revolutionary' than the party leadership in the early post-war period pushing the party to the 'left', or were they largely apolitical 'opportunists' diluting the party's commitment to Marxism–Leninism? How, if at all, did rank-and-file members influence the strategies and tactics of the top brass and, finally, what role did the 'people' play in the dramatic 'February Days' and the seizure of power, not just in Prague but in other towns and villages? That said, we can attempt to examine the impact of the working class in the trade union and factory council movements and how the communists sought to channel these officially independent labour organisations; the degree to which the KSČ was able to penetrate everyday working-class life and local administration; and, finally, the less successful communist stance on the long-debated 'woman question'.

At the end of the war, labour leaders and many workers themselves expressed a fierce desire for unity to reconstruct the nation and state on new foundations.[60] Organisationally, this sense of solidarity manifested itself in the creation of a single 'Revolutionary Trade Union Movement' (*Revoluční odborové hnutí* – ROH) to be led by a Central Trade Union Council (*Ústřední rada odborů* – ÚRO). The early post-war weeks and months also saw the establishment in large numbers of enterprises of extremely powerful factory councils (*závodní rady*), the prime tasks of which were to represent the interests of the workforce, oversee renewal of production and purge workplaces of 'collaborators' and discredited officials, especially in former German-owned plants. These spontaneous developments reflected the revolutionary élan of many workers and were initially beyond the control of any political party. The relationship between the burgeoning factory councils and trade unions was never adequately addressed, but it was the firm belief of the communists that the latter should be superior to the former, and that both should be subordinate to the economic and production goals of the new National Front government. This meant, in essence, bringing the factory councils and unions under KSČ control in line with the Stalinist notion of labour organisations as 'transmission belts' for party directives. In practice this entailed overcoming syndicalist tendencies, limiting the independent powers of the factory councils, and centralising and bureaucratising the unions. This process was in part enabled by the predominance of communist trade unionists in ÚRO, notably the experienced Antonín Zápotocký, who was elected its chair on 7 June 1945, and by communist leadership of the main unions such as the miners and metalworkers. Indeed, the history of working-class institutions in the years 1945–48 shows the incremental hegemony, many would say manipulation, of the KSČ so that by the time of the February crisis the party leaders could rely on mass displays of organised, almost ritualised, support.

However, this image of cynical communist manipulation is not quite the full picture. The KSČ was the most organised and disciplined party, it espoused clear, decisive and in many ways moderate policies on labour and economic issues, while the Social Democrats, who were to the 'left' of the communists in their demands for the wide-scale nationalisation of industry, and the National Socialists proved largely incapable of elaborating coherent alternative proposals, more often than not deferring to communist union leaders. The communists also enjoyed a near hegemonic role in crucial industrial areas, such as 'Red Kladno', and powerful positions in the Ostrava-Karviná steel and coal belt, even in the traditional Social Democratic stronghold of Plzeň.[61] But more than this, as Lenka Kalinová has demonstrated, the KSČ, through its dominance in the trade union movement and at the factory level, sponsored cultural, sporting and educational activities for workers creating a rich collective social life. For example, by the end of 1946 over 1,500 factory clubs were in existence arranging hundreds of stage and film performances, organising trips to cinemas and theatres, distributing free tickets to employees and setting up amateur theatre, musical, sporting and physical training events in which large numbers of workers participated. Young worker-members of the Union of Youth spent much of their free time on 'brigades', and unions established so-called 'schools of labour' offering specialist tuition for thousands of functionaries. In helping to develop these cultural, sporting and educational opportunities, the communists were in part able to harness the post-war optimistic moods and satisfy common strivings for a better existence after the suffering, fear and poverty of the war.[62] In short, it can be argued that the KSČ successfully engaged in the 'politics of the everyday', forging an embedded working-class culture and powerful sense of identity. To this extent, it was a mass party not only in terms of membership, but also in that it penetrated, and not always in negative ways, the lives of millions of 'ordinary' people. The benefits were reaped in February 1948.

The communists also took pains to influence and direct the daily administration of local, district and regional government. The key institutions here were the National Committees (národní výbory) which on communist insistence were created throughout the country in the immediate aftermath of the war as popular democratic bodies responsible for a very wide range of social, welfare and security activities, including the purging of Germans and 'collaborators' from the public services. Originally conceived on a parity basis among the political parties, these organisations were relatively soon dominated by the communists, who by May 1946 had 46.6 per cent of local Czech National Committee chairmen in their ranks.[63] The internal organisational structure of the KSČ was likewise designed to be democratic with a network of regional, district and basic branches in factories and localities where ten-member sub-groups were envisaged as 'a two-way channel of communication between the leadership and the members' enabling rapid mobilisation of the entire party.[64] Broad internal party discussions on key issues, such as the 'Czechoslovak road to socialism', also offered ordinary members the opportunity to air their views, doubts and grievances. However, in practice, as in all communist parties, the higher organs tended to dictate to the lower and there was a strong emphasis on party discipline and Leninist 'centralism'. One reason for this was that many new recruits had either transferred from other parties, were unschooled in Marxism or were outright careerists. Indeed, in the second half of 1947 the party executive noted a growth in passivity among members and a lack of experienced political organisers.[65] It remains speculation, but in these circumstances the temptation to trust in the 'leading core' and use the mass of members as political ballast and muscle must have been very strong.

It is interesting that the communists were far less dominant in the Czech women's movement.[66] Women had played an important role in the domestic and foreign resistance during the war and entered the workforce in very large numbers. Partly in recognition of this, all parties in the National Front government proclaimed their commitment to the extension of women's rights and vied actively for the female vote. The Košice Programme offered the prospect of broad gender equality and spoke explicitly of equal pay for equal work, a radical provision that was indeed enacted in July 1945 but rarely implemented in practice. The communists, like the Social Democrats, emphasised productive labour as the source of genuine female emancipation and promised to ease women's lives by material improvements and socialised child care. The National Socialists and People's Party, while accepting the importance of women in 'building the new republic', attempted to chart a middle course and were keen to uphold more traditional values on marriage, motherhood and the family.

Although the KSČ was able to recruit impressive numbers of women into its ranks, particularly in the main urban areas, so that by 1947 there were almost 450,000 female members, it came up against two prime obstacles in its efforts to influence the women's movement. The first was the latter's organisational diversity, and the second was the spirited stance of non-communist activists, such as the National Socialists Milada Horáková and Františka Zemínová, who were often more resilient and vocal in their opposition to communist encroachments than their male counterparts. Unlike the trade unions, there was no single women's movement. Instead, several competing bodies sought the right to speak for women – the National Women's Front (NWF), the Council of Czechoslovak Women (CCW), the Women's

Commission of the ROH and even the United Union of Czech Farmers. Relations between, and within, these organisations were often extremely tense and female communist leaders found it very difficult to impose their agendas, especially in the NWF and CCW led by Horáková. This had to wait till after the February takeover when a united Union of Czechoslovak Women was created under KSČ auspices.

The Seizure of Power

In January 1947, seven months after their electoral triumph, the communists announced that their strategic goal was to gain an outright majority of 51 per cent in the next polls scheduled for May 1948. This was significant in two ways. First, it appeared that the KSČ leadership was continuing its parliamentary 'Czechoslovak road to socialism', but, second, it proved highly divisive for the party's political partners, including the Social Democrats, who jumped on the contradiction 'between the aim of electorally defeating all rivals and the aim of establishing close cooperation between parties' in the National Front.[67] The central component of Gottwald's new government, the Two-Year Plan for the economy designed to restore, or even slightly surpass, pre-war production levels starting in early 1947, also caused ructions in the coalition. The National Socialists and the People's Party were ideologically equivocal about state intervention in the economy and the dangers of 'totalitarian monopolisation' in the nationalised industries, and sought to maintain a balance between state, cooperative and private enterprise, which the plan basically accepted. Hence, the overall atmosphere between the two camps, communist and non-communist, and to a certain extent in society at large was gradually becoming more tense and conflictual, although it seems prudent to argue that none of the parties wished to disrupt the National Front and none possessed a clear vision of how to achieve their aims. Each responded to events as they arose which tended to preclude cast-iron political plans.

All commentators agree, however, that from mid-1947 and the onset of the Cold War these antagonisms hardened into a full-fledged political battle. The will for compromise dissipated, moderate voices were sidelined and from August–September onwards, as crisis followed crisis, the KSČ and the National Socialists consciously engaged in an increasingly bitter and raw campaign for political power. Activists in both parties, radicalised by rapidly worsening internal and external political and socio-economic conditions, were genuinely fearful that each side, backed by foreign allies, was striving to alter fundamentally the direction of Czechoslovak political life. Communists became convinced that ubiquitous 'reactionaries' among the National Socialists, the People's Party and the Slovak Democratic Party were in league with 'American imperialists' and were seeking to create an anti-communist 'bloc', smash the coalition, reverse the achievements of the 'national democratic revolution' and restore the 'old' capitalist system. The non-communists believed that Gottwald and his colleagues had turned into puppets of the Kremlin, had never renounced their goal of a one-party monopoly and thus were endeavouring to usher in Soviet-style 'totalitarianism', a term that was used more and more often. Even the Social Democrats began to speak of 'communist terror'. We do not need to discuss in any detail all the various sites of contention between the two protagonists – they included controversial communist policies like the millionaires' tax to overcome the gross food supply and other economic difficulties which hit the country in summer 1947; the 'Slovak conspiracy'; determined efforts to organise and finance pro-KSČ 'left-wing fractions' and informers in rival parties; the attempted assassination of three non-communist ministers by parcel bomb; and the mass mobilisation of public opinion through the trade union, factory council and peasant movements behind an extension of nationalisation, social security provision and land reform. Such extra-parliamentary pressure was abhorred by the non-communists.[68]

Historians agree that the origins of these sharp struggles lay primarily in the stiffening resolve of Stalin to consolidate his grip on Central and Eastern Europe, but the precise role of the Soviet authorities, both in the autumn crises and more controversially in the February events, remains a mystery. Neither is there clarity on the overall direction and thinking of key actors, let alone the mass of citizens. However, Martin Myant has recently constructed a forceful argument on KSČ perspectives which is worth citing at length:

> it is difficult to speak of a single communist strategy in late 1947 and early 1948. There were distinct, but overlapping, conceptions of the exact aim and of how to achieve it. One approach [Gottwald's] focused on elections, but increasingly sought means to influence their outcome, at least to ensure communist dominance. Others [Ďuriš] sought to use some of the same means to transform the power structure without regard to elections and that meant more decisively eliminating other political forces from any chance of sharing power.

The most radical options came from elements in the communist-controlled police and security forces, who wanted 'to settle matters quickly with a putsch'.[69] There were militant moods, too, among lower-level regional and district party functionaries. The party was not a complete monolith: more flexible approaches continued to circulate, but they were increasingly eschewed in favour of harder-line alternatives.

The cabinet crisis that resulted in the communist takeover was precipitated by the decision of Václav Nosek, the communist Minister of the Interior, on 12 February 1948 to suspend eight non-communist security police commissioners and replace them with communists. The National Socialist, People's Party and Democratic Party members of government regarded this as the last in a long line of abuses of power by communist ministers which could no longer be tolerated. Therefore, they demanded the reinstatement of the eight dismissed police officials. The communists prevaricated, Nosek claiming to be ill, whereupon after extremely heated exchanges in cabinet 12 non-communist ministers resigned on 20 February having consulted with President Beneš two days before.[70] They were given the impression that the President would refuse to accept their resignations and call elections. The confused situation was further complicated by the unannounced arrival in Prague on 19 February of the Soviet Deputy Foreign Minister, Zorin, and the US ambassador, Steinhardt. Much speculation has surrounded Zorin's visit and even with the opening of relevant archives the motives and consequences of his trip are obscure. According to documents in the Soviet Foreign Ministry archive, he told Gottwald 'to be harder' in the push for power, 'not to give in to the right-wingers' and to overcome his 'parliamentary illusions'. There is no evidence that Zorin offered Soviet military assistance, though Gottwald may have requested this. Whatever the case, on 22 February Molotov informed Zorin by telegram that 'we consider as unsuitable' any movement of Red Army troops in Germany and Austria towards the Czechoslovak borders. Nevertheless, the potential Soviet threat remained hanging, a fact Gottwald apparently brought to Beneš's attention.[71]

The unexpected resignations momentarily caught the communist leaders unawares, but they very soon responded with an all-out mobilisation of their supporters in the trade union, factory council and peasant movements. Congresses of these communist-dominated bodies, which had been arranged for weeks, hastily adopted thousands of resolutions demanding that the cabinet proposed by Gottwald should be ratified by the President. On 21 February and thereafter, huge street demonstrations in all the major cities and towns were organised to back up the calls. A one-hour general strike of over 2.5 million workers took place on 24 February. A People's Militia was formed of armed communist industrial workers. Non-communist ministers were debarred from their offices by essentially illegal 'Action Committees'. The first arrests and 'cleansing' of 'class enemies' began, sometimes spontaneously at the local level. Unbelievably, the National Socialists did virtually nothing to influence the course of events, some ministers even retiring to the tranquillity of their country homes outside Prague. The best the democrats could muster was a march of a few hundred students to Beneš's residence. After six days of anguished delibera-tion, the aged and ill president finally accepted the resignations and signed Gottwald's proposal for a new hand-picked government. He surely knew it was a fateful decision.

Chapter 3:   Stalinism Reigns, 1948–53

In the months and years immediately after the February takeover, the Czechoslovak communists embarked on their prime goal of 'constructing socialism'. The burning political task was to consolidate and extend the party's monopoly of power and the mandatory model was a Soviet-style de facto one-party dictatorship: in short, Stalinism. A pivotal component of this intense drive was the coercion of 'class enemies'. To this end, state-led repression was unleashed by late 1948 and lasted until well after Stalin's death in March 1953. Many tens of thousands of Czechs and Slovaks were persecuted and imprisoned in labour camps and top-ranking communists and non-communists were arrested and executed after infamous sham show trials. The emerging Cold War, ingrained fears of a resurgent US-sponsored German revanchism, and even belief in the 'inevitability' of a Third World War imparted a clear, albeit grossly distorted, ideological imperative to Stalinist terror: the 'construction of socialism' had to be as rapid as possible and this required the removal of all 'aliens' and 'anti-socialist elements', who by definition were suspected of allying with the 'imperialist war-mongering' West. In this menacing atmosphere, political pluralism and the rule of law were effectively renounced as 'bourgeois' institutions and power was concentrated in the hands of the few men (never women) who composed the Communist Party's Presidium, or Politburo. Private enterprise and ownership of the means of production were virtually eliminated; the nationalisation of heavy industry, begun after 1945, was expanded; the economy was placed on a war-footing; and agriculture was subject to recurrent collectivisation campaigns. Finally, a leadership cult was created around Gottwald to bind the 'nation' together, and intellectual and artistic life was constrained by the theory and practice of 'socialist realism'.

Emphasis on the terroristic and undemocratic essence of the state, however, should not obscure the fact that Czechoslovak Stalinism was a contradictory political, economic and socio-cultural phenomenon which elicited divergent and hybrid responses not only from different social strata, but also often *within* individuals. On the one hand, the swift steps towards a one-party state, the growth of a seemingly omnipotent secret police, the rise of bloated bureaucracies, the Soviet-inspired 'militarisation' of the economy, the repression visited on many 'ordinary' citizens and the draconian labour discipline undoubtedly contributed to embedded alienation and resentment. Similarly, the sustained efforts to collectivise agriculture embittered the majority of farmers, especially the more prosperous. Indeed, poor socio-economic conditions continued to be at the heart of popular discontent with the system, and this malaise signified for many workers, and one suspects some lower-level party and trade union functionaries, that government policies were failing and in need of reform.

On the other hand, important components of communist strategy, such as large-scale nationalisation of industry, security of employment, a highly egalitarian wage structure, extended social benefits and 'democratised' educational and cultural opportunities facilitated a fragile bond between worker and regime based on the strident 'class perspective' that pervaded Stalinist rhetoric. This 'bridge' linking state and society was reinforced by the manipulation of ritualised public discourse and terminology. Upward social mobility for hitherto disadvantaged groups was a particularly noteworthy aspect of 'Stalinisation' with hundreds of thousands of 'traditional' workers moving into non-manual administrative jobs to be replaced by even more 'new' workers from largely non-proletarian backgrounds. It seems reasonable to conclude that these beneficiaries of the system formed a solid, if not permanent, social base of support for the regime.

That said, most scholars agree that after 1948 the Stalinist command model of socialism was imposed on a Czech and Slovak society whose political culture was perceived to be essentially democratic, pluralist and humanist. But how far did Stalinism represent a sharp rupture with dominant past practices? By what means did the new communist government consolidate its monopoly rule? What were the origins and processes of Stalinist terror in Czechoslovakia, and how did the population respond to state repression? Why did most citizens conform to 'imported' political values and policies? What role did cultural politics play in the 'struggle for socialism'? What did it mean to live and work under Stalinism? What was the extent of 'resistance' and how far was it politicised? How can we best conceptualise state–society relations in Stalinist Czechoslovakia and begin to analyse the nature and meaning of popular opinion? These are among the key questions to be explored in this chapter.

Elite Purges and Mass Repression

Between 1948 and 1954, Czechoslovak society was subjected to multiple forms of repression by the newly installed communist regime. No stratum of society escaped the depredations. Ever since, experts have attempted to explain the origins, processes and outcomes of these deeply troubling events. A recurrent question haunts historical scholarship and indeed the Czech and Slovak collective consciousness: why did political violence on this scale take place in a country with the democratic credentials of Czechoslovakia? Does the comforting answer lie in external pressures exerted most obviously by Stalin and the Soviet political and secret police hierarchies? Or was there a disconcerting internal determinant at play, sometimes referred to as 'indigenous Stalinism'? Or were the broader geopolitical conflicts and constraints of the emerging Cold War more relevant? Other no less intractable issues abound. Who were the prime targets? By what mechanisms were the repressions actually carried out, and who organised them? What was the political impact and longer-term significance of the Stalinist terror? Most intriguingly perhaps, what was the popular reaction to the purges, particularly of leading communists such as Rudolf Slánský, who was condemned to death in November 1952 on trumped-up charges?

Origins: Exogenous and Indigenous Factors

The generic term 'Stalinist terror' is often used to describe the process of state-led violence in communist regimes. Specifically, it refers to the murderous elite purges and mass repressions that engulfed Soviet officialdom and society in the late 1930s and beyond, and is intimately associated with the aims and policies of the Soviet dictator, Josef Stalin. Many of the methods and mechanisms perfected in Stalinist Russia in the 1930s – a pervasive secret police service, sham show trials, forced labour camps, deportations of peoples, state propaganda campaigns – were transposed to the infant communist regimes in Eastern Europe after the Second World War, culminating in the persecutions of the late 1940s and early 1950s.[1] Fundamentally, 'Stalinist terror' denotes the conscious attempt by communist leaderships to crush civil society and its autonomous institutions. The overall aim, even if not always fully achieved, was to entrench the parties' monopoly of power by eliminating alternative independent sources of authority and allegiance, notably opposition groupings, class networks, military cliques and the organised churches.

The origins of these violent campaigns lie in a complex combination of externally generated longer and shorter-term pressures and deep-seated indigenous social and ethnic conflict exacerbated by war, foreign occupation and post-war fears and retributions. I will examine the former first. A key question here is: how can we begin to understand the collective psychology of communist leaders who implemented, rationalised and justified what we term 'terror' and 'mass repression', but which they called 'class justice' and the elimination of 'enemies'? First, the process of the 'Stalinisation' of communist parties, initiated by the Comintern from the mid-to-late 1920s, signalled an unswerving commitment to, and ultimate dependence on, Moscow in terms of party strategy, selection of leadership cadres and financial backing. Second, emergent Stalinism exacerbated the communists' almost hermetic way of life and their self-identification as 'outsiders'. The Stalinist project demanded that comrades 'work on themselves' to internalise the values of total party loyalty and Bolshevik self-sacrifice and 'vigilance', and to expunge deviant 'bourgeois individualistic' thoughts and actions. Crucially, this 'hermeneutics of the soul' inculcated a mental landscape of criticism, self-criticism and conspiracy in which 'enemies', both within and without, were deemed ubiquitous. Stalin's terror of the late 1930s immeasurably strengthened such attitudes.[2] To the extent that this mindset was appropriated by East European communists, particularly those who had lived in exile in the Soviet Union such as Gottwald and Slánský, its persistence helps to explain the events of the late 1940s and early 1950s. Finally, it may well be obvious, but it is worth stressing nonetheless, that communists were not liberals – they were Marxist revolutionaries who were intent on rapidly reforging the world and this necessarily entailed recourse to coercion.

These long-standing external factors were compounded by shorter-term exogenous catalysts. Here, it is tempting to see a monolithic hand at play: Stalin and the Soviet political and secret police bosses carefully orchestrating the purges in order to 'Sovietise' the country, remove all 'Titoist', 'bourgeois nationalist' and 'Zionist' conspiracies and challenges to the infant 'socialist camp', and thus secure the international and ideological position of the USSR in the dangerous uncharted waters of the Cold War. Tito's defiant attitude towards Soviet strictures was particularly alarming, threatening as it did the Kremlin's dominance of the embryonic communist systems throughout the region. These goals were given added urgency in Czechoslovakia's case by its exposed geopolitical location at the frontline of East–West frictions and intrigues. To be sure, such analyses are well-founded and, at one level, highly persuasive. Stalin's actions were undoubtedly informed by the darkening international conjuncture and the belief that war between socialism and capitalism was inevitable. It should also be recognised that Western and émigré spies really did exist and attempted to recruit agents in Czechoslovakia, compounding communist fears and insecurities. Therefore, society needed to be 'protected', mobilised and prepared for the decisive battles ahead and the political trials of 'renegade' communists and 'anti-state' oppositionists were an indispensable method of inculcating uniformity and passivity among potentially unruly Soviet bloc allies.

Moreover, Stalin's pet theory that the class struggle would heighten and 'bourgeois' resistance intensify as socialism approached provided the ideological underpinnings of terror by exposing the machinations of the 'class enemy' as the root of all problems. Hence, 'class justice' had to be applied, meaning that farmers, businessmen and artisans opposed to communist economic policies were perennial regime targets. For instance, kulaks (an imported Russian word signifying better-off peasants) were systematically harried, just like they were in the Soviet Union, as a means of redistributing their wealth and property for the benefit of state-directed industrialisation programmes. And there were other perceived economic benefits to be derived from the use of terror, not least in the form of forced labour extracted in the numerous camps established in all of the new socialist dictatorships. Another factor was the attempt to identify scapegoats for economic and political failures, or to mobilise supporters of communist regimes against 'spies' and 'class enemies'. Stalin's suspicion of communists who had spent the 1930s and early 1940s in exile in the West, who had fought in the Spanish Civil War, or who had been in Nazi concentration camps, also contributed to the search for 'enemies'. Finally, with or without Soviet involvement, there were inevitably local power struggles and personal score-settling going on among party, state, economic and cultural elites.

It is also often affirmed that Stalin's increasingly anti-Semitic tendencies in the last years of his life, associated with crass 'anti-cosmopolitanism' and the notorious 'Doctors' Plot', impacted on Czechoslovak and wider bloc developments. Indeed, such sentiments were given full reign in the late 1940s and early 1950s when the KSČ unleashed a vicious 'anti-Zionist' campaign dutifully following Stalin's shift to a pro-Arab and anti-Israeli foreign policy. This drive effectively degenerated into an anti-Semitic onslaught most grossly manifested in the Slánský trial in which 11 of the 14 defendants were officially designated 'of Jewish origin'. There is little doubt, then, that the Soviet dictator bears ultimate responsibility for the repressive campaigns in Czechoslovakia and elsewhere, though his exact role is almost impossible to verify, subject as he was to vacillation, obfuscation and tactical change.

The bottom line, however, was Stalin's *Realpolitik* and never-ending quest for Soviet state security. As ever, domestic developments in the countries of Eastern Europe in these years can never be divorced from wider international relations. As the Cold War intensified from 1947 and the Stalin–Tito split in 1948 opened up fractures in the Soviet bloc, the imperative for near monolithic homogeneity became ever more urgent in the Kremlin – unity meant strength. This, in turn, demanded an assault on omnipresent 'class enemies', 'spies', 'saboteurs' and 'traitors' within and outside communist ranks. These 'enemies' were identified primarily on 'traditional' Soviet lines: kulaks, priests, private entrepreneurs, anti-communist 'terrorists', 'Mensheviks' (Social Democrats), *ancien régime* military, police, judicial and state officials. But these actions were not simply vindictive and arbitrary campaigns aimed at bolstering the cohesion of state and society in dangerous times. For the Stalinists were motivated by an *idée fixe*: prophylactic strikes against multifarious 'anti-social elements' would 'purify' society and lay the class foundations for the overriding task of 'constructing socialism', as they understood it. In this sense, a distorted Marxist ideological utopianism underlay mass repression and it is clear that many communists, particularly at a leadership level, regarded political violence as the sharp end of class war and as an indispensable weapon in the struggle for the 'radiant future' purged of 'alien dross'.

However, regardless of the explanatory potency of this exogenous interpretation, it is in my opinion inadequate. Even if we accept that the purges were initiated and coordinated in Moscow, they often fell on fertile soils, were adapted for domestic purposes and were not always amenable to strict party control 'from above'. In the specific case of Czechoslovakia, we have seen the immense relevance of the Munich 'betrayal', Nazi occupation, wartime horrors and particularly the widespread post-war retributions and cleansing of the Sudeten Germans, all of which made plausible the notion of the 'enemy within' and engendered pressures 'from below' for restrictive practices. Internal tensions and conflicts could be, and were, used to 'solve' power struggles, organisational rivalries and personal jealousies among the Czechoslovak political and cultural elites, target class and in some instances ethnic 'enemies', identify scapegoats for the gross economic and material hardships, serve as a reservoir of forced labour for developmental and military goals, and act as propaganda and educative tools for the masses. Coercive policies emerged initially as a response to the sense of crisis that afflicted the regime as early as the autumn of 1948, the origin of which was the failure to satisfy unrealistic economic targets and aspirations. Ultimately, however, mass repression had a direct political goal based on an ideological imperative steeped in Stalinist brutality: to bolster the legitimacy of the infant communist state by declaring a 'class war' on the 'bourgeois', 'impure' and 'socially harmful elements' who stood in the way of the communist project.

In sum, repression was closely related to the intense drive of the new rulers to 'construct socialism'. The unpalatable truth is that many Czech and Slovak communists, from all ranks of the party, condoned this violent campaign; some actively participated in it. Prime responsibility for the carnage most assuredly resides with the leading cohort, but it is hard to avoid the conclusion that many lower-level functionaries and ordinary members, and not a few non-communist citizens, were complicit by their 'silence', illiberal attitudes and tacit consent. Indeed, the social acceptance of political and ethnic violence after 1945 helped to lay the foundations for Stalinism. In the controversial words of the Czech writer, Dušan Hamšík: 'we are all collectively responsible for the political trials – the nation as a whole, as a continuum'.[3]

Processes and Mechanisms

The immediate political goal for the KSČ after the 'victorious February' was to consolidate its power. To this end, within a few months approximately 28,000 employees were removed from state and public administration, including in the army, secret services and judiciary. Leading non-communist officials, especially National Socialists and Slovak Democrats, were summarily dismissed, their parties infiltrated and effectively decimated, by communist-dominated

'Action Committees' which were given the power to purge mass organisations regardless of normal legal procedure. Economic and cultural institutions were also targeted. Dozens of university professors were dismissed, as were many students, who tended to be most vocal in their opposition to the infant regime. Many National Committees, the organs of local and municipal government, were purged of non-communists or disbanded. As early as March, April and May 1948, 'espionage' trials were held of high-ranking National Socialists and Slovak Democrats. Less violently, the Social Democrats were politically emasculated by a merger with the KSČ in June 1948, by which time Czechoslovakia had become in essence, if not formally, a one-party state.[4] In the following months and years, persecution affected all sections of society: communists, non-communists and anti-communists, Czechs and Slovaks, men and women, young and old, urban and rural. Numerically, it is still impossible to arrive at precise overall figures as the term 'repression' covers a wide variety of meanings and measures: non-judicial murder, judicial execution, detention in labour camps or prison, enforced military service, expulsion from the party, loss of employment and status, and a host of other social and material restrictions including evictions from dwellings, exclusions from schools and universities, arbitrary reduction or cessation of pension payments and confiscation of personal property. Neither is it always evident whether a victim was targeted specifically for 'political' or 'anti-state crimes'.

Post-1989 archival findings indicate, however, that approximately 90,000 citizens were prosecuted for 'political crimes' in the years 1948–54, including at least 19,100 Slovaks. In addition, over 22,000 people (about 7,000 of whom were Slovaks) were incarcerated in 107 labour camps, almost 10,000 suspect soldiers and conscripts were condemned to back-breaking work in special construction battalions, and as many as 1,157 people perished in detention.[5] The most awe-inspiring labour camp was the Jáchymov mine complex in north-western Bohemia, which produced highly valuable uranium for the USSR and became a living hell for thousands of inmates. It is also widely agreed that in the period October 1948 to December 1952, 233 death penalties were pronounced, of which 178 were carried out. This figure included Milada Horáková, a National Socialist parliamentary deputy and the first, and only, woman to be executed in Czechoslovakia on political grounds. More death penalties were approved in 1953 and 1954, a total of 181 being passed between 1953 and 1967. Tens of others were shot while trying to escape from prison or attempting to flee the borders. Among the communist elite,

278 high-ranking party functionaries were convicted, although communist victims represented a tiny fraction of the total sentenced (some have estimated a mere 0.1 per cent). In addition, party purges and expulsions reduced the size of the KSČ by several hundred thousand in the years 1949–54.[6]

What were the mechanisms by which this terror was perpetrated? During the Prague Spring of 1968, the reformist party leadership under Alexander Dubček ordered an official enquiry into the Stalinist repression of the late 1940s and early 1950s. The archival based findings, known as the Piller Report after the chair of the commission, were not published at the time, but the damning account concluded that the purges were conducted by three main bodies: the political institutions, the state security service (*Státní ezpečnost* – StB) and the judiciary. In the first category, determining roles were played by named individuals: most consistently Party Chairman and President of the Republic Gottwald and Prime Minister Antonín Zápotocký, but also 'at times' other top figures, such as Antonín Novotný, Viliam Široký and Karol Bacílek. Gottwald 'usually' took the decision to arrest leading officials, he was informed of the course of interrogations and he 'intervened in the preparation of the big trials'. He and his closest colleagues also approved the indictment and length of sentence in all the major political trials. To this extent, 'he bears full and major responsibility for the trials'. The significance of these political actors and institutions lay in their ability to issue specific directives and articulate ideological justifications for the repression, while at the same time extending their domination over the judiciary and, more ambivalently, the secret police. Underlying these personal responsibilities, according to the report, was the 'deformed political system', notably the monopoly of power of the Communist Party and the way its 'leading role' in political and social affairs was exercised. Hypertrophied centralisation and bureaucratisation meant that power became concentrated in ever fewer hands and any independent control over that power by parliament and the judiciary was eliminated. In turn, fiercely applied party discipline ensured 'unquestioning obedience' among subordinates, many of whom genuinely acted in good faith.[7]

The state security service, or more accurately those departments of the service devoted to preparing and staging the trials, played a pivotal role in the whole terror process, becoming in typically Stalinist fashion a virtual law unto itself. The falsification of written evidence, verbal and physical abuse of prisoners and the extortion of 'confessions', all of which were sanctioned by the political leadership, were routinely employed by StB agents, such as Bohumil Doubek and Karel Košt'ál. From a broader perspective, it has been claimed that the secret police heavily influenced the political conception of the main trials and that leading communist functionaries themselves were at times fearful of the StB. Indeed, Kaplan has argued that the security service:

> acted as the driving force of the entire mechanism for the manu-facture of political trials...most importantly, its actions determined the decisions of political institutions, [and] it pursued its own objectives or those of its Soviet colleagues in selecting future victims and preparing trials.[8]

The reference to 'Soviet colleagues' is noteworthy. Having been invited to Czechoslovakia by Gottwald in autumn 1949, many Soviet agents worked in the central and regional security administrations right through to the mid-1950s. As representatives of Moscow, they wielded enormous power and prestige: 'their advice and instructions had the weight of orders' and most Czech and Slovak officials, up to and including the Minister of National Security, accepted their prescriptions as correct.[9] Furthermore, Soviet advisers introduced harsher forms of interrogation, recommended the composition of groups to be tried, intervened in the formulation of the indictments and, it appears, injected distinct anti-Semitic overtones in the prepa-ration of the Slánský trial.[10] In a real sense, they were Stalin's eyes and ears in Prague.

The third component of state coercion was the judiciary. Although the Piller Report absolved the judicial profession as a whole from implication in the terror and suggested that it played a relatively minor part, the principal function of the relevant judicial organs was not inconsiderable: to legalise the trials and publicise the proceed-ings in line with party directives. As such, many judges, prosecu-tors and defence lawyers were unable or unwilling to uphold the independence of the courts and oversaw 'a system of administering justice behind closed doors', in effect condoning gross violations of the law bordering on arbitrary misrule. Top officials in the Ministry of Justice, the Supreme Court and the Prosecutor's General Office enthusiastically endorsed this politicisation of the judiciary and initi-ated key repressive legislation, including the ignominious Act on the Protection of the People's Democratic Republic No. 231/48. In sum, the Piller Report concluded that 'an instrument of power had come into being, accountable to no one, beyond all control and outside the law; it had placed itself above society and usurped a power to which it had no right. Its very existence was unconstitutional'.[11] And it was this supreme 'instrument of power', founded on a firm alliance of monopolistic communist political hegemony and untrammelled secret police authority, which unleashed the mass repressions.

These campaigns took two main interrelated forms: socio-economic and political. Crucial components of the former were the special 'operations' (*akce*) organised by the party leadership and supported by the Ministries of the Interior, Defence and National Security. 'Operation B', lasting from May 1952 to July 1953, targeted 'anti-state elements' who were to be evicted from the major cities. Several thousand families were affected.[12] 'Operation K' was aimed at resettling so-called '*kulaks*', a total of 8,246 people being hit between November 1951 and summer 1953.[13] 'Operation P' was directed at the Roman and Greek Catholic churches under the terms of which virtually all bishops and thousands of priests, monks and nuns, especially in Slovakia, were demoted, interned in assembly camps or placed under house arrest. People deemed of 'bourgeois' and 'petit-bourgeois origin', both urban and rural, were systematically harassed. For instance, plans were enacted in April 1950 to liquidate private craft businesses, and by 1958 such firms had been cut from 247,404 to just 6,552. In the countryside, Soviet-style collectivisation of agriculture and accompanying 'elimination of the kulaks' were initiated in April 1949 and reportedly hit over one million farmers, drastically reducing the amount of farm-holdings above 20 hectares.[14] Even industrial labourers, the social backbone of the system, were far from immune from persecution. Kaplan has maintained that initially workers comprised approximately 30 to 40 per cent of prisoners in the labour camps.[15]

Political repression was endemic between 1948 and 1954. The first mini-wave of trials occurred in September and October 1948 and involved primarily young people accused of writing and distributing anti-state propaganda and leaflets. It is estimated that up to 1,800 were sentenced.[16] Thereafter, other categories of society were earmarked for attack, affecting in some cases KSČ members: army officers and former participants in the anti-fascist resistance; officials of non-communist parties, notably National Socialists and Social Democrats; so-called 'Trotskyites'; 'external enemies' connected in some way with Western agencies and organisations; and economic officials, managers and white-collar workers. Some of these mockeries of justice – the great 'show trials' of non-communist politicians, Catholic bishops and communist luminaries – had national, even international, significance, and were carefully staged performances designed to expose 'the enemy', intimidate the population and act as educative and propaganda tools. Other trials were secret in nature, generally having local and regional connotations. The victims were invariably non-communist citizens often charged under the Act on the Protection of the People's Democratic Republic. It has been calculated that between 40,000 to 45,000 people were sentenced in accordance with this law and the Penal Act of 1950. It should be noted that at a regional and district level, local Communist Party officials composed 'security groups' which appear to have had a degree of autonomy from the 'centre' in deciding repressive policy.

Popular Responses

The most infamous case of Stalinist terror in Czechoslovakia concerned Rudolf Slánský, the second-in-command of the communist system. A brief study, based largely on archival sources, of his show trial illustrates not only the stifling degree of centralised control exerted by the communist authorities, but also the multifarious responses and level of criticality exhibited by 'ordinary' citizens to the purges that rocked Czechoslovak political life.[17] From the end of World War II to September 1951, Slánský was general secretary of the KSČ and without doubt one of the most powerful figures in the country. Reasons for his arrest, on Stalin's orders, in November 1951 are still obscure. According to the Soviet dictator, he had 'committed a number of errors in promoting and posting leading personnel' which had allowed 'conspirators and enemies' to go on the rampage in the party.[18] Beyond this, Stalin's broader geopolitical concerns, Slánský's Jewish background and relative unpopularity in the KSČ, and inner-party elite rivalries all served to make the ex-general secretary a perfect scapegoat for the socio-economic travails afflicting the communist regime.

Physically and mentally tortured for many months by Czech and Soviet secret police interrogators, Slánský eventually confessed to having acted as the head of a fictitious 'anti-state conspiratorial centre' composed of 14 prominent party and state leaders, 11 of whom were 'of Jewish origin'. The men were charged inter alia with high treason, espionage, sabotage, and economic and military subversion with the ultimate aim of tearing Czechoslovakia from the Soviet camp, undermining socialism and restoring capitalism. Amid tumultuous public fanfare, the falsely condemned were brought to trial on 20 November

1952 having diligently memorised predetermined scripts. After a week's ordeal, Slánský and ten others were sentenced to death and three received life imprisonments. All 11 were hanged in the early hours of 3 December, and their ashes unceremoniously scattered on an icy road near Prague.[19]

At one level, the Slánský trial and its reception exemplify all too clearly the centralised organisational grip and ideological manipulation of the top party leadership. After Slánský's arrest, Gottwald and a handful of his closest aides were informed in minute detail about the progress of the interrogations, and in the weeks before the trial they decided the date of the proceedings, the composition of the court and the sentences to be administered. The mass media covered the proceedings on a daily basis, newspapers were reportedly sold out immediately, and the public followed the trial on state radio, and, subversively, on foreign stations such as Radio Free Europe, with intense interest. Contrary to all legal norms, the guilt of the accused was assumed. Between 20 November and 2 December 1952, 8,520 resolutions and telegrams flooded the Central Committee and the state court. The wording and structure of these communications were formulaic and stock phrases – though not always entirely identical – recurred, suggesting orchestration from above.[20] In them, many thousands of factory workers, collective farmers, clerical and institute employees, teachers and even schoolchildren from all over the republic expressed their outrage and righteous indignation at the 'crimes' of the 'Slánský gang'. Some were accompanied by long lists of hand-written signatures. While a minority of the resolutions explicitly demanded the death penalty, the vast majority called for 'the strictest punishment' of the 'traitors', 'villains' and 'imperialist agents'. The 'masses', then, seemingly endorsed the party's version of the affair and positively welcomed the harsh sentences.

However, a closer reading of the archival sources reveals a more variegated picture. Local party functionaries and secret police agents despatched daily reports to their superiors indicating that many citizens, including party members, adopted non-conformist and sceptical attitudes to the trial. For example, some, generally older, workers refused to accept that Slánský, a long-serving 'co-fighter' with Gottwald, was capable of betrayal. He was rather 'a lightning rod who is blamed for all mistakes and scarcities while the guilty lot stay clean'. A few brave souls doubted the charges brought against him and one party official expressed surprise at Slánský's demise, regarding him as a 'model Bolshevik worker'. The conduct of the trial itself came in for scathing criticism among the more independent minded. For them, it was 'a show (*divadlo*) rehearsed in advance', 'a well-staged comedy', 'a filmed circus' and 'farce'. One citizen complained: 'you can't listen to such crap (*kraviny*)'. It was commonly suggested that 'drugs', 'pills', 'injections', 'narcotics' and 'chemicals', even beatings, were responsible for the abject performances of the accused.[21]

Anti-Semitic outbursts were depressingly legion, ranging from unreflective knee-jerk stereotyping to quasi-Hitlerian vituperation. Several representative comments will suffice: 'we worked' while these 'Jewish pigs fleeced us of our money'; 'Jews always shirk honest labour and do well for themselves'; 'what else can you expect from Slánský, a Jew who's never known manual work and has always been affluent'. Among the more violent diatribes are the following: 'All Jews should be shot'; 'Hitler shot lots of them, but still not enough'; 'I'd like to get my hands on this Slánský and tear him limb from limb'; 'they should hang him immediately'; this 'stinking Jew' should be 'cut into strips'; these 'scoundrels' should be 'cut to pieces'.[22] These vicious sentiments confused and worried some party officials and even Gottwald felt constrained to offer publicly a distinction between ideologically sound 'anti-Zionism' and crass racist 'anti-Semitism'.[23]

Less common, but one suspects more disturbing to the party elite, were those voices which implicitly and explicitly criticised leading figures in the KSČ for their gullibility and lack of vigilance in the Slánský case. Even party members were not afraid to express their distrust of specific ministers and Central Committee dignitaries, up to and including Gottwald and Zápotocký, who were on occasion openly blamed for ignoring warning signals from below. How come these people are so divorced from rank-and-file complaints? Why are party 'comrades' isolated from the workers and never move among them? Surely, 'this is not a communist attitude'? Why aren't leaders subject to rigorous 'cadre review' like everyone else? Shouldn't Gottwald carry out 'self-criticism'? Shouldn't there be a 'screening' of all responsible figures in party, state and economic life in order to guarantee that they have the appropriate 'class origins' to defend workers' interests? Proletarians understood that the 'higher-ups' must have decent houses and other amenities if they are to represent the republic, but 'luxury and gross differences' should not be permitted.[24] Secret police agents reported that factory workers were apparently 'signing resolutions demanding the resignation of the entire government and the establishment of a new government composed of people whose past life is unambiguous and well known to the public'. Likewise, regional party officials in Brno noted ominously that workers were calling on 'members of the CC [Central Committee]

KSČ to give up their functions'. A perspicacious Prague security agent stated the obvious: 'among some workers, even party members, faith in the government and the CC KSČ is shaken'.[25] It appears, then, that the Slánský trial was used by discontented and frustrated citizens to vent their anger against the communist regime per se, not just against the few designated 'enemies'.

What do these diverse popular responses tell us about the impact of terror in Czechoslovakia? As far as the KSČ is concerned, it seems that internal party discipline generally held firm, but the leadership could never blithely rely on strict Leninist dictate among the rank and file. Ordinary members, and not a few lower-level functionaries, aired views that were disquieting to the centre and were critical by name of top party and state bosses. The accountability and trustworthiness of the executive were cast into doubt, the reality of 'inner-party democracy' was impugned and the gap between 'us' and 'them' clearly identified. In the process, it is possible that the administrative competence and loyalty of some party-state cadres were undermined. These unintended consequences of the leadership's policy of repression hint at the muted limits of 'Stalinisation' at the base of the Czechoslovak party, even if we accept that the KSČ elites were growing increasingly accustomed to obeying Moscow's orders.

At a societal level, given the scale and range of the repression there can be little doubt that most citizens lived in fear and were scarcely able to voice their opinions openly. Nevertheless, attitudes towards the Slánský trial, as we have seen, ranged from strident, sober and selective support to passive compliance and resigned accommodation, to apathy, doubt, guarded dissent and overt opposition. In the absence of hard statistics and regardless of the ostensible loud consensus behind the party line, it is impossible to assess the relative weights of these positions. However, the numerous signs of non-conformism suggest that public backing for the trial was exaggerated and that the communist authorities were never able to manipulate completely popular opinion and eliminate negative comment. We are palpably not dealing with a fully fledged 'totalitarian' system capable of moulding public discourse at will. A minority was not afraid to speak critically, even if many others, enthusiastically or passively, played by the rules of the game. Not everyone, it appears, was intimidated by the terror.

In summary, elite purges and mass repressions in Stalinist Czechoslovakia were multifaceted processes with distinct, but closely interrelated, exogenous and indigenous origins and multiple politico-ideological and socio-economic aims. Precisely because of this complex web of causes and effects, they cannot be interpreted as merely a product of 'evil' megalomaniac men bent on creating a 'totalitarian' order. Neither were they simply imposed by Moscow on a resistant party and society. Neither is there a single overarching explanation for their emergence. Stalinist terror in Czechoslovakia is best located in a framework which emphasises both longer and shorter-term factors: the pre-war 'Stalinisation' of the KSČ and the creation of a mentality of ubiquitous 'enemies'; the traumatic experiences of the Munich 'betrayal', Nazi occupation, the Holocaust and, notably, post-war ethnic and class retributions, all of which went some way towards tearing the fabric and cohesiveness of Czechoslovak society; and the sense of internal crisis and external pressure generated by the failings of the infant communist regime in an intense international atmosphere of breakdown between two hostile camps. In addition to these 'objective' circumstances, the goals, ambitions, perceptions and misperceptions of concrete actors should never be ignored – individual agency is crucial. Stalin, Gottwald and other Czech and Soviet political and security bosses operated in an almost Byzantine network of personal rivalries and clandestine conflicts, and the elite purges are explained, in part at least, by these ultimately impenetrable intrigues and cabals. In short, structural and contingent factors combined to produce a toxic form of lawlessness, which bred mistrust and suspicion, engendered widespread feelings of fear and legal insecurity in the population, and undermined public faith in the constitution and politics in general. The wounds were deep and are still apparent to this day, an ugly and unwanted reminder of a dark past which implicated and tainted too many people.

'Constructing Socialism': Politics, Culture and Labour

State-sponsored coercion, exclusionary policies and the inculcation of fear were not the only methods adopted by the communist authorities after February 1948. 'Socialism' in its Stalinist guise also had to be created in more inclusive productive ways. A solid base of social support needed to be forged. It is true that the Soviet model was de rigueur and that Muscovite shibboleths and blueprints could never be ignored, especially after the Stalin–Tito split in mid-1948. But the limitations of this 'Stalinisation' process should be noted. First, 'Stalinism' and 'totalitarianism' were not the conscious and self-proclaimed aims of the Czechoslovak communist leaders. These are pejorative terms given, no doubt often for good reason, to communist policies and actions by Western and émigré academics, politicians and journalists. Second, 'Stalinisation' was not directly imposed by 'Big Brother' to the east. As Mary Heimann points out: 'it was Czech and Slovak Communists, not Russians or Soviets, who turned post-February Czechoslovakia into the Stalinist hell that it rapidly became...No one forced [them] to hold up for emulation the Soviet example in everything'.[26] Third, this 'copying' of the Soviet model was far from straightforward. The party in nearly all fields and endeavours had to adapt its Stalinising ambitions to the contours and divergences of Czech and Slovak society and, importantly, 'since the KSČ was itself formed by this society, there was always a danger that rather than itself transforming society, society might transform the KSČ'.[27] Finally, before pressures to Sovietise the Czechoslovak political system became acute from autumn 1948 onwards, there existed a restricted space for alternative paths and tactics, even a measure of inner-party debate and disagreement on the way forward. Not everything was decided in advance; and the party was not a total monolith.

The Contradictions of Stalinist Politics

For several months after February the party leadership pursued what one expert, Robert K. Evanson, has termed 'an undogmatic, quasidemocratic course', which bore similarities with the concept of a separate 'Czechoslovak road to socialism' of the years 1946–47.[28] Broad immediate goals included:

> attempts to garner support or cooperation from a wide assort-
> ment of social forces, efforts to maintain continuity with par-
> liamentary democratic traditions and other popular aspects of
> [Czechoslovakia's] political past, a gradual approach to economic
> socialization, and sharp restriction of the use of terror against the
> regime's opponents.

According to Evanson, Gottwald's early 'carrot and stick' strategy sought to 'win the voluntary support of the masses' and 'persuade the public that only socialism would bring social justice and prosper-ity'. To this end a 'policy of inclusion' was adopted for the most part, which identified all but arch 'reactionaries' as potential allies of the regime. This was most clearly manifest in the vast party recruitment drive from March to October 1948, which saw membership rise to a massive 2.6 million people, over 20 per cent of the population. Tens of thousands of civil servants, army officers and professional soldiers, lawyers, former adherents of non-communist parties, workers, even small craftsmen, shopkeepers and pensioners swelled the ranks of the KSČ. No doubt many newcomers were far from convinced Marxist–Leninists – careerism, opportunism, self-protection and a fair degree of intimidation often proving prime reasons for 'jumping on the bandwagon'. But the party leaders appeared to be declaring that the KSČ was an inclusive 'all-people's party'. In the state, regional and local bureaucracies, co-optation of administrative personnel was often the preferred method of ensuring support rather than purging. The majority of 'bourgeois' judges retained their positions, although university professors and students, particularly in the arts and law faculties, were treated less leniently.

Evanson also emphasised the communists' post-February 'policy of continuity' as an important component of their attempt to gain legitimacy. By taking steps, however circumscribed and tentative, to identify the new regime with the democratic political culture of the Czechs and Slovaks, it was hoped that public consent would consolidate and any latent opposition dissipate. For example, the Constitution ratified on 9 May maintained several features of the 1920 'bourgeois' Constitution and hence was 'an elaborate hybrid, a combination of Western parliamentarism and sovietism…[and] a remarkably moderate document'.[29] The parliamentary system, separation of powers and the highly popular and prestigious office of the presidency were upheld, Gottwald taking on the latter role after Beneš's resignation in June; two non-communist parties, the People's Party and the revamped Socialist Party, were permitted a legal exist-ence; certain civil and judicial rights were formally preserved; private property and ownership of land up to 50 hectares were protected; and religious worship was safeguarded. The new electoral law of April 1948 also included democratic conventions, and at first the KSČ Presidium even seemed prepared to permit open competitive slate elections scheduled for 30 May. However, probably under external pressure, this decision was soon reversed in favour of a united list of candidates, which was dominated by communists and their support-ers. Yet 'rather than claiming in ritualistic Soviet fashion a virtually unanimous electoral victory…the regime acknowledged an opposi-tion vote of over 10 per cent'.[30] Other signs of relative official temper-ance were the popular National Insurance Law, also passed in April, which expanded the pre-existing welfare state and improved the system of cash benefits,[31] negotiations between the government and the Catholic Church, which continued well into 1949 before breaking down in bitter acrimony and ultimately vicious state repression of the clergy, and the fairly broad scope that was afforded the People's Party until the end of 1948.

The new regime's treatment of the remnants of the expelled Sudeten German minority – around 170,000 people – also demonstrates the contradictory character of communist policy in the era of high Stalinism. According to recent research undertaken by Matěj Spurný, already by late 1948 'the now stabilized Communist Party dictatorship brought an end to direct ethnically legitimized coercion [against the Germans] and introduced a measure of liberalization', in which 'assimilation and integration slowly replaced' repression and segregation. Mixed marriages were permitted and citizenship was often granted to hitherto stateless Germans, to whom basic civil rights were extended. This certainly does not mean that Sudeten Germans became fully trusted equal co-citizens: most remained impoverished, resentful of their loss of identity and often subject to abuse and hostility by their Czech 'neighbours'. Many chose to escape the degradation by emigrating to West Germany whenever the opportunity arose. Nevertheless, Spurný's conclusions are far-reaching, controversial and, I think, largely convincing. First, he argues that in the years 1945–47 'when most German-speaking inhabitants of Czechoslovakia were being displaced, the extent of violence committed by the state and its security and other bodies was far greater' than in the 1950s, when the targets of persecution changed and the total degree of 'state-induced violence decreased gradually'. Indeed, 'there was no more repression and explicit discrimination against stateless Germans after the spring of 1949'. Second, the principle of national 'purification' and segregation was considered 'normal' by most Czechs and Slovaks and what is more 'even in the 1950s the government's repressive measures were often a reaction to a broad and persistent social demand' emanating 'from below'. Finally, Spurný infers that there was an important ideological determinant to the regime's more moderate policies towards the German minority: 'the party's quest for legitimacy'. That is, the overall goal was to 'gain the Germans for our state', integrate them into the 'construction of the socialist homeland', and thus vindicate 'the existence of the socialist dictatorship;...show that the Communist Party could construct a community, open to everyone who wanted to take part, including those who had been marginalized and discriminated against; and...prove that this new society was better than anything that had gone before'.[32] Ideologically, it mattered to the communists that 'socialism' had to be seen to be superior to capitalist democracy and that the population should be turned into loyal citizens.

Education and Cultural Politics

In their early educational policies, the authorities also aimed to establish a firm foundation of social support by appealing to hitherto under-privileged strata. The dual goal was to eliminate the power and influence of the old 'bourgeois' elites and replace them with an upwardly mobile 'proletarian' intelligentsia.[33] The question was, having purged the existing 'bourgeois' universities soon after the takeover of power, what would the new 'socialist' university look like? Ways had to be found to boost the number of grammar school (*gymnasium*) and university students from working-class and peasant backgrounds, a strategy that the communists had almost entirely over-looked in the 1945–48 period. The results were patchy: in 1947–48, 18 per cent of Czech university students came from working-class and peasant families, but by 1953–54 this figure had risen to only 37.3 per cent. Preparatory 'worker courses', which were designed to fast-track ambitious and bright labourers into higher education, also met with modest returns. The relative failure of this affirmative action agenda reflected both the lack of enthusiasm for fundamental educational transformation which persisted among inexperienced communist planners and strategists well into the 1950s, and the 'intensely anti-intellectual' atmosphere that pervaded the KSČ at all levels. The will simply did not exist to alter radically the educational system, in which practical apprentice-type schooling at secondary level was particularly striking. It also had much to do with traditional working-class culture and notions of social status: 'workers continued to think of higher education as something alien, and the middle and upper classes continued to think of [it] as their birth right'. The longer-term his-torical significance of these deep-rooted social mentalities and of the party's political inertia was that largely 'unproletarianised' university students and dissatisfied intelligentsia 'spearheaded the move for political change' in both 1968 and 1989.

If we turn to communist cultural policies in the years 1948–53, we likewise see a complex dichotomous pattern of strict control 'from above' partially tempered by adaptation 'from below' and fierce organisational and personality conflicts. The prevailing lodestar of Stalinist culture was the enigmatic concept of 'socialist realism'. First enunciated in the USSR in 1934 and forcefully reiterated in 1946 by Andrei Zhdanov, Stalin's main overseer of the arts and culture, socialist realism sought to depict existing reality through the lens of the bright utopian future. Literature, painting, film, even architec-ture and music, had to be optimistic, readily comprehensible to the 'masses', shorn of elitism and 'bourgeois abstract formalism', and ever mindful of the party 'line'. Artists and intellectuals were to learn from the 'people', work for the good of the collective and in this way contribute to the 'democratisation' of the nation's culture. Thus, the struggle for a truly inclusive popular culture was an absolutely vital part of the overall struggle for socialism. These Soviet-inspired principles were to be applied in post-February Czechoslovakia. But there were several conundrums: could 'socialist realism' be transposed lock, stock and barrel from Moscow, or did it need to be 'naturalised' and accommodated to the divergent Czech and Slovak milieux? Who would define its content and limits: party apparatchiks or intellectuals themselves? Was it a static unchanging entity, or, if not, how should it evolve? How should the new regime treat the cultural avant-garde, many of whose leading representatives before the war had been leftists, some even communists, but who had not liberated themselves totally from the pursuit of 'artistic freedom' and an objective 'truth' over and above the 'truth' of Marxism–Leninism? As ever, there were no straightforward answers. Generalised models and broad maxims emanating from the USSR were all very well, but they had to be adapted to meet local conditions if specific detailed policies were to be hammered out and agreed.

The standard account of Stalinist cultural politics has it that 'socialist realist artists in the Eastern bloc were passive "transmission belts" relaying official party strictures to a recalcitrant public on behalf of the Party leadership'. Tight state censorship reigned. All intellectuals who did not debase themselves before the altar of 'socialist realism' were purged or silenced. Culture was a battleground between 'the heroic anti-communist "dissident" [and] the worthless political "collaborator"'.[34] While over-simplified, this is not an entirely wrong interpretation. As we have seen, KSČ leaders were deeply wary of the 'ideologically erratic stratum of the intelligentsia' and did indeed place them 'under the unwavering surveillance of the "revolutionary class"…with methods of practical application ranging from being publicly discredited and bans on publication through denial of employment and even prison sentences of many years'. For example, by the end of 1948 over 30 authors had been expelled from the Syndicate of Czech Writers for their alleged active opposition to the new order. A few intellectuals were reduced to suicide and others were bought off by sinecures and flattery, the price of which was unrelenting conformism.[35] Not surprisingly, the cultural artefacts that emerged from this oppressive atmosphere were 'comparatively bland' and for many scholars it appeared that 'Stalinism was nothing more than an artistic caesura between the artistically vibrant interwar Republic and the Prague Spring of the 1960s'.[36]

However, a closer examination reveals unexpected nuances. First, as in politics, so in culture, communist rule in the months immediately following the seizure of power was 'fragmented, haphazard, and improvisational'. It was not evident exactly what 'socialist culture' would entail and the authorities 'made no effort to impose socialist realism as state policy', a stance which persisted until autumn 1948. Only in January 1950 did the party impose 'official guidelines for an overarching theory of socialist realism and communist cultural criticism'. This was accompanied by 'political purges and smear campaigns against artists and intellectuals deemed antithetical to socialism'. The broad aim was to engender 'socialist unity'; the unanticipated result was 'a series of vicious arguments over *how* this new Party line should be interpreted, and more importantly *against whom*'. Hence, there were debilitating, even life-threatening, clashes among, on the one hand, powerful officials in the Ministry of Information and Enlightenment, and, on the other, their counterparts in the Cultural and Propaganda Division of the party Central Committee. The former might be termed 'moderate Stalinists' and the latter 'radical Stalinists'. The eventual victory of the 'moderates' by early 1951 gave some hint of a more 'tolerant attitude', even a very 'partial thaw...of the regime's cultural policies'.[37] It is crucial, then, to take on board that the party did not speak with one voice.

Second, party officials often did not need to enforce a 'cultural line'. Many Czech and Slovak intellectuals willingly played their role in the establishment and consolidation of Stalinism. According to one of them, Antonín Liehm, the 'young Turks' gave succour to the infant regime by temporarily extirpating the 'intellectuality' and self-doubt from their middle-class minds, thereby forging an identity with the essentially proletarian communist movement. But their blind faith in socialism, which blurred the discrepancy between party and truth, between ideology and reality, with disastrous consequences, began to be shaken by what Liehm calls the paralysing 'bourgeois intellectual's guilt complex'.[38] By shedding this degrading sense of inferiority, born of their 'alien' class origins, and by regaining confidence in their own reason, self-dignity and personal experience, some intellectuals after 1953 gradually felt emboldened to criticise the stifling political, cultural and economic fetters of the Stalinist model. In doing so, they helped to prepare the path for an agonisingly slow process of 'de-Stalinisation', lasting from 1953 to the mid-1960s. Neither should it be forgotten that 'culture' and its practices were differentiated, so that 'the campaign to impose Soviet-model socialist realism in the plastic arts was met with embarrassment and its impact was limited. Even during the worst days of Stalinism many artists tended to go their own way'.[39]

The Czech–Slovak Imbroglio

The strained relations between Czechs and Slovaks have been described by one eminent historian as a 'chronic disease', eating away at the heart of Czechoslovak statehood and legitimacy.[40] The underlying conviction of the KSČ bosses, steeped as they were in Marxist internationalist precepts, was that national distinctions and tensions would be erased once the socio-economic level in the more agrarian Slovakia reached the 'higher' Czech industrialised levels. National conflicts were, in this schema, the product solely of the inequities of uneven capitalist development and exploitation. The rapid socialist modernisation of Slovakia, it was argued, would remove the material preconditions of Czech–Slovak hostility. Regardless of the impressive economic achievements wrought in Slovakia in the years 1945–89, the so-called 'Velvet Divorce' of 1992–93 strongly suggests that this theory did not quite work out as planned.[41] One important reason for this failure is that successive communist leaders, both Czech and Slovak, like their democratic counterparts in the interwar republic, grossly under-estimated the strength of the Slovaks' desire for meaningful self-governance and autonomy, albeit within the existing state. In the fraught Cold War atmosphere of the late 1940s and beyond, strict centralisation, firm unity and the forging of a singular 'national political society' were considered far higher priorities than pandering to out-dated Slovak 'bourgeois nationalism'. The policies and actions of the Stalinised KSČ in the period 1948–53 provide ample proof of these powerful centralising trends.

The Constitution of May 1948 seriously undermined the provisions of political and executive self-rule that had been granted to the Slovak National Council under the terms of the Košice Programme of April 1945. These stipulations, which sought to define clear limits to central government jurisdiction in Slovakia, had already been watered down by the so-called 'Third Prague Agreement' of June 1946, but the Constitution went much further. It identified a mere ten fields over which Slovak organs had competence, the most important being culture, school education and public health, but even here, in certain circumstances, the central authorities could intervene. What is more, Slovaks were left vulnerable to their worst fear – being out-voted by the more numerous Czechs, a situation known as *majorizácia*. In short, 'there was no policy area left in which Slovak administration could exercise unchallenged authority'. This baleful state of affairs was compounded by the decision of the KSČ Central Committee in late July 1948 to create a 'single political leadership in the form of a unified statewide' party.[42] This resolution signified the end of the Slovak Communist Party as an independent, nominally co-equal, entity. The party organisation in Bratislava would retain the name 'KSS', but its Central Committee would be subordinate to that of the 'superior' KSČ in Prague. All these developments prompted one émigré Czech scholar to conclude that the 'status of Slovakia from 1945 to 1954 is thus a story of a gradual but steady decline of Slovak self-government and autonomy, and of a corresponding continuous increase in centralization'.[43]

These constitutional and organisational amendments, though highly significant, were but the tip of the iceberg. Already in September 1948, Viliam Široký, a leading Slovak communist and staunch 'Pragocentric', had warned about the dangers of 'bourgeois nationalism'; that is, a heretical ideological 'deviation' among some Slovak communists to over-estimate expressions of 'narrow-minded' national sentiment to the detriment of state-wide 'proletarian' interests. It was a charge that had its origins in the fierce conflicts between Czech 'centralisers' and Slovak 'autonomists' which had convulsed the KSČ since 1944–45,[44] and it became a heinous offence that would have murderous resonances by the early 1950s. At that time, the high-ranking Slovak communists Vladimír Clementis, Gustáv Husák, Laco Novomeský, among others, were expelled from the party accused of planning a separatist programme, even of plotting the secession of Slovakia from the republic. Clementis was executed as one of the 14 defendants in the Slánský trial. Husák and Novomeský fell victim to the last major show trial of the Stalinist era in Czechoslovakia, held as late as April 1954. They were sentenced to life and ten years imprisonment respectively for the dubious crime of being 'Slovak bourgeois nationalists'. Such travesties of justice rankled deeply among Slovaks, communists included, and repeated demands for judicial and political rehabilitation were to play a key role in the tortuous 'de-Stalinisation' process from the mid-1950s onwards.

'Socialist' Work

According to Marxist theory, under socialism unalienated free workers would enjoy the fruits of their labour unfettered by capitalist exploitation. Czechoslovakia, as a heavily industrialised and urbanised country with a highly organised educated workforce and a hefty proportion of its economy nationalised by 1948, should have been an ideal showcase for the Marxist experiment. Communist leaders were not alone in their utter conviction that the benefits of socialism would soon become apparent once a rationally planned state-run economy had overcome the chaos, venality and unpredictability of the capitalist market. Nothing better epitomised the communists' confident vision of the transformatory power of socialist ideology than the ubiquitous propaganda image of the class-conscious and diligent skilled male worker enthusiastically building the new society. However, the harsh truth by the early 1950s was one of flagrant imbalances in production and investment, steep price rises, depreciated real incomes, a lack of decent housing and a concomitant plunge in living standards, all of which demonstrated definitively that the cherished hopes and expectations of abundance under socialism had been far from fulfilled. The crass imitation of the Stalinist 'command economy' – the virtual elimination of private ownership of production, retail and distribution;[45] the fixation with armaments and iron, steel and coal outputs; the forced collectivisation of agriculture; the transfer of trade from the West to the Soviet bloc; and the micro-management of the economy by central ministries staffed by ill-trained bureaucrats – had reduced the much-vaunted and diversified Czechoslovak economy to a state of semi-crisis. My aim here is not to assess the economic factors behind this unanticipated outcome, but to elucidate the impact of Stalinist policies on the shop-floor experience of Czechoslovak workers and on their relations with the socialist state.

Without doubt life was extremely tough, and occasionally very dangerous, for the vast majority of Czechoslovak industrial workers. The Soviet-inspired all-out drive to 'militarise' the economy rapidly in preparation for the feared outbreak of war engendered intense pressures on the labour force. Imported Stalinist production incentives were introduced: 'output quotas; piece rates and bonuses; speed-ups, in which quotas were increased without commensurate rewards; "socialist competition" among factory groups; "voluntary" overtime and holiday contributions; and extended workweeks'. The largely successful attempt to turn trade unions into party 'transmission belts' and 'organs of discipline and productivity rather than worker representation' meant that labourers had precious few formal mechanisms of redress for the inevitable grievances that festered in the factories. The strained situation was exacerbated by the existence of police informer networks, a system which ensured that many employees found their way into the nightmare of a Stalinist prison or labour camp for relatively minor 'offences'. The introduction of rationing at the start of 1949, and again in summer 1951, and successive price hikes did little to alleviate the dismal prospects for the Czechoslovak working class.[46]

Women workers, in particular, commonly suffered from the 'dual burden', toiling long hours in the factory and yet being expected, in a patriarchal society, to carry out the bulk of domestic familial duties. They were still largely employed in traditional female industries, such as textiles and food, which were lower paid and had lower status; they were still open to abuse and condescension by their male co-workers and bosses; they seldom reached managerial and other upper-level positions of authority; they were marginalised by the party's 'cult of masculinity'; and they certainly never attained the rarefied realms of equal pay for equal work, despite the regime's progressive rhetoric. It is true that socialised child-care facilities were massively extended, the number of crèches growing from 268 in 1948 to 1,155 by 1955, and important social legislation and a new family code were passed, but in general state planners looked on women as a cheap labour reserve and gender equality in the workplace was never fully achieved.[47]

Workers were not, however, entirely defenceless. In the desperate struggle for survival, many resorted to absenteeism, engaged in mass job fluctuation, launched strikes and production slow-downs, feigned illness, or stole state property, all of which were regularly lamented in the media. They also devised informal strategies and practices in the factories and mines of 'working the system' to their advantage in an attempt to ease the burden of breakneck industrial growth. These local improvisations and mechanisms were based on inherited cultures of labour and workers' ingrained sense of a moral economy, which often flew in the face of new 'socialist' forms of production, like 'Stakhanovism'. This Soviet expedient of 'shock work' and personalised norm-busting was bitterly, and fairly successfully, resisted by the majority of Czech workers, whose collective ethos and commitment to wage and status egalitarianism was affronted by the individualisation of work relations. Significantly, there was more than a measure of collusion between shop-floor operatives and lower-level officials in the trade unions, factory councils and enterprises. For instance, 'unions often falsified records to reclassify workers into higher wage categories, covered up absenteeism, and issued phoney shockworker booklets which entitled the holders to free market goods at rationed prices'.[48] In response to these informal arrangements and working-class recalcitrance, the authorities were sometimes forced to make concessions, such as introducing greater democracy in factory council elections in the early 1950s. One of the leading historians of the Czechoslovak labour movement, Peter Heumos, has termed this process 'the "flexible management" of the government administration', indicating that the regime's room for manoeuvre in the workplace was relatively limited and open to adaptation.[49] It also suggests, importantly, that the 'mitigation of the worst features of economic Stalinism…probably lessened the degree of the workers' alienation' and opposition to the system.[50]

Anti-Communist Resistance

Regardless of the ambivalences, contradictions and negotiations of Czechoslovak Stalinism, the turmoil created by the policies of the communist regime after February 1948 generated widespread popular discontent. The prime example of overt resistance was the workers' uprising in the Czech industrial city of Plzeň in early June 1953, just three months after Stalin's death. 'Resistance' is a topical, but decidedly ambiguous and polemical concept, lacking definitional clarity. It is debatable whether historians can identify precisely which acts constitute 'resistant' behaviour, or can penetrate the subjectivities of resistance and disentangle individual impulses in chaotic situations like strikes or mass riots. Stark binaries such as 'resistance' versus 'conformity' or 'coercion' versus 'consensus' only go so far in explaining the complexities of state–society relations under Stalinism. In highly authoritarian systems such as Stalinist Czechoslovakia, where the state itself was instrumental in turning 'normal' deeds into criminal offences, it is tempting to evince 'resistance' not only in brazen acts of anti-government violence, but also in common practices such as low labour productivity, listening to jazz or the ubiquitous political joke. But the implication that all those workers who operated a 'go-slow' or flitted from job to job or engaged in anti-Gottwald banter in the pub were putative 'resisters' is surely problematic. While remaining at all times sensitive to the barbarous nature of the Stalinist system, we should not, I think, posit an undifferentiated oppositional Czech society locked in some unequal 'heroic' confrontation with an inorganic illegitimate state. A more nuanced understanding of state–society interactions and individual subjectivities, going beyond out-dated binaries by identifying the sources of consent, accommodation and conflict, will help us to grapple better with the enigmatic and recalcitrant notion of 'resistance' in communist Czechoslovakia.

Contrary to the stereotypical picture of Czech passivity, indifference and buffoonery, expressions of popular anger, opposition and even armed resistance were not unknown in the years of Stalinism. Anti-state conspiratorial groupings, sometimes with links to émigré organisations, undoubtedly existed, the most celebrated case being that of the Mašín brothers, Ctirad and Josef, who between 1951 and 1953 carried out several politically motivated violent acts, including murder. In the Czech Republic today, the brothers are regarded as either anti-communist heroes or common criminals. However, many of these 'anti-state organisations', one suspects, were figments of the imagination of over-zealous secret police officers. More common were anti-communist leaflets and posters – 'The KSČ is Leading Us to Destitution and Poverty', 'The Death of Stalin Means Death to Communists', 'Long Live the USA, Death to Communism' – which appeared sporadically in various Czech and Slovak towns.[51] Blue-collar workers were not slow to vent their resentment over high work norms, gross food shortages, Soviet-style 'socialist competition' and cuts in customary social and labour benefits. Between 1948 and 1953, a total of 218 strikes broke out in the country's principal industrial areas, including in Slovakia.[52] Most were short-lived particularist affairs, but two mass demonstrations did occur in Moravia, the first in Brno in late November 1951 when an estimated 6,000 workers marched on the city centre briefly bringing public life to a standstill.[53] The second took place in the town of Prostějov on 10 April 1953, when a crowd of around 3,000 protesters attacked the seat of municipal authority after the statue of Tomáš G. Masaryk had been demolished by local communists.[54]

The degree and durability of this popular unrest should not be exaggerated, nor should it automatically be seen as politically motivated. Indeed, Heumos has concluded that strikes were usually of a defensive character, focusing on 'social issues' with 'political demands' playing a 'marginal role'.[55] What is more, as he has also tellingly suggested:

the focus on social relations is not to be understood...as a history characterized by the actions of the state...and the often oppositional reactions of those who were simply acted upon. Cooperation with the political system could coexist with actions that could be described as deviant, just as accommodation and the pursuit of individual interests could reinforce conformity. Patterns of behavior that were unambiguous were only found occasionally.[56]

Nevertheless, it is certainly the case that major work stoppages and large-scale public disorder alarmed party dignitaries and imparted a sense of looming social crisis, not least because they indicated that political discontent could rapidly emerge from socio-economic concerns.

This was precisely the pattern that would be followed in the most overt and menacing form of popular resistance in Czechoslovakia in the 1950s – the Plzeň workers' revolt of June 1953. This little-known event might accurately be termed the first anti-Stalinist rebellion in communist Eastern Europe, coming as it did two weeks before the more serious East German uprising which demanded Soviet military intervention. The immediate catalyst for the trouble in Czechoslovakia was a currency reform promulgated by the government on the evening of Saturday 30 May, which effectively wiped out people's savings and resulted in heavy price rises. By stipulating that existing Czechoslovak crowns would be exchanged for the new currency at a ratio of 5:1 for the first 300 crowns, and thereafter at the extortionate rate of 50:1, the decree was widely regarded as 'state theft', or in the collective memory as 'the robbery of the century'. Particularly badly hit were large working-class families, pensioners, invalids and better-paid employees with bank deposits. In response, on 1 and 2 June at least 32,000 workers nationwide, including in Prague, went on strike, demonstrated and in one or two places temporarily overran the local authorities. The most threatening events occurred in Plzeň, where around 2,000 workers from the huge Škoda engineering and armaments plant, bolstered by hundreds of school and college students, apprentices, brewery workers and curious on-lookers, took to the streets. The town hall was ransacked, busts of Lenin, Stalin, Gottwald and Zápotocký were hurled into the square to the great delight of the protesters, portraits of Beneš were brandished, politicised slogans were heard – 'Down with the communists!'; 'We want free elections!'; 'We want a new government!' – and fairly widespread violence broke out, requiring the deployment of the army and other special units to put down the rebels. There were no fatalities, but many scores of people were injured, including as many as 50 policemen and other officials, and hundreds were arrested, many of whom were sentenced to hefty terms in prison and labour camps.[57]

Several important issues emerge from the Plzeň events about resistance in Czechoslovakia. First, it appears that communist workers, even some lower-level party and trade union functionaries, participated in the disturbances together with non-communists, suggesting that working-class solidarity took priority over Leninist party discipline.

Second, the near total ineffectiveness of Plzeň's party, police and security bodies in quelling the uprising implies a deep malaise at the heart of regional governance, which in turn raises questions about the 'totalitarian' nature of Czechoslovak communism. Third, the overwhelming majority of demonstrators, around 80 per cent, were industrial workers. The sources are silent, however, on whether these workers were skilled, semi-skilled or unskilled. Only one Czech historian has broached this issue and she deduced that the demonstrations were strongest in factories with a relatively permanent cadre of 'class conscious' engineering workers, but archival sources indicate that all categories of workers participated, including technical, research and service staff.[58] Fourth, judging from court statistics approximately 65 per cent were young, between the ages of 17 and 30 – Plzeň was in essence a revolt of the youth. Finally, and more surprising perhaps, a substantial minority of participants were women – about 14 per cent of those convicted were female, which may be indicative of the everyday frustrations, travails and harassment suffered by women workers. The worrying conclusion, no doubt, for leading representatives of the regime was that relatively large and diverse strata of the population were discontented and potentially open to oppositional activity. Something had to be done.

That the outpouring of pent-up worker anger in the nationwide demonstrations had seriously shaken regional and central authorities is proven by the harsh repression meted out after the events. This 'strong hand', as Zápotocký termed it,[59] was primarily designed to teach workers an enduring lesson, and it did have the desired effect of curbing industrial activism: there were only 45 strikes in Czechoslovakia in the years 1954 to 1956, compared to 146 in 1953 alone.[60] But more than the exclusionary 'stick' was used, suggesting that the regime had more productive and inclusive ways of forging a measure of political legitimacy. Already in spring 1953 a reform-minded strategy, the 'New Course', had been devised in Moscow and in the next few years it was applied in varying degrees throughout the Soviet bloc. By reducing huge state investments in the military and heavy industry in order to expand consumer and agricultural production, the difficult balancing act of the 'New Course' was to ameliorate general standards of living without unduly risking security. Indeed, under Nikita Khrushchev, the emerging force in the USSR by the mid-1950s, socio-economic advancement became one of the focal ambitions of the Soviet regime, epitomised by an article published in Moscow in 1957 which insisted no less that 'the essence of the Great October Socialist Revolution was an improvement in the material conditions of the workers'.[61]

In Czechoslovakia, the equation 'socialism = better living standards' was partially achieved in the years after 1953 under the new party First Secretary Antonín Novotný, who took over following Gottwald's death in March of that year. Retail prices were lowered six times during 1953–56; personal consumption rose by 14 per cent in 1954, its highest post-war level; real wages increased, as did pensions and some social benefits; and the construction of 40,000 new homes was projected for the year 1954. Electrical appliances such as fridges, washing machines, radios and by the late 1950s televisions gradually became more available and affordable, and the provision of foodstuffs was relatively adequate, certainly in comparison with the dire situation in Hungary and Poland.[62] Indicative was the rhetoric about 'socialist technology', encapsulated in the production of the 'people's car'. As we have seen, life was onerous in the early to mid-1950s, but there were a few signs of improvement for the future.

However, the 'New Course' was ambivalent. On the one hand, it fostered hope among the people and 'changed [the] attitude of a large section of the population towards the regime', but on the other, the 'overwhelming majority of the Party aktiv retained their opposition to the changes'.[63] The socio-economic concessions and the more nebulous political changes, focused on an 'anti-bureaucracy' drive, introduced by the Novotný regime went some way to assuage popular discontent and thus acted to shore up the communist system, while the limitations placed on the New Course by the neo-Stalinist leadership were welcomed, and in part conditioned, by the 'conservative' party apparatus at all levels. In these circumstances, the authority of the party was cautiously restored after the disruptions of June 1953, political centralisation persisted intact, the power-holders remained overwhelmingly united and to a certain extent expectation, mingled with a measure of passivity, was engendered among a confused and divided citizenry. These complex domestic developments and moods were accompanied by an equally ambiguous foreign scene in which anti-West German and US propaganda sat uneasily with a relaxation of international tension, which by 1955 was associated with the 'Geneva spirit'.

The overall question of the nature and scale of popular resistance in communist Czechoslovakia in the 1950s is not resolvable with any certitude and conclusions must be weighed judiciously. That said, I fully agree with Padraic Kenney that we should 'discard...the old myth that opposition was natural and inevitable'.[64] In this spirit, I would argue that defiant acts such as the Plzeň uprising should not be automatically construed as evidence of ubiquitous political and ideological resistance to the existing order or be viewed teleologically as the first in a line of mass revolts culminating in the *annus mirabilis* of 1989. The Plzeň revolt, ignited by a ruinous currency reform, was more a reflection of the disastrous socio-economic conditions and the breakdown in relations between party and workers at the point of production. It also seems likely that the conventional, and still influential, wisdom that the Stalinised KSČ in this period was a fully fledged 'totalitarian' party permeated with Leninist 'democratic centralism' and 'iron discipline' is in important ways wide of the mark. If not ramshackle, the party, especially at the regional and enterprise level, was dysfunctional and divorced from its own grassroots members, let alone from the mass of non-communists. Finally, and most saliently, the Plzeň events represented the initial turning-point in the party's tentative and belated realisation that fresh methods had to be found to improve state–society relations. This was achieved, though never permanently, first by means of a New Course, then by what became known in the West as 'de-Stalinisation', and in the longer term by a 'softer' strategy of 'socialist consumerism'. All these phenomena found their expression in the eventful decade 1953–67.

In conclusion, after February 1948 the new communist rulers of Czechoslovakia, often under pressure from Moscow, took decisive steps to create a highly repressive, strictly centralised and politically monolithic Stalinist system. In the process, civil society was dealt a severe blow and many tens, probably hundreds, of thousands of people were stripped of their human dignity and freedoms. This is the bottom-line, which can never be overlooked or attenuated. However, this almost entirely pejorative image of a brutal, efficient and functional 'totalitarian' behemoth is complicated by two main caveats. First, as Fred Eidlin argued in the late 1980s:

> This is not a regime controlled by an omniscient, omnipotent elite single-mindedly united in pursuit of clearly defined goals. Rather it is one in which the ruling elite is ridden with conflicts and personal rivalries, continually faced with apathy and hostility among the rank and file membership of the party. It is a power monopoly in which top decision-making bodies are unable to…keep track of the execution of their own decisions.[65]

The resulting 'organised chaos' in the party, which often went hand-in-hand with regional and local modifications of central directives, was accompanied by a second important trend identified by Spurný in his analysis of the regime's treatment of the German minority: the 'ambiguous' policies of 'care' and 'control'. These, he maintains, were 'two interconnected responses to the insecurity of the 1950s', the first of which 'is often excluded' from discussions of the Stalinist polity.[66] Paternalistic 'care' for citizens, and not just Sudeten Germans, was evident for instance in the changes to the social, educational and cultural systems, several of which we have examined. Indeed, according to one expert, some of these amendments, 'especially the National Insurance Law, corresponded to new international tendencies and even to the aspirations of the majority of the population'.[67]

The broader conclusion is that Czechoslovak Stalinism engaged not only in exclusionary class-based violence, but also sought inclusive devices, which affected different social strata in different ways. Upwardly mobile worker-promotees, impoverished collectivised peasant-farmers, self-satisfied bureaucrats, repressed 'class enemies', privileged 'shock workers', starving labour camp internees, enthusiastic communist youth, compromised or silenced intellectuals – all endured, survived and helped to fashion the system and its discourses in numerous ways, not all of them negative. This plurality of lived experience meant that Stalinism was a murderous inferno for many, but was 'socialism in the making' for others. It is more than likely that individuals had multiple reactions to Stalinist policies, internalising and welcoming some, repudiating and rejecting others, doing their best to adapt, ignore or circumvent yet others. In sum, Stalinism was not simply imposed 'from above' by an 'alien' force completely and irrevocably divorced from Czechoslovak political culture and social processes. It was, to a limited extent at least, the product of the inter-mutuality and reciprocal accommodations of state and society.

Chapter 4: Social Crisis and the Limits of Reform, 1953–67

There is a temptation to view the period 1953 to 1967 as a 'quiet era' for communist Czechoslovakia. After the horrors and upheavals of Stalinism, the KSČ leadership under First Secretary Antonín Novotný remained united and judiciously managed to limit the impact of the potentially damaging 'de-Stalinisation' measures imported from Moscow. Murderous elite purges came to an end and Czech and Slovak citizens appeared 'passive', having been coerced or co-opted into sullen silence. Moreover, there were signs of relative political and economic stabilisation: the worst excesses of mass repression were ameliorated, living standards perceptibly improved and the country portrayed itself as a modernising and 'progressive' state, epitomised by the triumph of the Czechoslovak pavilion at the Brussels World Fair in summer 1958. Indeed, the new Constitution of July 1960 formally announced that Czechoslovakia was the first people's democracy in Eastern Europe to attain the lofty goal of socialism – the state was now officially called the Czechoslovak Socialist Republic (ČSSR). Czechoslovakia may have been a solidly conservative pro-Soviet acolyte, but nothing untoward appeared to ruffle the image of tranquillity, conformity and measured advance.

However, bubbling below the surface were political, socio-economic and intellectual processes that scholars with the benefit of hindsight have conventionally termed 'the origins of the Prague Spring'. Historians of the 1950s and 1960s, tantalised by the allure of the reformist innovations of 1968 and the subsequent Soviet invasion, have understandably focused their attention on the pivotal question: why did the Prague Spring occur? When, and why, did the seemingly impregnable Stalinist system start to implode? Why after 1956 did reformist ideas begin to influence fairly broad strata in the party, its bureaucracies and society as a whole? This chapter concentrates on these vital problems by examining the slow pace of de-Stalinisation in Czechoslovakia after 1953, the dilemmas of rehabilitating the victims of Stalinism, the on-going tensions between Czechs and Slovaks, the consequences of economic stagnation in the early to mid-1960s, the intellectual challenge to the political and cultural norms of the regime and the emergence of an anti-Novotnýite coalition in the party hierarchy by autumn 1967. In addition, the origins of the Prague Spring must be elucidated by incorporating into the narrative such under-explored, but essential, themes as state–society relations, the strategies adopted by the communist leadership in its constant quest for political legitimacy, lifestyle and 'socialist consumerism', and the 'Westernisation' of youth and popular cultures. As in previous chapters, the aim is to provide a more balanced and inclusive interpretation of the period by offering 'from above' and 'from below' perspectives.

Abortive De-Stalinisation

The historiographical consensus is that the Novotný regime was tardy in introducing de-Stalinisation policies after the Soviet dictator's death in March 1953. It is true that a measure of liberalisation did occur: most labour camps were closed down, several leading victims were quietly released, grandiose show trials were eventually eschewed, punishments were less severe, conditions in prisons improved and limited attempts to rehabilitate the martyrs of Stalinist repression were undertaken. But state-sponsored repression did not cease, persecution, harassment and arrests, though at a reduced level, remaining an integral part of state governance well into the 1960s. The final big show trial, as we have seen, came as late as April 1954 when leading Slovak communists were sentenced to lengthy terms of imprisonment for 'bourgeois nationalism'. Grotesquely, a towering statue of Stalin was erected in Prague as late as May 1955. Even Khrushchev's ground-breaking 'secret speech' at the twentieth congress of the Soviet party in February 1956, in which he famously denounced aspects of Stalin's despotic rule and 'cult of personality', did not put an end to the depredations. What is more, political power became increasingly centralised in the hands of Novotný, who in November 1957 added the Presidency to his position as party First Secretary. The lack of meaningful political and attitudinal change in Czechoslovakia was graphically illustrated in the momentous year 1956. At a time when Poland

and Hungary were racked by internal party convulsions and popular anti-Stalinist uprisings, the KSČ and Czechoslovak society appeared quiescent, cohesive and ideologically orthodox. The consequences of this stability were signal. For if the Czechs and Slovaks had rebelled in the autumn of 1956 like their Polish and Magyar neighbours, the very existence of the Soviet bloc could have been put in serious jeopardy. Hence, the stakes were extremely high for both Moscow and Prague. Why, then, did the country appear to be 'dead calm' (*mrtvý klid*) in 1956?[1] And how did Czechs and Slovaks respond to the slow pace of 'de-Stalinisation', and in particular the delayed release of political prisoners?

The following archival-based case study of the reactions of party members and society to the challenges thrown up by de-Stalinisation, the Hungarian uprising and the tortuous rehabilitation process raises important interpretive points about popular opinion and state–society relations. To be sure, the problematic and fragmentary nature of party and secret police sources do not permit any sweeping generalisations and all conclusions must be circumspect. That said, it is clear that state–society relations were rarely straightforward: they were contradictory, dynamic and tense, often antagonistic. But the 'people' were not perpetually at loggerheads with the 'regime'. There is more than superficial evidence of a mutually supportive nexus, of a certain shared socio-cultural, even ideological, terrain on which citizens sought to empower themselves and shape and make sense of the world around them. In the process they appropriated and reformulated aspects of the official ideology in line with their daily experiences and personal views. I call this convoluted amalgam 'critical loyalty'.

Drawing on the work of Third Reich, East German and Soviet specialists,[2] my basic argument is that there existed several 'bridges' linking party-state beliefs, values and mentalities with those of substantial social strata. Fundamental communist ideological assumptions on class divisions, hostility towards 'enemies', the 'superiority' of the working class and the necessity of defending the 'socialist state' from its 'revanchist' neighbours appear to have influenced fairly broad sections of society. This was an intermediate and shifting set of shared perceptions, identifications, images and fears, some of which were short term and provisional, others longer term and more durable, some ideological, others practical, some more embedded, others fragile and contingent on changing circumstances. But it seems to me that the boundaries between 'us' and 'them' in post-Stalinist Czechoslovakia were not always as sharp as some scholars

have insisted and the state had more productive ways of generating
legitimacy and compliance than intimidation and sheer coercion.
That manifestations of outright 'resistance' and overt anti-communist
action in Czechoslovakia in 1956 were minimal compared to Hungary
and Poland – in Muriel Blaive's words 'the anatomy of a non-event' –
suggests that most citizens at best accepted or at worst tolerated the
socialist framework of the republic as a home-made project rooted
in the 'national democratic revolution' of 1945–48.[3] The majority of
Czechs and Slovaks, I contend, favoured meaningful democratisation
and change within the existing system. These conclusions, in turn,
reveal the social underpinnings of both the twisted path of de-Stalinisation and the eventual emergence of the Prague Spring reforms.

A 'Non-Event'?: Czechoslovakia in 1956

The 'crisis of communism' in 1956 severely tested Novotný's rather
colourless regime, but it emerged from the tremors largely unscathed,
at least in the short term.[4] The tentative signs of political de-
Stalinisation in the USSR after the passing of the 'Great Leader',
notably the release of prisoners and the closing of labour camps,
represented an acute dilemma for the incumbent Czechoslovak party
bosses. As Mary Heimann succinctly explains:

> to admit their own guilt in creating and perpetuating what were
> suddenly being called Stalinist 'deformities' might end up costing
> them their necks; yet to continue to defend the status quo would
> make them vulnerable to the charge of 'deviating from the Soviet
> model', the very crime for which they had persecuted their former
> colleagues.[5]

There is no doubt that the 'big four', party leader Novotný, newly
elected President of the Republic Antonín Zápotocký, Prime Minister
Široký and Slovak Party First Secretary Karol Bacílek, were deeply
implicated in the elite purges and mass repressions of the Stalinist
era. They were well aware of the illegal interrogation methods used
by the secret police and of the gross irregularities of the main show
trials. As such, their power positions were directly threatened by any
open investigation into the barbarities of the years 1948–53. After all,
were they not the real guilty ones?
    The strategy they adopted in an attempt to extricate them-
selves from this tight predicament was to recognise certain past
'excesses', offer one or two high-ranking sacrificial lambs and enact

token democratisation measures while more genuinely pursuing the Moscow-inspired 'New Course' with its emphasis on improving mass living standards. This would, it was believed, circumvent the need for substantive reforms. But cynical opportunism, careerism and obfuscation were not the only factors that hindered the de-Stalinisation process in Czechoslovakia. It would appear that many communists, particularly in the party apparatus, sincerely believed in the guilt, or at least complicity, of some of the main victims of Stalinist terror. It was almost impossible for diehard militants to acknowledge that the party – the repository of 'historical truth', progress and enlightenment – had *got things wrong*. This ideologically conditioned, essentially 'Stalinist', mentality played an important role in delaying what was arguably the most significant de-Stalinisation measure: the release and rehabilitation of victims. One might also speculate that at the micro-level the willing or unwilling involvement of ordinary citizens – friends, neighbours, co-workers – in the persecution of the Stalinist years may have negatively influenced the popular reception of de-Stalinisation. Why dig around in the dirt when so many people had colluded with the authorities and so many had stepped into dead men's shoes?

In late February 1956, Khrushchev's 'bomb' – his attack on the God-like Stalin – unexpectedly shattered this fragile conjuncture, shaking the Czechoslovak party rigid.[6] Shell-shocked KSČ leaders did their best to contain the whirlpool of doubts, vacillations and strictures among rank-and-file communists often directed towards local and central luminaries. Both the immediate and longer-term response of the party executive in 1956 was that although ideological and political 'mistakes' had been made in the previous years, the party's 'basic line' was, and remained, fundamentally correct and inviolable. But the new spirit emanating from Moscow could hardly be ignored. Hence, in early March regional meetings of the party *aktiv* were arranged at which lower-level officials were informed about the results of the Soviet congress. At these passionate and heated gatherings, disoriented party members posed rather too many disconcerting questions about Stalin's historic 'errors' and the effect of his cult on Czechoslovakia. Who in the present executive was trustworthy, should party members continue to believe in the Central Committee and how, given the continuity of personnel, would future policy improve on past mistakes?[7]

Intense discussions peaked in April when high-ranking figures in the Politburo and government, including Novotný, came in for stinging rebuke 'from below' for their 'luxurious lifestyle', 'bourgeois manners' and arrogance. If such negative views about individuals were not bad enough, there were signs that faith in the party elite as a whole had been undermined. It was even contended that 'a class struggle exists today in the party' pitting 'ordinary workers' against 'the top functionaries, the so-called red aristocracy'. The dangerous heresy of pro-Titoism reared its head and Czechoslovakia's uneasy relationship with the USSR was also aired, rank-and-file communists in central Prague putting it very starkly: 'the ČSR is an ideological and economic colony' of the Soviet Union.[8] For a short period in spring 1956, then, the KSČ appeared rudderless, lacking in concrete directives from above, either from the leadership in Prague or Moscow. The resultant political and ideological space allowed party members to grope towards their own conclusions about Stalin and Stalinism. Profound bemusement, uncertainty and recriminations were engendered. Indeed, the straightforward word 'chaos' may not be too much of an exaggeration to describe some members' reactions as seen in the words of one party stalwart: 'today I cannot trust the Central Committee...there is chaos in the heads of communists'.[9]

This inner-party turmoil quickly spread to the intellectuals. In April, at the writers' congress several respected Czech authors took advantage of the more self-critical atmosphere and delivered scathing speeches on past party interventions in creative life, reinstating the challenging notion, first articulated in the national awakening of the nineteenth century, that writers were the 'conscience of the nation'.[10] This formulation undoubtedly represented a veiled ideological threat to the party's hegemony in national culture and as such was fiercely resisted by the leadership, which in the course of the next few months gradually tamed the intellectuals' 'congress front'. Slovak writers also entered the fray, bemoaning the lack of freedom of expression compared to Poland and Hungary.[11] In May, university students likewise challenged the status quo, but their actions, though equally symbolic and certainly more visible, proved ultimately just as ephemeral as the pen-smiths'. The students' protest found its most overt and bizarre expression in the traditional Majáles demonstrations in Bratislava and Prague on 12 and 20 May respectively, during which the authorities were openly lampooned in a colourful and carnivalesque atmosphere. Some scholars have concluded that the students' demands, which were an admixture of the academic with the political, represented an 'abortive revolt' against the system. However, there is little evidence to suggest that they were motivated by ardent anti-communism. Indeed, one of the Prague ringleaders later recalled that 'we didn't intend to make any sort of organized resistance against the Communist regime', a stance encapsulated in a slogan shouted at the May Day rally: 'we don't want to rebel, we want discussion'.[12]

Despite these strivings for greater democratisation among ordinary party members and sections of the intellectual elite, the KSČ as a whole remained essentially united and the leadership was able to contain the debates within desired limits and isolate, and eventually reject, the more radical demands. By mid-May, they were sufficiently confident to undertake a counter-offensive. This retrenchment, combined with a series of moderate 'de-Stalinising' devices, such as limited economic decentralisation, administrative de-bureaucratisation, a measure of enhanced autonomy for Slovakia and a theoretical commitment to 'socialist legality', meant that the Politburo never lost control of the situation, even at the height of the 'cult' controversies. A crucial factor in this stabilisation was the existence among many party officials and members of a tenacious predilection for 'Stalinist' conventions and ascriptive class designations which later in the year helped to bind the party together during the turbulent days of the Hungarian uprising. As one party instructor in Brno put it: 'love for comrade Stalin is great'.[13] The KSČ was certainly never a monolithic 'Stalinist' party, but a persistent 'indigenous Stalinism' ran through its core in the 1950s and beyond by which 'the more democratic and national aspects of communist tradition were…submerged by the dominant Stalinist patterns of thought and behavior, and communists were torn between conflicting loyalties and clashing precepts'.[14] This dichotomy helps to explain the longer-term mentalities and collective psyches behind both the prosecution and eventual refutation of Czechoslovak Stalinism.

How did non-party popular opinion develop in 1956 and what historical significance can be attached to it? Contrary to stereotypes, Czech and Slovak citizens were not entirely passive in 1956, at least judging from party and police archival sources and perlustrated private letters. They eagerly engaged with events and expressed a plethora of divergent views ranging from strident support for the Hungarian 'freedom fighters' in their unequal struggle against the invading Red Army to fervent backing for the official party line on the 'counter-revolutionary putsch' in Budapest. There was much anti-communist and anti-Russian invective: 'we will hang the red dogs', 'we should shoot the communists', 'why don't the Russians fuck off!'[15] An 'ex-fascist' worker surely put his finger on the regime's worst fears when he declared: 'it's a pity that these events did not occur all at once. First there were disturbances here in Plzeň, then in Poland and now in Hungary. It would be different today if they had all happened together'.[16] There were widespread demands, too, for greater democ-ratisation on the part of workers, professionals, students and rank-and-file party members, one Slovak labourer insisting that 'there's no democracy in the USSR and it's the same here'.[17]

Clearly, it was dangerous to be caught uttering such iconoclastic thoughts. According to a confidential party report on the Hungarian uprising, in the whole republic from late October to 5 November 1956 there were 665 politically motivated criminal prosecutions. Exactly one-third of the judicial cases took place in Slovakia, which bordered Hungary and was home to a substantial Magyar minority, and almost one-half of those condemned were classified as manual labourers (dělníci).[18] A typical sentence appears to have been several months in jail and a hefty fine.[19] From these statistics, it seems safe to assume a fairly high level of anti-regime sentiment, although one that is hardly indicative of mass unrest and pervasive opposition. Indeed, most arrests were for verbal drink-related infringements and minor 'provocations', which were consciously politicised by the authorities.

It is equally obvious from the archival record, however, that nega-tive opinion was tempered by more regime-affirming views, and not just from party members. Czech political émigrés no less saw many positive socialist aspects of the system – full employment, nationalised industry, state-controlled prices, sickness insurance, pensions, and child and maternity allowances. In August 1956 these ideas were sum-marised thus· ''t cannot be presumed that the people would agree to the re-establishment of a regime similar to that in power between the two world wars. Practically nobody thinks in terms of returning to a capitalist system'.[20] Even British diplomats in Prague noted that 'pro-Communist sympathies, which were strong immediately after the war, have not been entirely spent'.[21] Several letter writers were passionate about the superiority of socialism over capitalism, epitomised by the words of one female author: 'I stand with my heart and mind behind the socialist system'. A husband writing to his wife asserted that this sentiment was fairly widespread: 'not only party members, but also non-party people, remain firmly behind the policies of the KSČ'.[22] The improving socio-economic situation was also noted by many citi-zens, one non-communist worker maintaining that 'what's happened in Hungary and Poland is impossible here because we have a united party and government backed by the working class'.[23]

Anxiety among Czechs and Slovaks over perceived German and Hungarian 'revanchism' ran deep. The fear of German irredentism was especially pronounced in north Bohemia among Czech settlers who had replaced the expelled ethnic Germans in 1945–46. For example, a railway worker from Ústí nad Labem revealed his dread of retaliation: 'the Germans will come to our republic and throw all us Czechs into the Elbe', no doubt a symbolic reference to the Ústí massacre of July 1945.[24] In Gottwaldov, 'some non-party and party members…say that now we will again be surrounded by enemies as in 1938'.[25] A police report from early November 1956 spoke of citizens fearing a West German 'attack on the GDR and then Czechoslovakia'.[26] It was an embedded historical memory which regime propaganda actively fostered and reflected. As a young émigré said, one of the most refined and popular communist arguments was against the so-called 'German danger' and threat of retribution.[27]

Magyar revanchism was likewise broadly feared and rooted in the historical consciousness of Czechs and particularly Slovaks. There was a host of rumours about 'Hungarians occupying Slovakia' and concerns that 'Hungarian irredentists are working at full speed'.[28] These were accompanied by a widespread rejection of the 'gross bestiality' and 'chopping off of heads' that was perpetrated, according to the Czechoslovak media, by the insurgents in Hungary.[29] Hence, the suppression of the Hungarian uprising by the Red Army in early November 1956 seems to have been welcomed by many Czechoslovak citizens, not so much because it represented a victory of 'progressive forces' over 'counter-revolution', but because it ended the barbarous violence and sense of uncertainty and prepared the way for 'normality'. As one letter writer vividly put it: 'thank God we have beaten these Hungarian counter-revolutionaries, bandits, fascists, terrorists and imperialist elements and there is peace…Now we can calmly get back to work'.[30] Regardless of the crass ideologised terminology, it was a sentiment that was not lost on relatively large numbers of people.

Novotný's depressingly conservative and lacklustre regime thus survived the turmoil of 1956 for a variety of reasons: internal party discipline was maintained despite the initial disarray caused by Khrushchev's attack on Stalin's 'cult of personality'; no popular reformist Władysław Gomułka or Imre Nagy existed in the KSČ leadership to challenge the incumbent neo-Stalinists; socio-economic conditions had improved since the upheavals of June 1953 and there was hope for future advances; all sources of real or potential opposition to the regime were isolated and intimidated; and the 'critical loyalty' displayed by many citizens to the regime signified that the lingering bonds between state and society had not been entirely destroyed by the years of Stalinist repression and material hardship.

A similar conclusion can be drawn by an examination of the long drawn out rehabilitation process in Czechoslovakia.

Rehabilitation of Stalinist Victims

The legacy of Stalinist terror in Czechoslovakia, as elsewhere in Eastern Europe, was far-reaching. Mass repression struck at the very heart of the legitimacy of the regime and its leading representatives and therefore in many ways the painfully delayed release and reha-bilitation of victims in the post-Stalinist period lay at the root of the social crises that culminated in the reforms of the Prague Spring. Indeed, a complex amalgam of moral disgust with the judicial crimes of the 1950s and a sense of guilt felt by many for contributing to past evils underlay the growing opposition to the Novotný regime. What mattered was unearthing the 'truth' about the discredited past in an effort to cleanse the body politic. It was this longing for the return of legal norms, the end of arbitrary rule and of the concentration of power in a few hands that gradually bound the majority of citizens to the reformist movement. As Milan Hauner has noted: 'the central element in this process of trust-building between the reformist lead-ership and the population was precisely the desire to visualise social-ism without secret police and torture chambers, [and] the need to rehabilitate the thousands of innocent victims who suffered during the 1950s in the Czechoslovak variant of GULAG'.[31] But even the dis-tressing re-evaluations of the past associated with Alexander Dubček's 'socialism with a human face' did not adequately fulfil the demands for moral rehabilitation and justice on the part of the unjustly con-demned. Such closure had to await the collapse of the communist regime and the ongoing legal amendments of the 1990s and 2000s.

The rehabilitation of political prisoners in the 1950s and early 1960s, spurred by developments in Moscow, unfolded in two phases. The initial stage occurred in the mid-1950s when the KSČ Presidium belatedly established a party commission to review the cases against leading communists. The second phase began after Khrushchev's renewed 'de-Stalinisation' drive in 1961–62 and culminated in two other inconclusive party revisions of the trials. These official reviews were in part occasioned by a deluge of petitions from both promi-nent and lay victims and were punctuated by a series of presidential amnesties which cumulatively saw the conditional release, but not full rehabilitation, of many thousands of people, 'ordinary' criminals as well as communist and non-communist political prisoners.[32] The three party review committees created to investigate the Stalinist trials – the Barák Commission in 1955–57, the Kolder Commission of 1962–63 and the 'Barnabite' Commission of summer 1963 – were all unsatisfactory compromise affairs designed to limit the impact of rehabilitation on the reputation of the incumbent leaders, notably Novotný, and of the KSČ and regime as a whole. Some sentences were reduced, several leading victims were quietly released and the Kolder Commission's report, ratified by the Presidium in April 1963, even 'described the main trials as fabrications and completed the judicial [though not political and moral] rehabilitation of all the condemned', Slánský included.[33] However, the partial rehabilitations and amnesties from the mid-1950s onwards represented a distinct double-edged sword for the communist authorities. On the one hand, they were a palpable risk for the party leadership, creating turmoil, doubt and heretical ideas in the heads of lower-level functionaries, ordinary members and intellectual strata, particularly in Slovakia. But on the other hand, there is evidence that sections of the rank-and-file and, more importantly, non-party citizenry at times identified with the goals and ideological suppositions of the regime, thereby indirectly contributing to abortive de-Stalinisation.

Ostensibly, top secret KSČ reports on responses to the piecemeal revisions reflected the disciplined stance of party functionaries and activists. But a closer reading reveals that an ideological can of worms had been opened. Already in spring 1956 in the wake of Khrushchev's 'secret speech' party officials and rank-and-file members began asking many highly sensitive questions: 'how should party members explain the violently forced confessions of the Slánský band' and 'what will happen to those who broke socialist legality' in Czechoslovakia by carrying out 'Gestapo methods'?[34] Others demanded: 'who is culpable for the tyranny?' and seemed to point the finger at Novotný and Bacílek, 'who were the main accusers in the Slánský trial'.[35] The new requirement for an objective 'truth' struck at the very heart of the party's claim to a monopoly of knowledge and doctrinal purity and hence must have been considered a dangerous heresy. The 'answers' provided by the leadership to these unwelcome queries were clearly inadequate as, seven years later, in April 1963 at the time of the Kolder report, the same issues were again troubling district officials and the rank-and-file: 'how was it possible to commit such gross errors and breaches of socialist legality...Did the party leaders really not know of the incorrect investigation methods of the security organs'? What role did the present members of the Central Committee play in the early 1950s and have they performed real self-criticism? Some speakers linked the 'cult of personality' and lack of inner-party democracy with contemporary economic problems in the country and called for broader improvements in KSČ policy.[36]

Indicative of the subterranean upheaval in the party, especially among the cultural intelligentsia, was the on-going Czech–Slovak impasse. In retrospect, it appears that 1963 was a pivotal year for Czech–Slovak relations. In April, Dubček replaced the despised Bacílek as First Secretary of the Slovak party and thereafter oversaw a partial, but nonetheless significant, revitalisation of political and cultural life in Slovakia, which some observers have termed the 'Bratislava Spring', pre-dating its Prague equivalent by several years. As a result, tensions grew between the conservative Novotný and the cautiously moderate Dubček. Their personal rivalry was, however, the tip of the iceberg. In 1964, the Security Services drew up a classified 'Information Report on the Situation in Slovakia' surveying reactions to the rehabilitation of Gustáv Husák and other prominent Slovak communists sentenced in April 1954 on the spurious and inflammatory charge of 'bourgeois nationalism'. The document painted an alarming picture of Slovak political life. Like all official files, great care is required in assessing its provenance and content, but the report strikes a chord in its depiction of Slovak nationalist sentiment. It stated that the Slovak intelligentsia and 'cultural workers' positively evaluated the rehabilitation of Husák and the 'bourgeois nationalists', supported their activities in the 1940s and 1950s and viewed their rehabilitation as a starting point for further political change. There were also demands for Husák's return to responsible political functions in the Slovak Communist Party. But more disconcerting for the leadership in Prague were the suggestions that the entire Czech–Slovak relationship needed to be re-examined, that there was 'broad support' for Slovak national emancipation and that Slovakia faced a renewal of religious life and church activity.[37]

Indeed, a federal solution was a long-standing goal of many Slovaks and was forcefully reiterated by the eminent historian Miloš Gosiorovský, whose pro-federalism memorandum of March 1963 heavily influenced Slovak party and intellectual elites, some of whom addressed a letter to the Soviet Consulate in Bratislava in June stating that the 'whole economic, political and cultural life of Slovakia is basically directed from Prague'.[38] Profoundly angered by the impact of Gosiorovský's bold initiative, Novotný delivered an offensive anti-Slovak speech in Košice which did much to inflame passions. What is more, it seems some Czechs regarded Slovak proposals for a democratisation of mutual relations as a form of separatism – 'the Slovaks wanted to break away' ('*Slováci se chtěli odtrhnouť*'), an attitude that would reappear five years later during the Prague Spring.[39] The point is that these 'nationalist' aspirations did not remain confined to a small band of educated intellectuals in and outside the party. They resonated with many 'ordinary' KSS members and Slovak citizens. To this extent, the fear of the central authorities was that the release and full rehabilitation of the 'bourgeois nationalists' would boost notions of federalism, strain Czech–Slovak relations and represent, no less, a potential threat to the integrity and unity of the state. Certainly, the Czechoslovak secret police, the StB, went to great lengths to monitor the activities of former members of the wartime Slovak nationalist party and the perceived remnants of its armed wing, the Hlinka Guard.

A brief study of the presidential amnesty of May 1960 also reveals that the regime had good cause for concern over the release of so many internees. Under the terms of the amnesty, introduced as part of the celebrations marking the fifteenth anniversary of the country's liberation by the Red Army, 7,168 inmates were freed from detention, of whom 5,677 were political prisoners. According to the Deputy Minister of the Interior, over 3,800 were workers, farmers and 'working members' of the bourgeoisie, 2,620 were 'kulaks' and other 'bourgeois', and around 650 were 'anti-social parasitic elements'.[40] Returnees were effectively on probation, received meagre compensation, if at all, were debarred from public life and often denied appropriate employment, most being assigned menial jobs. Before their release they had to sign a document saying they would never speak about their experiences in prison or camp, although some did. Hence, in the opinion of one Czech specialist, the presidential decree created 'a new category of "former persons" – the so-called "amnestants"'.[41] The bulky security service reports on these amnestants clearly indicate that although the communist authorities had decided to set free several thousand Stalinist victims they still regarded them as 'enemies' whose activities had to be closely followed.[42] The StB motto appeared to be: 'once an enemy, always an enemy', a tacit recognition that the years of detention had failed to 're-educate' the prisoner. For example, police files are replete with reports that ex-prisoners were engaged in 'hostile activities', especially former priests in Slovakia stigmatised as 'reactionary Catholic fanatics', banned sectarians such as Jehovah's Witnesses and ex-members of non-communist opposition parties.[43] An official police report into the May 1960 amnesty summed up the regime's concerns: 'vacillating elements' among the released believe a political 'reversal' is possible in the near future not only in Czechoslovakia, but also in other socialist states including the USSR.[44] The 'typical view of the amnestied was distrust and an overwhelmingly hostile attitude towards our [socialist] order'.[45]

Popular perceptions of the amnesty, as depicted in the Security Services archive, also gave the authorities cause for disquiet. Although many citizens welcomed the amnesty and some, in line with the official rendition, regarded it as a manifestation of 'socialist humanism' and the moral strength and political vitality of the system, people of 'bourgeois origin' were said to 'trivialise' the guilt of the returnees, churches provocatively offered thanksgiving services and believers considered the amnesty 'an act influenced by God' and saw no positive part played by the state. The remnant German minority took advantage of the concession to push for improvements in their conditions and there were several reports of 'reactionary doctors' writing supposedly false certificates for amnestied prisoners freeing them from unsuitable work.[46] In some communities, especially in the rural areas of south Moravia, returnees were 'heartily greeted by persons with negative attitudes' to the regime.[47] To this extent, the amnesty had potentially oppositional implications and citizens' responses to it were unpredictable and uncontrollable.

The Security Services archive, however, is full of sources which are best interpreted as evidence of an underlying affinity between diverse sectors of society and the communist regime. Although police documentation is doubtless exaggerated, over-ideologised and self-aggrandising, it does impart a revealing glimpse into the social resentments and cleavages that rumbled below the surface of daily life. For instance, in a Prague paper mill employees complained that workers remain in prison while the 'gentlemen factory owners' (*páni fabrikanti*) are set free.[48] Similarly, citizens in Ústí nad Orlicí disagreed with the amnesty, saying a labourer who steals 2,000 crowns of property from the socialist state must serve his entire sentence, while 'enemies' are released for 'anti-state crimes'.[49] In the Kolín chemical works, it was stated that 'mainly workers should be liberated…not members of anti-state groups', while at the Tatra factory in Česká Lípa there was 'sharp criticism' about the fact that 'workers remained in prison, while class enemies were set free'.[50] A Slovak editor lamented that 'out-and-out fascists, bloody [Hlinka] guardists, people who have blood on their hands, people who have murdered and killed' have been included in the amnesty and 'they will now poison our political life'.[51]

Individual 'class aliens' were also targeted. In Beroun district, local people opposed the reappointment of a Catholic priest to 'spiritual service' as 'he belongs down the mines', and one resident complained that the 'amnesty had released all the scum (*lumpové*)'.[52] Inhabitants of Třeboň were annoyed by the reappearance of a notary who had 'robbed the people' and in Česká Lípa 'citizens were seriously agitated by the return of Josef Kulhánek, a downright [American] agent and leader of an anti-state group'.[53] Residents in Havlíčkův Brod proposed that all returnees should be removed to another housing estate as if they were blighted by disease. One local family had four amnestants, one of whom was 'well known as a foreign intelligence agent', and their return 'would mean nothing good for the community'.[54] This sense of illiberalism and class resentment seems to have permeated much of the population. For example, citizens in Prague's 11th district 'protested' about the fact that some amnestants had been provided with accommodation without having to take their turn on the housing list.[55] Workers in central Bohemia were angry that returnees were being re-awarded their academic titles, civil and voting rights, and were even granted paid holidays. 'In the entire Chrudim district', people criticised the fact that the crimes of the returnees are 'forgiven' and that they can lay claim to pensions. In addition, in one local community 'citizens disagreed with the release of the majority of amnestied persons', saying their time in prison was too short to re-educate them. They were 'outright enemies of the system'.[56] In the north Bohemian region, it was even reported that in general 'ordinary workers' were of the 'firm opinion' that the 'scale of the amnesty was too democratic' and the liberation of 'hardened anti-state elements' would not 'pay off', as witnessed in Hungary and Poland in 1956.[57]

The overall picture of communist politics and state–society relations in the decade after Stalin's death is thus opaque and contradictory. On the one hand, measures to reform and democratise the system were strictly limited, reflecting the vicissitudes of de-Stalinisation in the USSR under Khrushchev. The embedded conservative proclivities of the KSČ leadership alienated and confused many lower-level officials, party members and citizens, particularly the intelligentsia, who were impatient with the slow pace of change. Czech–Slovak tensions continued to fester, oppositional currents existed and the regime's reluctance to rehabilitate Stalinist terror victims represented a canker on the body politic. On the other hand, party discipline ultimately remained firm, a resilient vein of 'indigenous Stalinism' afflicted a substantial stratum of the rank-and-file and, importantly, the dominant social attitude of 'critical loyalty' signified that state–society relations were, to a certain extent, mutually reinforcing. This strained reciprocity was based on a relatively broad acceptance of the fundamental principles of socialism and the recognition of socio-economic advancement, profound apprehensions about state security in the face of perceived German and Magyar 'revanchism', shared class or 'workerist' perspectives and resentments, revulsion over the barbarity of the 'counter-revolutionary' violence in Hungary, and distinct currents of populist illiberalism, authoritarianism and even forms of neo-Stalinism. But these bonds of minimal trust were to be severely tested in the early to mid-1960s by the poor performance of the economy and frustrated social aspirations.

Economic Crisis and Social Flux

The Novotnýites could justifiably pat themselves on the back for surviving the 'crisis of communism' in 1956. Their hard line against 'counter-revolution' at home and abroad had proven to be 'correct' and won Soviet plaudits. Understandably, this uncompromising stance was deemed worthy of continuation, and in the wake of the crushing of the Hungarian Revolution an almost immediate backlash took place in Czechoslovakia in the form of a vicious campaign against Yugoslav inspired 'revisionism' and its intellectual proponents. What is more, several recalcitrant Slovak writers were scapegoated in 1957, the drive to collectivise agriculture was stepped up, an anti-religious crackdown was set in motion, a mini-purge of managers, professionals and officials was launched in 1958 and the 'Soviet model' continued to be lauded and copied. This triumphalist mood was buoyed by apparently sound economic growth figures in the late 1950s. National income rose by 7–8 per cent a year, industrial output by 11 per cent and labour productivity by 7 per cent.[58] In this atmosphere, meaningful reform was firmly off the agenda. On the contrary, the regime appeared confident, stable and resistant to change, typified by the new Constitution of July 1960, the ratification of which signified formally that the socialist goals of the 'victorious February' had been fulfilled. The road to communism lay ahead, or so it seemed.

Economic Stagnation and Reform

The sense of self-assurance and the impressive production statistics were, however, hopelessly inapposite. Economic crisis struck with a vengeance by 1962–63 providing a mighty impetus for reform, particularly when linked to destabilising political phenomena such as renewed pressures for de-Stalinisation, incompetent bureaucratic over-centralisation and the ever-present 'Slovak question'. In addition, structural social transformations, rising educational levels and related aspirations for a higher quality of life and improved consumption and cultural participation engendered powerful currents in favour of a more 'modern' and humane form of socialism in tune with the demands of a rapidly changing and diversified society. Inside the KSČ, a wide range of intellectuals, academics, technical and professional experts and, not least, younger apparatchiks began to push for substantive change. Novotný and his cohorts, notably chief ideologue Jiří Hendrych, paid lip service to economic, social and cultural reform, but more often than not dragged their feet fearing that innovations in the socio-economic field would inevitably lead to demands for a far-reaching political metamorphosis, and with it their demise. They were not wrong. The debilitating intra-party battles between 'conservatives' and 'reformers', which characterised the 1960s and culminated in Novotný's ouster in January 1968 and the subsequent Prague Spring, had commenced.

By 1963 the once vigorous industrial economy of Czechoslovakia was showing virtually zero growth, an unprecedented disaster for a socialist state.[59] In that year industrial output fell, as did GNP by over 2 per cent; there was an acute shortage of consumer goods; housing construction was still not meeting demand; the balance of trade was negative; labour productivity was disconcertingly sluggish; and agricultural production, though improving, remained below that of 1936! The situation had been catastrophic since the summer of 1962, when the third five-year plan had to be abruptly terminated and replaced by an emergency one-year plan to stabilise the economy. But neither did this ill-conceived improvised project work. What was the problem? International factors – the Berlin and Cuban missile crises and a loss of trade with China – and climatic conditions outside of the leadership's control undoubtedly played their part, but the real issue was the nature and scale of the Stalinist 'command economy' constructed since the late 1940s. Specifically, the reformers sought a decisive move away from the hyper-centralised basis of state planning and its irrational investment policy, which in their view had engendered the crises of 1962–63. A shift from 'extensive' to 'intensive' growth was needed and this in turn required a fundamental reassessment of the role of the market in a socialist economy. The overall aim was to modernise and perfect that economy, making it more responsive to society's needs.

Since the late 1950s, and more substantively in the early 1960s, a group of official economic theorists led by Professor Ota Šik had

begun to advocate a moderate decentralisation of the planned economy allowing for greater enterprise autonomy, a recalculation of the
pricing and wage systems, and most controversially the introduction
of regulated 'commodity money relations', later dubbed the 'socialist
market', to satisfy consumer demand and activate light and tertiary
industries. Even the accursed word 'profit' was used. For the more
radical reformers, these innovations demanded a re-examination
of the input of the state in the socialist economy. By the mid-1960s,
Šik and others were arguing that the government should perform a
macro-economic function, overseeing the basic structural and financial tasks of the economy, while leaving the micro-economic functions to lower level organisations and enterprise managers. There
was even talk of self-managing workers' councils on the Yugoslav
model. Ultimately, these reforms, soon to be described as a potential
'third way' between laissez-faire capitalism and the centrally planned
Soviet-style economy, threatened a root-and-branch reordering of
the party's 'leading role' in society and hence struck at the heart of
the entrenched power structures and vested interests of the *apparat*.
Indeed, by 1967 Šik concretely broached the taboo of linking economic reform to political change and personnel turnover at the apex
of power.

It is therefore hardly surprising that Novotný and his supporters,
while recognising the need for a measure of creative thinking, did
their best to dilute the essence of the economists' proposals and
delayed their implementation until 1965. As the First Secretary said:
'no, comrades, we shall not allow liberalising, let alone capitalist
influences in our economy'.[60] The Novotnýites' basic goal was the
preservation, or at best 'improvement', of the existing system, and
anything that promised to boost the regime's legitimacy in the face of
economic decline was worthy of consideration. But the conservatives,
including many trade union officials and blue-collar workers, feared
the possible consequences of reform: inflation, greater wage differ-
entials and de-levelling, job losses and unemployment. More than a
few in the party apparatus resisted any change whatsoever. Hence,
recalcitrant and inert middle-level bureaucrats and many of their
superiors were determined that the reform process should be long
and slow. Under these unpredictable and inauspicious circumstances,
it was extremely difficult for the innovators to enforce substantive
decentralisation and pluralisation of the economy. It is even argued
that in some ways the Czechoslovak economy became *more* centralised
after 1965 and the introduction of market procedures was scarcely
begun. Those reforms that were implemented were experimental and

piecemeal. By mid-1965, for instance, only '20 per cent of industrial output was being produced in enterprises operating under experimental conditions'. Despite renewed formal commitment to an accelerated programme of economic transition at the party congress in June 1966 and some signs of growth thereafter, the speed up 'brought the whole process of reform to a point of crisis in 1967'.[61]

Social and Political Critiques

To understand this wider crisis of the *ancien régime*, it is essential to take on board the concerted and mutually supportive nature of the reformist onslaught on the defects of the Novotný 'system'. It was not only party economists who struggled against embedded conservatism. Social theorists, political scientists, philosophers, lawyers and many other professionals grappled their way towards a broad-ranging critique of the existing power hierarchies. The underlying proposition was that the old Stalinist model of 'total' party dominance in all fields of human endeavour – political, socio-economic, cultural, moral – was becoming increasingly out-dated in an era of mass education, social diversification and the so-called 'scientific and technological revolution' (STR). According to Radovan Richta, the eminent Czech social theorist of the STR and main author of the highly influential text *Civilization at the Crossroads* (1966), 'science is now penetrating all phases of production and gradually assuming the role of the central productive force of human society...Socialism stands or falls with science'. The enhanced economic position of science necessitated 'radical changes in education, the increased technical competence of workers, better utilization of the technical and scientific intelligentsia and adequate rewards for their work...and improved methods of consultation with scholars...An atmosphere of free discussion and conflicting views was a prerequisite for the maximum development of science' and thus 'democratic forms of participation' were required if socialism was to survive and prosper.[62] All this massively impacted on the key political issue: the leading role of the party. For what would remain of the party's monolithic position if critical voices were permitted, if enterprise managers, experts and state officials were appointed for their 'technical competence' rather than ideological commitment, if intellectual work was valued more than manual labour, and if it was recognised that stratified, even conflictual, interests existed in Czechoslovak society, which may eventually require multi-party representation and mediation? The contradictions and dangers were legion and traditional Marxist theses rarely provided adequate answers. More relevantly, neither did the inept and indecisive Novotný leadership.

In the realm of political theory, reformers such as the party-trained lawyer Zdeněk Mlynář were tentatively re-evaluating the relationship between state and society and reflecting on the party's leading role. Starting from the premise that the Stalinist system implanted in Czechoslovakia after 1948 had negated the rule of law and individual rights, Mlynář and other temperate iconoclasts argued that a 'new political system was needed which would shift the balance from coercion to persuasion and would establish democratic procedures for reconciling conflicting [social] interests'. Crucially, Mlynář, while accepting the single-party framework, contended that the KSČ's leading role was not won 'once and for all by a single act or organizational form', but had to be 'constantly re-formed by the practical policies of the party', which should 'defend all-society needs'. What is more, these needs and interests would be formulated and expressed by invigorated social 'pressure groups', which by operating within the confines of the National Front would impact on the state machinery.[63] This was, in essence, a democratised vision of a semi-pluralistic polity in which citizens, through their public organisations, would exert an influence on regional and national affairs. Mlynář's ideas were undoubtedly circumscribed, subject to internal contradictions and limited largely to party intellectuals and theorists, but, like Šik and Richta's, they represented a dynamic challenge to the stagnation and inefficiency of the Novotný status quo.

A telling example of the incompetence of the existing order with far-reaching consequences was the low level of educational and professional quality of its 'cadres'. It was calculated in the mid-1960s that 'only 11.9 per cent of "leading officials" had higher education, while 60.3 per cent had only primary or junior specialised education, the remaining 27.8 per cent having secondary and senior specialised training'. What did this mean on the ground? According to the respected sociologist, Pavel Machonin, a mere 48 per cent of enterprise managers and deputy managers and 38 per cent of foremen were adequately qualified for their posts and almost half a million people occupied jobs for which they were unqualified. Two major interrelated conclusions can be drawn from these statistics. First, ideological criteria too often won out over educational and technical prowess in the appointment of higher-ranking officials. This deeply ingrained party attitude, mirroring Novotný's personal anti-intellectualism,[64] was summed up by Josef Toman, the chair of the State Committee for Organisation and Management: 'a leading economic worker must above all be a man devoted to the cause of socialism'. But for reformers, such as the released Slánský trial victim Evžen Löbl, the 'creative thinking and business acumen' necessary for reviving the laggard economy 'cannot be commanded' and stifled by party loyalty.[65]

Second, the 'party ceiling', supplemented by cronyism and self-perpetuating networks, signified a distinct lack of upward social mobility for many tens of thousands of highly educated younger people. By the mid-1960s, one in six graduates 'had to take jobs below the level for which he or she was qualified' and hence had to endure lower wages. Despite the radical rhetoric of gender equalisation, women's earnings were still approximately two-thirds of men's. This disenfranchisement and social alienation also affected those young manual workers who were 'trained in the use of new technologies, but had few opportunities to ply their skills'. Thus, there was a growing disillusionment with the promises of official ideology, particularly among the youth who had 'no experience of the capitalist system but had not profited from the socialist one'.[66] In sum, the authorities did not trust their own 'socialist' intelligentsia and the latter were wary and dismissive of the 'establishment'. This was bad enough, but the underlying frustration was that Novotný's regime, lacking in conceptual clarity and sense of purpose, was simply unable to face the challenges of 'modernity', of renewing the 'humanist' socialist project and therefore risked lagging far behind the ever-changing capitalist world.

Towards a 'Socialist Consumerism'

To portray Czechoslovakia in the late 1950s and 1960s as simply a microcosm of economic doom and socio-cultural gloom is, however, misleading. It is vital to acknowledge the contradictory nature of development under Novotný. There were several pluses among the many negatives. For example, total expenditure on pensions and sickness, maternity and family benefits was at its highest level in 1965 and there was almost universal access to state welfare schemes.[67] Significant strides were made in such important areas as social housing experiments and industrial, creative and advertising design, reflecting the input of modernist architects, designers and cultural and technical specialists, some of whom had been active in institutes and workshops since before the war.[68] Even the fashion industry was not overlooked.[69] Various new individualistic, rather than Stalin-era collectivist, forms of leisure activity, tourism and mass entertainment were beginning to transform popular attitudes and activities by the early 1960s. This was typified above all by the production of afford-able televisions and cars, the number of TV licences rising from 172,000 in 1957 to 1.5 million in 1963.[70] Indeed, regardless of the leadership's enduring commitment to conventional forms of heavy industry and to 'quantity over quality', the regime could not be immune to the Khrushchevite rallying cry of improving the living standards of all citizens as a key indicator of de-Stalinisation and the superiority of socialism over capitalism. There was a Cold War in domestic appliances as much as in military hardware.[71] The turning point in this partial shift to a 'modern' consumerist lifestyle was the triumph of the Czechoslovak exhibition at the World Fair in Brussels in the summer of 1958. The inventive and expensive Czechoslovak pavilion was 'flooded by crowds of visitors', who were, judging by their hand-written comments, genuinely enchanted by the combina-tion of 'technology, works of art, stage design constructions, striking graphics, photography, [and] light effects with musical accompani-ment', all of which coalesced in 'an emotionally charged whole'. Even the *New York Post* enthused: 'In the Czech pavilion the product was pleasure…poetry and humor'. As a result, it was awarded the overall Golden Star and 56 Grand Prizes.[72]

The unexpected success at Brussels was symptomatic of a Czechoslovak society and cultural scene on the cusp of transforma-tion. It was also indicative of the state's constant search for new sources of political legitimacy. As Pavel Kolář has argued, 'in the post-Stalinist era self-presentation through nationalist propaganda became essential to the legitimation strategies of the East European regimes'. In Czechoslovakia's case, one could extrapolate that the World Fair project 'drew on the traditional self-description of Czechs as a democratic and peaceful nation'[73] by conveying the message of 'a successful, harmoniously developing, industrially and cultur-ally advanced, and socially fair society'.[74] Linked to this notion of 'socialist patriotism' was the authorities' attempt to recontextualise traditional production techniques, such as glass-making and folk craft, as a means of 'owning the past, using these elements to support [the regime's] narrative of cooperative production and the march to a better socialist future'.[75] More ideologically dubious and potentially damaging was the tentative quest for a 'socialist consumerism' which, while based on 'Western' stereotypes of material prosperity, style and leisure, presupposed that 'only Socialism could build a "humanist superstructure" that was connected chiefly with a broader approach to culture and…with the possibility of fully achieving one's personal development'.[76] Only socialism, it was insisted by party theoreticians and reformers alike, could deliver rational forms of the 'good life' for all, as opposed to satisfying the irrational egotistical urges sponsored by capitalism which benefited merely the few. This idea that socialist society represented a qualitatively superior alternative to the capitalist environment was particularly pronounced in the burgeoning area of 'free time' since only socialism allowed for the 'maximum all-rounded development of the human personality' and for the creation of the socially committed individual.[77]

The proposition of a rational socialist consumerism embedded in notions of the collective good and capable of enhancing the life of every citizen was not without its adherents among the population, but it was increasingly compromised by contact with Western standards and images. After 1962–63, liberalised travel regulations and mutual academic and cultural exchange agreements permitted many tens of thousands of Czechs and Slovaks to visit capitalist states which, accompanied by a similar influx of Western tourists, had the effect of exposing the relative lack, and inferior quality, of Czechoslovak consumer products. It also engendered a creeping 'Westernisation' of youth sub-culture, which, though adapted to indigenous conditions and norms, deeply worried conservatives in the political and cultural hierarchies. For what was happening, as Peter Bugge makes clear, was 'an intense "*Kulturkampf*"'...around the dichotomy "ideological–non-ideological"'. That is, were the new forms of mass leisure, popular entertainment and non-committed art 'innocent and legitimate supplement[s] to the constructive efforts of the Czechoslovak people in building socialism...or...potentially subversive phenomen[a] undermining the serious, unequivocal and authoritative voice of the Party'?[78] Ideological and cultural mandarins were hopelessly divided on this quandary and hence the authorities rarely spoke unanimously. In these circumstances, everyday life in the cultural field was a permanent cycle of conflict-ridden discussions and stand-offs between younger generally radical artists, their elder professional colleagues and various party-state cultural and censorship functionaries. But compromises were possible.

The classic example was the ultimate Western import: rock music. Unsurprisingly, official cultural bodies were highly suspicious of this alien and potentially destructive hydra, but the eventual response of the party was to appropriate and 'nationalise' it for socialist culture, just as it had for jazz and other genres of 'Western' music. Although attempts were made to limit rock's more extreme manifestations, such as sexual licentiousness, petty criminality and the appearance of long-haired bearded *chuligáni* (hooligans), 'the early 1960s brought an explosive growth in the number of rock bands [and]...the first regular venues'. The end result was that by mid-decade 'rock music came to count as a legitimate form of musical expression in socialist Czechoslovakia'. As Bugge concludes:

> the period from the late 1950s to the end of the 1960s therefore stands out in the history of Czechoslovak culture under communism as a time when the borders of what counted as official became wider, and cultural phenomena rapidly changed status from forbidden to tolerated or even propagated.[79]

This process of gradual transformation can also be evidenced in the so-called 'New Wave' that emerged in Czechoslovak cinematography and literature from the early 1960s, which leads us to the broader question: what role did intellectuals play in undermining the neo-Stalinist system?

Intellectual and Political Ferment

The piecemeal subversion of the Novotný regime carried out by party reformers in the realm of economics, politics and social theory was strengthened by a coterminous assault in the highly significant intellectual and cultural arena. Indeed, after the economic crises of 1962–63 had shaken the party rigid it was this collective front of vocal internal opposition which ultimately sapped the power and will of the Novotnýites. As described in previous chapters, many Czech and Slovak intellectuals had played a prominent role after 1948 in the establishment and consolidation of the Stalinist cultural policy of 'socialist realism'. And yet a few years later these same writers, poets, journalists and publicists were striving to remake the monstrous system they had helped to create. How to account for this mutation from convinced Stalinist in 1948 to timid critic in 1956 to outright reformer in 1968?

'The Killing of Words'

As we noted above, ever since the nineteenth-century cultural and linguistic renaissance Czech intellectuals had been commonly regarded as 'the conscience of the nation' in the battle against 'superior' foreign foes, be they Habsburg 'Germanisers', Nazi occupiers or Soviet overlords. In the absence of an indigenous aristocracy Czech intellectuals

'became the spiritual elite of a subjugated nation, and eventually transformed themselves into a political elite'. Hence, throughout modern
Czech history 'the connection between culture and politics [has]
had an organic basis'.[80] Given the politicised role and long-standing
authority of Czech intellectuals, it was inevitable that the controversies
between them and the communist regime would not remain simply
an academic issue, but would take on distinct political overtones. The
situation in Slovakia was similar. Greatly boosted by the Khrushchev
'thaw' and the revelations of criminality under Stalinism, Czech and
Slovak writers, journalists, academics and their radicalised students
began to seek a meaningful democratisation of the system and its
cultural practices. This 'loyal opposition' – in the sense that many of
the protagonists were party members and overwhelmingly strove for
a new alternative model of socialism – launched a prolonged struggle
with the party-state bureaucracy for the restitution of artistic freedoms,
academic professionalism and respect for basic human rights. This
largely behind-the-scenes war of attrition went on throughout the
1960s, but only in the crisis months of 1967 did the intellectuals, in an
uneasy alliance with party reformers, begin to win their cause.

   The seminal question must be asked: why was the ostensibly omnipotent party unable to prevent liberalising tendencies from flourishing in the arts, media and sciences? First, coercive administrative
methods had been dealt a blow by de-Stalinisation. No longer could
party apparatchiks automatically resort to the tried-and-tested tools
of demotions and expulsions, let alone arrest and imprisonment.
Novotný certainly never renounced the stick, but even when he did
attempt to stamp his authority on the cultural scene, as in 1963–64
after the reanimation of the 'Slovak question' and again after the
fractious fourth writers' congress in June 1967, intellectuals and their
supporters refused to buckle and continued the fight. Crucially, the
party was no longer united in its response to 'dissent' and hence the
intelligentsia, finely attuned to the subtle ideological manoeuvrings
in the party hierarchies, were learning to lose their fear. Second, as
the majority of cultural figures, or at least the older more influential
generation, were KSČ members, party functionaries regarded them
as real or potential partners and tended to rely on them to correct
any 'negative phenomena' that emerged among their radicalised
colleagues. Third, already by the late 1950s cultural institutions,
publishing houses and film studios had gained a measure of financial
autonomy from the state, and moreover by the time of the 'New Wave'
Czechoslovak cinematography was providing vital Western funds for
grossly depleted government coffers. Why ban controversial films if

they are earning precious dollars? Finally, it is too simplistic to view the cultural struggles of the 1960s in terms of 'democratic' writers and film-makers bravely resisting 'totalitarian' bureaucrats and ideologues in the name of Western-style freedom of expression and liberty. This undoubtedly was a compelling part of the story, but to a good extent both sides needed each other in a symbiotic relationship. Artists, scholars and the cultural elites in general relied on the patronage, resources and stability proffered by the party-state, while in an era of scientific and social transformation party leaders had to recognise, albeit reluctantly, the professional knowledge, status and intellectual space of the intelligentsia, as well as welcoming the financial benefits and academic kudos that accrued from cultural successes abroad.[81]

Unsurprisingly, one of the intellectuals' fundamental demands was for the easing, or outright termination, of state censorship, because for the Czech cultural elite, like the poet Miroslav Holub, the 'killing of words precedes the killing of people'.[82] The battle was waged primarily in the Union of Writers and its literary organs, the Czech *Literární noviny* and the Slovak *Kultúrny život*, both of which became real thorns in the side of the party's guardians of cultural orthodoxy. In Slovakia, intellectuals regularly included in their specific demands the need for greater national autonomy, but, contrary to received wisdom, there was no sharp dividing line between the 'democratising' Czechs and the 'federalising' Slovaks. Both focused on universal humanistic goals, even if their campaigns often ran on separate lines. An important milestone came in May 1963 at an international symposium on the hitherto banned works of the celebrated Czech–German author, Franz Kafka. The attempt to rehabilitate Kafka, whose interwar novels pondered humanity's alienation under absurd and inscrutable bureaucracies, 'represented the central point in a struggle to break out of the cultural isolation into which the Czechs had been forced during the period of Stalinism' and the conclusion that social anomie existed under socialism as well as capitalism was a veritable time bomb.[83]

By the mid-1960s, the literati were joined by a younger generation of like-minded theatre directors and particularly cinematographers, many of whom were to gain broad international acclaim for their allegorical, humorous, but rarely overtly subversive productions collectively known as the Czechoslovak 'New Wave'. The films of the New Wave, of which Jiří Menzel's *Closely Observed Trains* (1966) became the best known in the West, mirrored that sense of alienation adumbrated at the Kafka conference and felt by many Czechs and Slovaks in the face of the party's seemingly imperturbable and impenetrable power machine. At this level, the New Wave reflected the profound spiritual crisis at the heart of the Novotný regime. Indeed, the war of words between the central authorities and the cultural elites went beyond everyday politics, impacting on the very essence of the Czechs' and Slovaks' 'national, cultural, and linguistic survival' since 'truth could be arrived at only through free dialogue while bigotry and philistinism sabotaged the very existence of the nation'.[84]

Hostilities came to a head at the Fourth Congress of the Writers' Union in June 1967. Sharp criticism of the leadership's abuse of power and destructive policies by such respected authors as Milan Kundera, Ludvík Vaculík, Antonín Liehm, Ivan Klíma, Pavel Kohout and Václav Havel infuriated conservative officials. Kundera defended the intrinsic right of free speech thus:

> Any suppression of views, even when the views that are being forcibly suppressed are erroneous, must lead…away from the truth, for truth can be attained only through the interaction of views that are equal and free. Any interference with freedom of thought and words, no matter how discreet the technique or name given to such censorship, is a scandal in the twentieth century and a shackle on our emerging literature.

Vaculík was even more forthright:

> It must be acknowledged that over the past twenty years [under communism] not a single human problem…has yet been solved. What is more, I am afraid that we have not advanced on the world scene and that our republic has lost its good name. We have not contributed any original thoughts or good ideas to humanity.[85]

Novotný and his cultural and ideological 'tsar', Hendrych, were far from amused, but their subsequent heavy-handed attempts to repress freedom of expression and expel the recalcitrant writers only served to estrange the reformist and oppositional elements both in and outside the party.

'We Want Light!': The End of Novotný

Among the most alienated and troublesome strata of society were university students. Youth in general played a highly significant role in the 1960s, contributing in no small measure to the malaise of the regime. According to one contemporary Czech sociologist, most young people 'accepted socialism as a matter of fact, [but] they were much more prone than their elders to criticize the defects of the system, in particular the discrepancy between the ideal and the reality'.[86] This attitude also prevailed among many younger members of the party. Indeed, the authorities were deeply concerned about the contagious political apathy, uncertainty and lack of hope among this generation – by 1966 only 9 per cent of party members were 26 years of age or younger, and only 0.4 per cent were students. Affiliation to the Czechoslovak Union of Youth (ČSM) was in marked decline and surveys showed that most students devoted little or no time to political and public affairs. Piecemeal amendments to the functions and organisation of the ČSM did nothing to assuage student discontent, which focused primarily on practical issues such as compulsory Marxism–Leninism classes, poor accommodation and, before liberalisation measures in 1963, limitations on travel abroad. There were even youth demonstrations in October 1964 with many arrests, including young workers. By the summer of 1967 there were signs of contact between student activists and the rebellious writers and in late October students at the large Strahov dormitories in Prague spontaneously marched through the streets demanding 'We want light!' in response to repeated electricity cuts and, metaphorically, to the 'darkness' of the regime. They were met with considerable police brutality, which in turn further discredited the First Secretary and his out-of-touch minions. Hence, by the autumn of 1967 a broad anti-Novotný coalition was taking shape both within and outside the KSČ.

However, it would be wrong to oversimplify this struggle as one overtly pitting the 'people' against the 'system'. As H. Gordon Skilling wisely reminds us:

> the regime enjoyed substantial support, primarily in the apparatus, but also in the army and police, the people's militia, the state bureaucracy, and even among the broad masses. Neither the workers nor the peasants evinced active dissent, nor did the Slovaks as a whole, nor the Slovak party, openly resist Prague rule…Novotný lasted so long because he was in fact accepted by most of the people, despite widespread discontent and dissent in certain circles.[87]

The decisive factor in Novotný's demise was not mass pressure, but the loss of legitimacy among his own colleagues in the party leadership. His protracted removal between October 1967 and January 1968 after weeks of increasingly acrimonious disputes and political wranglings in the KSČ Presidium and Central Committee was carried out almost exclusively in the murky corridors of power and in near total secrecy. The main bone of contention was Novotný's concentration of powers. Šik's hard-hitting speech at the Central Committee plenum on 19 December did much to put the nail in Novotný's coffin. For the first time a leading official expressly called on him to resign as First Secretary.[88] The Slovaks weighed in with accusations of Novotný's perennial Czecho-centrism and anti-Slovak sentiment. The boss's anachronistic counter-accusations of the Slovaks' 'narrow national interests' demonstrated his unreconstructed neo-Stalinism and incensed his opponents. The denouement came on the night of 4–5 January 1968 when the embattled and out-voted Novotný was forced to hand over to a compromise candidate, the 46-year old Slovak, Dubček. Even the impromptu visit of the Soviet leader Leonid Brezhnev to Prague in December could not prevent Novotný's downfall. Although he did not wish to abandon Novotný entirely and sought a consensual solution, Brezhnev allegedly contributed to his fate with the words '*Eto vashe delo*' ('This is your affair'). No one knew it at the time, but the 'Prague Spring', one of the most significant events of the Cold War era, was about to begin.

When and why did the pre-1953 Stalinist edifice crumble? Four interlocking components can be identified in answer to this key question: external pressures from the Soviet leadership, known in the West as Khrushchev's 'de-Stalinisation'; underlying structural factors in the Czechoslovak economy, society and culture; internal debates, disputes and eventually full-blown conflicts 'from above' in the Czechoslovak party; and tensions and strivings 'from below' among different social strata and between Czechs and Slovaks. Specifically, the gradual complex process of decay started in earnest in 1956 after Khrushchev's 'secret speech' and was related largely to the need to reassess Stalinist terror and rehabilitate its victims. The reluctant, but sensational, exposure of police brutality and endemic illegality and the shattering of the myth of party infallibility were the most devastating consequences of de-Stalinisation. This was a massively risky undertaking, which was extended in 1962–63 also following intervention from Moscow. These cataclysmic revelations in turn engendered elite political rivalries and other profound disagreements at all levels of the party, pressures which were exacerbated from the early 1960s by unprecedented economic stagnation, rising Slovak discontent, intellectual and youth opposition, and broader social moods and attitudes, some of which supported and fostered reform, while others were 'conservative' and averse to rocking the steady boat of 'normality'. The former gradually won out over the course of the 1960s as political, socio-economic and cultural processes fostered change in an increasingly indecisive, bureaucratised and ossified *ancien régime*.

Two caveats, however, are in order. First, the conventional view of the 1960s and the origins of the Prague Spring as one of intensifying inner-party tussles between 'enlightened progressives' and 'unrepentant hard-liners' is only part of the story. On the one hand, few communist reformers were entirely cleansed of old patterns of thinking and action; on the other hand, some 'Stalinists' espoused new ideas depending on the issue. Moreover, 'society' can never be taken out of the equation. The demands, aspirations, hopes and fears of millions of citizens informed party policy and contributed in no small measure to the internal party debates and conflicts. Second, in important ways the 'Stalinist edifice' far from completely collapsed in the course of the 1960s. A resilient 'indigenous Stalinism', or more accurately 'neo-Stalinism', continued to exist throughout the party and, if my interpretation is correct, illiberal, populist, even authoritarian inclinations persisted among sections of society, which militated against fundamental political and social transformation and democratisation. These tendencies were certainly attenuated during the Prague Spring, but re-emerged under the post-invasion 'normalised' regime as we shall discover in the next two chapters.

Chapter 5: Czechoslovak Spring, 1968–69

The year 1968 was a pivotal moment in the contemporary history of Czechoslovakia, and indeed of Europe and the world as a whole. The unprecedented events of the 'Czechoslovak Spring' have been seen as part of a global phenomenon of radicalisation, protest and liberation in the late 1960s stretching from Paris to Chicago, from Belfast to Wuhan. In Prague, a new party leadership under Alexander Dubček initiated a series of reforms which collectively became known as 'socialism with a human face'. It was a bold peaceful experiment that attracted avid attention and its prime goal was to address the deep-seated crises that had afflicted Czechoslovak politics, economics, society and culture since the 1950s. The notion of a democratised and humanised socialism – or 'third way' between Soviet state socialism and Western liberal capitalism – appealed not only to disillusioned East European Marxists, but also to many on the left in the West, providing the ideological basis of the 'Euro-communist' trend of the 1970s and 1980s and influencing Gorbachev's path-breaking *glasnost* and *perestroika* in the USSR. The potential ramifications of the reforms, both at home and abroad, were indeed profound, not least because a new and in some ways spontaneous actor entered the fray – popular opinion and an embryonic civil society. However, it must be recognised that for the leading reformers the innovations had their limits – they represented precisely a 'democratisation' of the existing communist regime, not a conscious route to a fully fledged 'democracy'. Their architects, after all, were communists, not liberals. An important additional point is that the rubric 'Prague Spring', which is universally used in historiography and therefore unavoidable, is 'Czecho-centric' and rather misleading. The reforms not only affected the Czech lands.

They were as galvanising for Slovaks as they were for Czechs and hence I have entitled the chapter 'Czechoslovak Spring'.

Many of the projected reforms, in particular the abolition of media censorship, the activation of non-communist political and social groupings, and the demotion of conservative pro-Soviet officials and promotion of radical reformers, aroused deep concern among Soviet and East European communist leaders. Already by early spring the changes in Czechoslovakia were seen in Moscow, East Berlin, Warsaw and Sofia as opening the door to 'counter-revolutionary elements' and 'anti-socialist right-wing forces', whose ultimate aim was perceived to be the overthrow of communist rule. A series of bilateral and multilateral negotiations between the two sides proved unavailing, despite seeming binding agreements in late July and early August. To the utter bewilderment and anger of the vast majority of Czechs and Slovaks and the dismay of most foreign socialists, including a large number of communist parties, the reformist endeavour was abruptly curtailed by Warsaw Pact tanks on the night of 20–21 August. Although grassroots activism persisted until the summer of 1969, the Czechoslovak Spring had been effectively crushed and the country was about to succumb to 20 years of 'normalisation'. The essential questions I will address in this chapter are: what were the content and aims of the Czechoslovak reforms? What were their main contradictions and limitations? What role did the cultural elite and other sectors of society play in their formulation, and how were they received by the population? Why did the Soviet leaders deem the Dubčekite reforms a threat to the 'socialist commonwealth'? Why did they decide to undertake concerted military action against Czechoslovakia? What was the immediate political outcome of the armed intervention? And what were the first steps towards 'normalisation'? Throughout, I will demonstrate how the archival discoveries of the last 25 years have enhanced our understanding of this seminal turning point in Czechoslovak and European history.

'Socialism with a Human Face'

In early January 1968 not much was known about the new party boss, Dubček. Appointed without Moscow's explicit prior approval, he was a staunch communist, had spent his childhood and early youth in the Soviet Union and had been head of the Slovak party since 1963. He had only moderate reformist credentials before 1967 and was initially regarded as a trusted friend of the USSR – 'our Sasha'.[1]

Remarkably, however, Dubček soon became the personification of the Prague Spring, a 'heroic' almost mythologised figure. This worldwide image was in part fostered by his human warmth, sincere rather unassuming character and ready smile which contrasted markedly with his dour predecessors. It was as if he embodied the defining slogan of 1968: 'socialism with a human face'. But this does not mean that Dubček was a radical innovator who inspired all, or even most, of the specific reforms. Or that he was not prone to indecision and ill judgements, and on occasions lacked resolution and consistency. As one progressive reformer later put it, Dubček incarnated 'in contradictory fashion both continuity and discontinuity' with the old order; and a recent reassessment of his political modus operandi is more sardonic, labelling him 'the scheming *apparatchik*'.[2]

The phrase 'socialism with a human face' was apparently coined for Dubček by the reformist sociologist Radovan Richta, was first used by the party leader as late as July 1968 and gained far greater resonance after the crushing of the Prague Spring than during it. It reflected the renewed interest of party theoreticians, academics and other intellectuals, evident since the early 1960s, on Marxism's relationship with 'humanism' and on the position of the individual in socialist society. The concept was, perhaps intentionally, left vague and meant different things to different people, but its implications were explosive. In essence, it was an attempt to forge a humane, civilised and modernised socialism in tune with Czechoslovak political culture and contemporary conditions, and moreover one which was, implicitly at least, to be an improvement on the Soviet prototype. This new polity would be achieved by democratising the relationship between state and society, by reconciling individual liberty, reason and social justice, by permitting broader societal input in public affairs and by eliminating the openly repressive aspects of the regime. In this way, it also had a more immediate and pressing practical aim: to relegitimise the communist system in the eyes of its citizens. However, 'socialism with a human face' strongly implied that the existing regimes in Eastern Europe and the USSR were somehow 'inhuman'. As Brezhnev tetchily asked Dubček in May 1968: 'What's with this human face? What kind of faces do you think we have in Moscow?'[3] But the truly radical latency of the slogan was that no one knew precisely where it would lead – to a revitalised socialism which would strengthen KSČ rule or a multiparty democracy which would end it and remove Czechoslovakia from the Soviet orbit. The consequences of democratisation were manifold and unpredictable.

Communist reformers attempted to square this circle by repeatedly insisting that it was never their intention to diffuse power by creating a pluralist liberal democratic system. As Marxist theorists they argued that society's divergent interests could be recognised and institutionalised, but must respect the common socialist fabric of political discourse; that corporate and pressure groups should have access to the decision-making process to prevent the over-centralisation of authority, but could only legally exist in the framework of the communist-dominated National Front; and that no opposition parties should be allowed, as agreed unanimously by the KSČ Presidium in March 1968. Dubček and other moderate reformers emphasised again and again that the Communist Party would retain its 'leading role', but should rule by example, be prepared constantly to earn society's voluntary support, should set out the broad direction of macro-policy and perform a 'persuasive', as opposed to a 'coercive', role in resolving societal problems.[4] The crucial dilemmas, however, were how to reactivate public life and involve citizens in the management of the state *without* jeopardising the party's monopoly of power and how, in the absence of repression, to maintain control over a popular opinion that threatened to go well beyond limited reform. It was these contradictions, never adequately addressed by the Czechoslovak leaders, that aroused the Kremlin's grave suspicions.

From this brief overview it would appear that the Czechoslovak reform 'movement' was a monolithic bloc of like-minded liberalisers. This is a misconception. In reality, there were at least four strands to the movement and they can be termed 'conservative', 'centrist' and 'radical' reformers, all of whom found themselves in the same Communist Party, and non-party activists and intellectuals, who wished to accelerate and deepen the reform process. But even this categorisation is overly rigid as individuals could, and did, move from one grouping to another depending on the circumstances and specific issues. The boundaries were hardly precise and changed over time. As Prime Minister Oldřich Černík stated: 'the mass media divide people into progressive and conservative. Yet that dividing line runs through every person'.[5] It is also impossible to overlook personal rivalries and power ambitions between, and within, these loose coalitions. That said, there were definite nuanced differences. The conservatives, such as Vasil Bil'ak, Drahomír Kolder, Alois Indra and Oldřich Švestka, were content with piecemeal and limited reform, fearing that more drastic measures might threaten vested interests and privileges and undermine established Marxist–Leninist doctrine. By the summer, they had formed an insidious pro-Moscow 'fifth column' in the KSČ apparatus.

The centrists, including Dubček himself, Černík, Zdeněk Mlynář, Josef Smrkovský and arguably Gustáv Husák, favoured a more far-reaching liberalisation, but this was to be controlled from above, introduced gradually and not permit any space for 'anti-socialists' to threaten the 'leading role' of the party. The radicals, František Kriegel, Ota Šik and Čestmír Císař, sought a thorough democratisation of political, economic and cultural life and grew impatient with the slow tempo of reform, but they were reluctant to endorse multi-party democracy and the unregulated market. Non-party intellectuals, such as the playwright Václav Havel and the philosopher Ivan Sviták, argued cogently for the creation of a genuine opposition party as the precursor to a fully fledged democracy, but both, especially the latter, couched their demands in socialist rhetoric.[6]

This diverse composition of the reform movement helps to explain the contradictions that littered the Dubčekite programme. Kieran Williams admirably summarises these dichotomies and his conclusions are worth citing at length:

Lumped uneasily into one kitchen sink were liberal ideas of individual rights and constitutionally limited government, a functionalist, corporatist system of bargaining and decision-making, a managerial technocracy of semi-autonomous state enterprises, and a radical experiment in workplace democracy and humanized market...Party members were to find local solutions to local problems, yet were expected always to defer to central decrees. Other political parties were to enjoy independence and equality... but the communists would remain supreme and brook no opposition. A new model of socialism was to emerge that would offer far greater freedom and opportunity than capitalism could, and would thus contribute to the anti-imperialist struggle by luring Western states, yet, at the same time, the model was presented as suited to Czechoslovakia's unique national conditions and not intended for replication in other Soviet-bloc states. Censorship would yield to a new openness, but no one was to articulate an ideology hostile to communism. Market forces would replace rigid central planning, but there was to be no large-scale private ownership or decollectivization of agriculture. Groups would be allowed to pursue their interests and influence policy-making, but a powerful state would uphold higher communal goals.[7]

These limitations were clearly revealed in the foremost party statement on the aims of the renewed KSČ, the Action Programme adopted in April. Throughout January and February, there had been no major moves towards reform. Most of the Novotný team remained in post; there was no media discussion of the reasons for Novotný's ouster; Dubček made few public utterances outlining his vision of the future; and there were as yet no overt signs of disquiet among Soviet and East European leaders. It can therefore be safely assumed that the new leadership did not possess a pre-arranged detailed blueprint for reforming the country and that much would depend on the correlation of forces inside the party hierarchy and on the response of society to the new proposals. The immediate task that Dubček and his supporters set themselves was to codify a reformist package in an Action Programme, which would elaborate the party's position on fundamental political, economic, social and cultural problems, including the 'Slovak question'. Dubček put great store in this endeavour and after many delays the Action Programme was finally ratified by the Central Committee on 5 April 1968.[8] This important, eclectic and open-ended document, hailed by some as the *Communist Manifesto* for the twentieth century, was riddled with ambiguities and compromises, but attempted to institutionalise a division of power in the communist system; projected economic decentralisation; safeguarded democratic civil liberties, including the freedom of assembly, association and foreign travel; posited, uniquely for a communist regime, full political and civil rehabilitation of victims of Stalinist illegalities; and recognised the autonomy of artistic and cultural organisations. As such, the Action Programme was broadly welcomed by the Czechoslovak public, but it did not go down well in the Kremlin, Brezhnev ominously describing it as 'an expression of petty-bourgeois spontaneity' and 'a bad program that opens up the possibility of the restoration of capitalism'.[9]

This somewhat exaggerated assertion must be seen in the context of developments in Prague since March. The one initiative of the January–April consolidation period that really did strike at the heart of orthodox communist rule was the end of preliminary censorship of the media. The KSČ Presidium's profoundly controversial decision in early March effectively curtailing censorship was taken in the belief that 'we can win people over to the ideas and policy of the Party…only by truthful and complete information, and…scientific analysis'.[10] It was a bold and massively popular notion, but one which very rapidly brought about an unheard-of situation bordering on the complete freedom of expression in the press, television and radio. This was a veritable landmine as it offered the potential for unrestricted debate, a clash of views, even oppositional currents;

in short, an embryonic civil society. The party daily *Rudé právo* and other official newspapers suddenly became worth reading as mouthpieces of objective reporting rather than merely propaganda vehicles. Political humour and satire, characteristic of the Czechs and Slovaks, was almost ubiquitous and cartoons soon appeared lampooning communist officials and institutions.[11] A host of progressive publications, notably the Union of Writers' new weekly *Literární listy* (*Literary Pages*) and *Student*, began to address highly contentious themes.

An abbreviated list of these long-taboo subjects demonstrates the incendiary nature of the cessation of censorship: 'the many injustices of Stalinist terror and Pragocentrism, the Masaryks and the First Republic, and musings on such core concepts as democracy, socialism, power, freedom, and identity'. This 'frenzy of rediscovery' occurred 'increasingly beyond [party] control' and was accompanied by mass meetings, some broadcast live on television, at which citizens in a totally unprecedented manner grilled leading communists and drew up radical resolutions explicitly linking the 'new' socialism with democracy. Open and highly critical debates took place involving top-ranking victims of Stalinist repression. It was becoming clear that 'the party monopoly on ideas and history had collapsed'.[12] So much so that comparisons between Czechoslovakia 1968 and Hungary 1956 were starting to be drawn, not least in Moscow, Warsaw and East Berlin. The crucial difference, however, is that the 'collapse' in the former was relative: social and political disagreements did not boil over into anti-communist violence on the streets, the party itself did not disintegrate from within and all 'oppositional' ideas remained in the broad socialist framework, no one advocating the renewal of the 'old capitalist order'. Nevertheless, there were strivings in society which pushed the boundaries of the possible to the limit.

Social Activism and Public Opinion

The reform process itself was in large part a manifestation of the social tensions and structural transformations that had been maturing since the 1950s, many of which were discussed in the previous chapter. In the liberalising atmosphere of 1968 these social conflicts and anxieties gave rise to various unofficial groups and organisations which began to emerge from early spring. In this context, it is vital to remember that the Prague Spring was not just a series of reforms elaborated and implemented 'from above' by communist politicians. It was also an exhilarating mass undertaking 'from below', tentative at first, but ultimately involving millions of ordinary citizens, many of whom had divergent ideas and beliefs to the party power-holders. For the first time people were beginning to enjoy the fruits of democratic freedoms and it was an intoxicating cocktail. It has often been argued that the spearhead of Czechoslovak reform was the creative intelligentsia. The ideas of writers, journalists, academics, lawyers and philosophers helped to crystallise both the political attitudes of society and, to a lesser extent, the decision-making of party leaders. Generally, the intellectuals strove to radicalise the reform movement along more democratic lines and pressure the party elite to maintain the tempo of change. They were not a totally homogeneous body, but were united in the firm belief that the discredited bureaucratic system was obsolete and should be replaced by a democratic socialist order based on full and equal rights, some form of institutionalised opposition and above all complete freedom of expression.

How exactly did the intellectuals radicalise the reformist agenda? One of the most contentious documents of the Prague Spring was the 'Two Thousand Words Manifesto', written by the novelist Ludvík Vaculík and published on 27 June at a time when the conservatives appeared to be obstructing meaningful change. The manifesto, addressed to all Czechoslovak citizens, provocatively called for 'public criticism, resolutions, demonstrations...strikes, and picketing' to induce the resignation of corrupt and dishonest communist officials. Although Vaculík shunned all 'illegal, indecent, or boorish methods', his appeal for grassroots activism was bound to raise alarm, and fear, among domestic and foreign hard-liners, even many moderates.[13] For them, the manifesto simply confirmed that 'counter-revolution' was on the march. The creative intelligentsia also made their impact felt in organisational terms. In early April, 150 intellectuals established the Club of Committed Non-Party Members (*Klub angažovaných nestraníků* – KAN) as a pressure group to ensure that the KSČ fulfilled its reform pledges 'toward a common goal – socialism, on the basis of humanism and democracy'. Despite its loose organisational structure and relatively small membership, estimated at 4,000 in May and 15,000 in July, KAN, by its very existence as an independent association of non-communists demanding a say in political life, aroused profound concern among conservative elements both at home and abroad, as did two other controversial bodies: K-231 and the steering committee of the Social Democratic Party (SDP). The former, numbering as many as 130,000 people, was founded by ex-political prisoners and sought full judicial, political and moral rehabilitation for its members. K-231 was a serious thorn in the side of high-ranking conservatives as a permanent reminder of their personal involvement in the degradations of the Stalinist era. The potential reactivation of an autonomous SDP also signalled a threat to the KSČ and therefore its steering committee operated on the margins of legality.[14] The prime importance of these groupings and of the actions of the radical intellectuals is that they created severe difficulties for the Czechoslovak leaders in negotiating with their Soviet counterparts, who could claim with a degree of validity that Dubček was tolerating the formation of 'anti-communist' organisations.

Popular activism in 1968, however, went well beyond the strictly political. A brief list of the numerous associations, clubs and pressure groups established in the course of that year gives an idea of the extent of the emergent civil society in Czechoslovakia: the Society for Human Rights; Workers' Committees for the Defence of Freedom of the Press; the Bohemian and Moravian Student Union; the Federation of Railway Engine Crews; the Union of Bohemian, Moravian and Silesian Towns and Communities; the revitalisation of Roman Catholic, Evangelical, Jewish and other religious congregations and councils; the reactivation of Magyar, Polish, Ukrainian and Roma cultural bodies; and the renewal of cooperative movements and diverse charities.[15] In Slovakia, the Organisation for the Defence of Human Rights was established with almost 2,000 members. As one observer later put it: 'a whole infrastructure of autonomous organisations and institutions…came into being, laying the foundations for political and social pluralism'.[16] Youth and 'alternative' culture, student activism and artistic experimentation, which had already appeared in the early to mid-1960s, mushroomed in the liberalised atmosphere. These manifestations were not always directly or consciously 'political', but they did denote a striking sense of social transgression.[17] A new rock music magazine, *Pop Music Expres*, was launched in April 1968 and long-haired members of the Czechoslovak Hippies Club even presented a small gift to Dubček at the May Day parade![18] From the point of view of the political elites, these developments were deeply ambivalent. For the 'progressives', they represented meaningful democratisation, the increasing civic maturity of an engaged public and the congruence of the party's reform programme with popular opinion, albeit accompanied by a few regrettable 'excesses'. For the 'conservatives', they were damaging signs that society was moving beyond the control of the party, organisationally and ideologically.

Another worrying development for the hard-liners was the huge increase in foreign travel, both into and out of the country. Travel had been liberalised in 1963 with the result that, whereas in

1961 only 62,610 Czechoslovaks visited capitalist countries and 102,600 Westerners came to Czechoslovakia, the respective figures for 1967 were 261,081 and over 800,000. In the period January 1968 to April 1969 the number of trips to capitalist states rose to 690,622.[19] The fear was that the growing exposure of young people in particular to Western culture and consumerism would engender 'bourgeois individualism' and undermine 'socialist collectivist' values. Furthermore, the risk of 'enemy agents' freely entering the country was threatening the security of the state. As Brezhnev bluntly intimated at a bilateral meeting in early May: '40,000 people from West Germany cross the border of Czechoslovakia every day without any control…[they] travel around in their own cars to military units…and a good half are American or West German spies'.[20] Soviet tourists to Czechoslovakia during 1968 also frequently complained about the impact of political liberalisation and were humiliated by their treatment after the invasion, some even being called 'fascists' and 'Asians' by outraged Czechs and Slovaks.[21]

What role did the numerically strong working class play in 1968? The first thing to say is that it was impossible by 1968 to talk of a singular 'working class' – the process of stratification since the 1950s had internally divided the workers and fairly rapid scientific and technological change in the 1960s had fostered a large technical intelligentsia and a skilled educated sector of the workforce. That said, initially after January 1968 industrial workers were generally indifferent to reformist ideas, fearing in particular the impact economic reforms might have on employment, the 'de-levelisation' of wages and reduced state price controls. Many were unmoved by the notion of political democratisation espoused by a reshuffled set of party leaders and a few radical intellectuals – 'we've seen it all before!' For most blue-collar workers, the prime issues were higher living standards and wages, security of employment and the right to strike. Their scepticism towards reform was deepened by hard-line communist workers and party and trade union functionaries of working-class origin, not least Novotný, who consistently rejected democratisation and warned workers that their social benefits and job security would be lost under the reformists' proposals. However, by spring and summer there were signs of movement. The central trade union leadership was revamped and its mission of defending members' interests was restated; there was much discussion about the formation of Yugoslav-style 'workers'' or 'enterprise councils' and the possibility of worker 'self-management' in the factories; several short strikes were held; and even a few workers' committees to defend press freedom were spontaneously created. But it was the

Soviet invasion in August which galvanised Czech and Slovak workers into action. Indeed, together with the students they were the most active participants in the national civil resistance to the occupation and the embryonic 'normalisation' measures enacted from autumn 1968 onwards.[22]

Less well known is the revitalisation of the women's movement and the emergence of feminist discourse. Already in July 1967, the Czechoslovak Socialist Union of Women (ČSSŽ) had been established as an auxiliary of the KSČ and its membership grew to around 300,000 by early 1969.[23] Following the pattern in the trade unions and party itself, in April 1968 the ČSSŽ's conformist leadership fell prey to the post-January democratisation. The new pro-reform Central Committee 'began to challenge the gap between official declarations of women's *emancipation* and the reality of women's oppression by state policies' and sought 'a role for the women's movement as an equal partner in decision-making about the future of Czechoslovak democracy'. To this end, the weekly magazine, *Vlasta*, became a vehicle for open readers' discussions about feminism, socialism, democracy and women's rights, focusing on such key issues as the family and childcare, poor working conditions, women's earnings relative to qualifications, the extension of maternity leave and injustices and unfairness in the workplace. In the words of Jacqui True, 'for a while it seemed that the conversations in *Vlasta*...would actually empower women to take action and prod the socialist government to live up to its promises of gender equality'. These hopes were dashed by the Soviet military intervention and within a year the ČSSŽ Central Committee was forced to resign and the body became effectively a 'transmission belt' for the new 'normalised' party leadership.

The intriguing and important question of popular reactions to the reform process can be partly answered thanks to the existence of public opinion polls, which were regularly undertaken in 1968. Like all such surveys, the responses need to be carefully evaluated, not least because of citizens' reluctance to reveal their beliefs in a semi-public forum, but also because of discrepancies between the Czech lands and Slovakia, between different social groups, and between party and non-party members. Nevertheless, the polls and other forms of emerging popular opinion became 'a serious factor which the leadership could not ignore', even affecting the decision-making process and thus providing 'a sense of participation in politics and a feeling of influence on the course of events'. They also revealed the pluralistic nature of Czech and Slovak political attitudes, 'reflecting diverse interests and clashing beliefs'. The polls, however, show conclusively that 'a substantial majority' of the population 'supported the reforms', especially from March–April onwards when their direction became clearer.[24] For example, in June 1968, 89 per cent voted in favour of 'a continuation of socialist development' with only 5 per cent desiring a return to capitalism. The vast majority supported the abolition of censorship and the extension of individual freedoms. Citizens' trust in the KSČ grew between January and June from 23 to 51 per cent. The August invasion strengthened this tendency: over 97 per cent of respondents had trust, a minority 'with some reservations', in the Dubček leadership. It is true that 50 per cent believed that one or more new political parties should be established, but 70 per cent thought that an 'opposition party' should have a socialist programme. Not one respondent advocated an 'anti-socialist' party. Surprisingly, perhaps, 21 per cent opposed the creation of any opposition party.[25] In sum, it can be argued that a large majority of the population, communists and non-communists, wished to combine socialism and democracy and broadly welcomed the post-January reforms, although the precise direction and nature of those changes remained hotly contested.

Slovakia and Federalisation

The 'Czechoslovak Spring' was as much a Slovak as a Czech phenomenon. As one prominent Czech scholar-politician, Petr Pithart, has suggested: 'the Prague Spring not only had a Slovak beginning but also a Slovak ending'.[26] The intractable 'national question' had been bubbling away ever since 1945 and in the freer atmosphere of 1968 it exploded to the surface. The overriding demand that crystallised in Slovakia, both in the ranks of the party and outside, was for a federalisation of the country that would finally guarantee equal relations between Czechs and Slovaks, overcome the inherently undemocratic asymmetrical institutional model that had stifled the autonomy and authority of Slovak national organs, and hence contribute to the overall democratisation goals of the reformers. For the majority of Czechs, the federalisation of the state was a peripheral aim, not least because they had much to lose. Moreover, after the expulsion of the Sudeten Germans in 1945–46 Czech national identity was no longer under threat and they lacked empathy with the 'minority' national status of the Slovaks. However, in the face of this initial Czech indifference, even a measure of hostility, federalisation gained general acceptance as an inseparable component of the emerging new socialist democracy and as the optimal way of improving strained mutual relations. It was outlined in the party's Action Programme of April 1968, discussed at length thereafter in state and party commissions and in the media, and formally ratified in late October 1968.

But controversy surrounded the issue from the start. To many Czechs it appeared that the Slovaks were sacrificing the 'higher' goal of political liberalisation on the altar of federalism, as 'demonstrated' in the popular slogan: 'First federalisation, then democratisation'. In its extreme post-invasion populist variant, this sentiment came close to identifying the Slovaks once again as 'traitors', fulfilling their 'narrow' national interests on the backs of foreign tanks as in 1939 and undermining the common struggle against the Soviet 'occupiers'. Such attitudes, though rarely expressed at an elite level, revealed the depth and historicised nature of the chasm between the two peoples. The Slovak counter-contention was that there could be no meaningful democratisation without federalisation – the two were inseparable. If the latter was implemented on the principle of 'equal with equal' (*rovný s rovným*), as elaborated in the Košice Programme of April 1945, a more democratic polity would be secured for both Slovaks and Czechs. There was nothing new about this equation. As Carol Skalnik Leff has argued: 'federalization...had been the implicit or explicit Slovak formula for political security and national recognition almost from the inception of the state' in October 1918.[27] It was a formula, however, that since 1945 had been repeatedly emasculated by successive Czech politicians, communist and non-communist, most drastically by Novotný's centralist Constitution of July 1960, which effectively stripped Slovak national organs of any real power and approximated to the discredited 'Czechoslovakism' of the First Republic.

These painful historical memories tended to exacerbate the debates of 1968, one Slovak journalist asserting in April that if Czech prevarication tactics continued the Slovaks would have to go it alone 'even if this means separation and foundation of an independent socialist state'.[28] However, more sober voices generally prevailed on both sides. Husák, the Slovak 'bourgeois nationalist' imprisoned in 1954 and positioning himself as a respectable 'centrist' in 1968, emerged as the main advocate of federalisation and played an important, and essentially moderating, role in the raging polemics. He told a regional party assembly in Bratislava that 'federalization means nothing more than applying democratic principles in the field of nationality policy' and sought to dispel Czech suspicions by insisting it would not threaten the unity of the state.[29] Even the hard-line First Secretary of the Slovak Communist Party, Bil'ak, championed federalisation, but largely as an opportunistic method of delaying democratisation. Several leading Czech political and cultural figures, among them Smrkovský, the new chairman of the National Assembly, the historian Milan Hübl and the constitutional specialists Jiří Grospič and Zdeněk Jičínský, acknowledged the necessity of federalisation, as did Dubček himself, who saw national equality as a guarantee of the stability of the common state.[30] Nevertheless, by the summer of 1968 many Slovaks were still concerned that the Czechs were dragging their heels, were at best only partial converts to federalism and were in no hurry to pass the federalisation law which had been slated for October.

Slovak anxieties, aside from the timing of the bill, were manifold. Would the Czechs agree to create their own Czech National Council and Czech Communist Party parallel to the existing Slovak bodies? Would they insist on 'one man, one vote' in the new federal system, thus exposing Slovaks once again to *majorizácia*, or out-voting by the numerically stronger Czechs? Would they accept parity of representation in all federal institutions? Would they advocate a 'rigid' federation stressing central government prerogatives and powers? Indeed, which precise areas would fall under federal jurisdiction and which to the devolved national organs? And, symbolically, what would be the new title of the state? Matters were not helped by the fact that there was disagreement on these substantive issues not only between Czechs and Slovaks, but also among Czechs and Slovaks themselves. Hence, compromises were required from all quarters in the arduous and urgent negotiations over the federalisation law. In the event, the bill, to be discussed in more detail in the next chapter, generally satisfied both sides, but in many ways it was completely overshadowed by the Soviet invasion and the renewed centralisation imposed by Prague in late 1970 dashed all hopes of tangible Slovak self-rule. It was a bitter pill, made worse in that the new man at the helm, Husák, was a putative Slovak 'nationalist'.

'Night Frost in Prague': Soviet Intervention

One of the great conundrums of 1968 is how and why the Soviet Politburo so rapidly changed their opinion of their erstwhile protégé, Dubček, and when and why they decided on the ultimate sanction of military intervention. The Kremlin's concerns over developments in Czechoslovakia were multiple and, if viewed from the broader perspective of the on-going Cold War, appear quite rational and legitimate. Looked at through Brezhnev's eyes, how could he not but be dismayed by the proposed reduction in the powers of the Czechoslovak Ministry of Interior and security police, the exposure of Soviet involvement in the judicial crimes of the 1950s, the espousal of genuine legality, mooted military reforms and the perceived threat to the installation of Soviet nuclear weapons on Czechoslovak soil, Prague's quest for limited autonomy in foreign affairs, and the KSČ's ideological 'deviations' from classical Marxism–Leninism? Above all, the end of censorship and the dismissal of trusted conservatives confirmed the Soviets' grave misgivings. Did not the logic of a democratised system and an open mass media mean the emergence of 'anti-socialist counter-revolutionary forces' both inside and out-side the Communist Party? If so, could Dubček or any successor be relied on to overcome the 'rightist elements' and maintain the party's 'leading role' in the future? If not, surely Czechoslovakia would be 'lost' to socialism and the threat of 'spill-over' to other East European socialist states, including the USSR, would be palpable? If so, would not the cohesion and unity of the entire Soviet bloc be plunged into turmoil, the inviolable gains of the Second World War be forsaken and the historic struggle between 'socialism' and 'capitalism' end in victory for the latter? The risks were extremely high.

Sources of 'Counter-Revolution'

One striking thing we now know thanks to recent archival discoveries is that fears were being privately expressed as early as mid-January 1968 and were beginning to crystallise into concrete forebodings by March. The first warning signals appeared within two weeks of Dubček's appointment as party secretary. On 18 January, the Soviet ambassador in Prague, Stepan Chervonenko, sent a long report to Moscow, which although generally positive about Dubček intimated that he was 'vacillating' and that the KSČ leadership as a whole was still 'weak and divided'.[31] At the same time, the East German boss, Walter Ulbricht, and the Polish party leader, Władysław Gomułka, informed Brezhnev of their anxieties, and Gomułka in a head-to-head conversation with his Czechoslovak counterpart in early February spoke of the likelihood of 'hostile elements rising against us'. Throughout the next seven months, Ulbricht and Gomułka, together with the Bulgarian supremo Todor Zhivkov, were among the most consistent and vociferous adversaries of the reform process in Prague and, indeed, were possibly the first to promote actively the idea of military intervention. Why? Because they were justifiably worried that the Czechoslovak initiatives would attract their restive populations and the Dubček leadership would prove powerless to prevent the spread of new ideas. Student riots and demonstrations in Warsaw and other Polish cities in which placards were borne aloft declaring 'Poland is awaiting its own Dubček' merely corroborated these apprehensions. In addition, Ulbricht had a specific concern: the unwelcome prospect of a rapprochement between Prague and Bonn which could conceivably end in a unilateral Czechoslovak recognition of the West German government.

While sharing East German and Polish disquiet, the Soviet leaders were particularly agitated by two phenomena in Czechoslovakia: the effective curtailment of censorship and the resultant free media and the demotion of trusted pro-Soviet figures in the party, security services and military. Combined with other troublesome developments, they indicated to Moscow that the Dubčekite leadership was losing control of the situation. The decision in March to end party regulation of the press, radio and television drove the Soviets mad. The Kremlin simply did not understand how ostensible Marxist–Leninists could relinquish authority over the mass media and permit 'anti-socialist' and 'anti-Soviet' outpourings. Why, for example, were articles being published and TV programmes aired which openly discussed Soviet involvement in the judicial crimes of the 1950s and in Jan Masaryk's death in 1948? Why was the press demanding that perpetrators of the repressions in the 1950s be purged from the party? Why were there sensationalist reports about top-level scandals? Why did sections of the media actively seek Novotný's removal as President in March? Why were anti-Soviet cartoons regularly appearing in the press? And why did Dubček fail to carry out repeated Soviet demands to sack the director of Czechoslovak state television, Jiří Pelikán, and other radical reformers? The Soviets were also worried by the prospect of mass actions, Brezhnev bemoaning at a Politburo session on 21 March that 'many of the rallies, meetings, core group gatherings, and so on are anti-Soviet', while Dubček simply says 'all is calm there; nothing will spill out into the streets'.[32]

To make matters worse, influential conservatives were being dismissed from their posts. Novotný was replaced by Ludvík Svoboda as President of the republic and the key portfolios of Minister of the Interior, Defence and Foreign Affairs and the party secretary for ideology all fell to prominent reformers. High-ranking staffing changes also affected the Czechoslovak People's Army. This personnel turnover undermined longstanding channels of Soviet influence and communication in the KSČ, the security services and military, compelling Brezhnev to lament 'that so many "good and sincere friends of the Soviet Union" had been forced to step down'.[33] And who knew where it would all end? New ideas went hand in hand with new leaders. Josef Pavel, the reformist Minister of Interior, characterised State Security as an 'enormous power apparatus which was to control everything and everyone'. Its strength therefore had to be reduced, it had to be removed from party jurisdiction and placed under the legal supervision of the government and the National Assembly. In addition, it was endlessly repeated that the courts and judiciary must be independent of the party and the secret police interference which had marked the dark days of Stalinist terror. Although Pavel's attempts to purge StB old-timers met with stiff internal, and probably Soviet, resistance and the official party report into the repressions of the 1950s went unpublished, moves to democratise the Czechoslovak security services and unmask direct Soviet collusion in the crimes of the recent past evoked great consternation in Moscow.[34]

Similar measures were proposed for the Czechoslovak armed forces, reforms which threatened to alter their position and status in the Warsaw Pact and simultaneously touched a particularly raw Soviet nerve: the storage of nuclear weapons on Czechoslovak territory. Although Dubček asserted again and again his country's total commitment and loyalty to the Warsaw Pact, some of his subordinates were less tactful. In July, the new Minister of Defence, General Martin Dzúr, and the head of the important Central Committee State Administrative Department, General Václav Prchlík, made highly controversial pronouncements on the Soviet-dominated command structure of the Warsaw Pact and called for 'representation on the basis of equal rights'. The Czechoslovak armed forces no longer wished to be 'mere passive members of the Warsaw treaty'. Other officers advised that Czechoslovakia, while remaining a firm partner in the Warsaw Pact coalition, should devise its own military doctrine and strategy. It was even mooted that there might be a 'bilateral or unilateral abolition' of the pact 'in the near future'.[35] Given these attitudes, it is hardly surprising that the Soviet top brass railed against the low morale and fighting capacity of the Czechoslovak army. Indeed, the Soviet Minister of Defence, Marshal Andrei Grechko, had already concluded that it was 'rapidly deteriorating' and was 'no longer capable of defending the border with the FRG [Federal Republic of Germany]'. What is more, talk of a separate Czechoslovak defence policy threw into doubt the secret agreements signed in 1963 and 1965 between Moscow and Prague which permitted the USSR to station nuclear warheads at three locations in western Bohemia.[36] All in all, it is clear that the Kremlin was deeply concerned that potential Czechoslovak military reforms would weaken the unity and coordination of the Warsaw Pact, thereby exposing the Soviet bloc to the old bugbears of American 'imperialism' and West German 'revanchism'.

Prague's evolving foreign policy was yet another bone of contention. Here again the Czechoslovak government constantly sought to reassure Moscow that the alliance with the USSR and other socialist states was built on 'firm permanent values' and reflected the 'vital interests and needs of our country' and the 'will...and feelings of our people'. Politically and economically, the links with the Soviet Union were regarded as beneficial for the country. Dubček specifically ruled out any notion of state neutrality or withdrawal from the Soviet bloc and it appears that public opinion, still wary of West German intentions, essentially endorsed this position. However, Czechoslovak foreign ministry officials and specialists argued that what was required in the socialist camp was 'unity in diversity' and this in turn meant that Czechoslovakia should seek a more 'active' diplomacy based on a greater degree of national sovereignty and independence. This extended to the highly sensitive issue of relations with West Germany. Although Prague's stance towards Bonn 'remained almost completely static' in 1968, the new Foreign Minister, Professor Jiří Hájek and Prime Minister Černík, noted and supported 'realist' tendencies in the West German government, no doubt a reference to the emerging *Ostpolitik* trend. Some commentators went much further, calling for 'our own German policy' and even prompt diplomatic recognition of West Germany, speculation which infuriated the Soviet and East German leaders. Any hint of a Czechoslovak 'special relationship' with Bonn was anathema to Moscow and East Berlin. In sum, the central dilemma for Prague's foreign policy-makers was how to maintain cordial relations with the USSR while harbouring real ambitions for limited autonomy.[37] No solution to this contradiction was found before the invasion.

It is surprising that recent literature on 1968 tends to underestimate the importance of ideology in Soviet calculations. For, as Matthew J. Ouimet has noted, 'the Kremlin's world view was steeped in Marxist–Leninist terminology that defined friends and enemies, threats and opportunities'.[38] Thus, on the ideological front Czechoslovak strivings to reform deeply entrenched Leninist principles and in particular to alter the conception of the party's 'leading role' were viewed as a negation of the very essence of Marxism–Leninism. Indeed, the whole attempt to build a 'new' model of socialism in tune with Czechoslovak specificities came to be viewed as an ideological deviation from a 'correct' and universally applicable Marxism–Leninism whose precepts were the preserve of the Soviet Politburo. Brezhnev informed his Central Committee colleagues in July that 'articles and speeches have appeared [in Czechoslovakia] criticizing Marx, Lenin, and Leninism'.[39] Even a high-ranking secretary of the KSČ's Central Committee, Císař, stood accused of writing one such piece provoking a biting rejoinder from a Soviet academician. Discussions in Czechoslovakia on the new party statutes were equally controversial. The Leninist canon of 'democratic centralism', which sought to maintain strict party unity, ensure that all leadership decisions were fully implemented and essentially stigmatised 'minority' opinion in the party as a dangerous 'fraction', was subject to serious revision and challenge. The intention was to democratise thoroughly the KSČ: elections to party posts were to be direct and secret, the monopolisation of power by the few had to be prevented, party members should be encouraged to contribute to policy formulation, lower bodies in the party should be given greater autonomy, minority rights should be guaranteed and the dominance of professional party functionaries over all aspects of public life should be attenuated. In Moscow's blinkered eyes, these innovations signified none other than an 'ideological preparation for counter-revolution'.[40]

These cumulative 'threats' to Soviet orthodoxy in both domestic and foreign policy spheres took on almost biological associations. Terms such as 'disease', 'contagion', even 'bacilli' were used by leaders of the anti-Dubček coalition as perhaps a subconscious justification for their worst nightmare: the 'spill-over effect'. For what if the Czechoslovak 'disease' should 'infect' the Poles, East Germans, Bulgarians and, heaven forbid, the peoples of the USSR itself? These were no idle fears. According to Mark Kramer, 'reports streamed into Moscow about disaffection among Soviet youth and growing ferment in several of the union republics, notably Ukraine, Moldavia, Georgia, and the Baltic states'. The powerful Ukrainian party boss, Petro Shelest, was adamant that publications sent across the Slovak border were radicalising Ukrainian intellectuals and nationalists, especially in the potentially unruly western regions which picked up Czechoslovak television and radio broadcasts. Even in Moscow, student and dissident activists were 'translating and disseminating a wide range of materials from Czechoslovakia'.[41] What is more, Brezhnev, Shelest and others came to believe that the Czechoslovak reformers were objectively to blame for this agitation, that they were 'interfering' in the internal affairs of their neighbours. It is alleged that Shelest even 'made shameless statements about the Czechoslovaks' attempts to wrest the Carpatho-Ukraine from the Soviet Union'.[42] No wonder Dubček and his colleagues found it impossible to reason with such dogmatic adversaries.

From 'Fraternal Warnings' to Armed 'Fraternal Assistance'

The rising alarm in Moscow and other East European capitals found its expression in multiple ways. The Soviet Politburo followed events in Czechoslovakia extremely closely, establishing a special nine-member 'commission' in May to maintain a daily vigil on developments. The Kremlin was also fed regular and contentious one-sided reports by the Soviet embassy in Prague and the KGB. There is as yet no evidence of substantive and consistent divisions among the leaders between 'hawks' and 'doves' or of any 'opposition' to the military suppression of the Prague Spring. However, Shelest recorded in his diary that the varying stances of leading protagonists 'prevented the Politburo from uniting firmly on how to deal with the question of Czechoslovakia'.[43] It is likely, then, that individuals and bureaucracies in the broader Soviet hierarchy also differed in their conceptions of the appropriate response. Certainly several very powerful figures were mortified by events in Czechoslovakia and from March onwards began to push for 'extreme measures', a euphemism for armed intervention. Others wavered between hard-line and moderate positions. Others still were more cautious and wished to see all avenues exhausted before embarking on a potentially risky Red Army undertaking. The decisive voice lay with Brezhnev as General Secretary. He preferred to pursue a 'political solution', but was quite willing to authorise the military option as a last resort. Hence, the consensual strategy adopted by the Kremlin from the spring of 1968 combined preparations for armed mobilisation with various forms of pressure and 'comradely persuasion' on the Czechoslovaks, including veiled threats of economic sanctions, concerted press and telegram campaigns, extended Warsaw Pact military manoeuvres on Czechoslovak territory, bilateral and multilateral meetings, and private conversations between Brezhnev and Dubček. Despite the latter's repeated assurances that Soviet concerns would be acted upon, by mid-August 1968 the Soviet leader's patience had finally run out.

The first signs of overt pressure came at a gathering of East European communist leaders in Dresden on 23 March. Thinking they had been invited to discuss economic matters, the five-member Czechoslovak delegation sat stunned as Ulbricht and especially Gomułka delivered them a 'cold shower'. The Polish boss insisted on the need for an immediate 'forceful counter-offensive...against the counterrevolutionary [and] reactionary forces that...are active on a grand scale in Czechoslovakia'.[44] He went on to draw an uncomfortable comparison with the situation in Hungary in 1956 which cannot have been lost on his Czechoslovak interlocutors. Brezhnev's tone was less shrill, but he demanded that Dubček explain what was meant by the term 'liberalisation of society' and also used the ominous word 'counter-revolution'. Even the generally conciliatory Hungarian party leader, János Kádár, impressed on the Czechoslovaks that resolute measures were necessary in this 'critical' situation. In an early indication of what was to become a growing and damaging trend, the reactions of the Czechoslovak representatives revealed certain nuanced differences, only Černík categorically asserting that the 'state of affairs in Czechoslovakia [is] overwhelmingly progressive and pro-socialist in character'. His colleagues, Jozef Lenárt and to a lesser extent Kolder, were more ambivalent, the former admitting that in certain circumstances 'counterrevolution...is possible'.[45] Such creeping divisions must have been music to Soviet ears, and indeed in the following months Moscow assiduously identified and courted 'healthy forces' in the KSČ on whom they could rely, the most influential being the hard-line Slovak party boss, Bil'ak.

The intense pressure on the Czechoslovak leadership continued throughout the spring and summer of 1968. In early May a bilateral meeting was convened in Moscow at which the Soviets made explicit their fears about the course of developments in Czechoslovakia, including American and West German attempts to undermine the regime and the domestic 'counter-revolutionary' groups and clubs which, according to Brezhnev, were 'raging in full force'. He concluded his tirade with the words: 'the main thing is to decide in what manner the cause of socialism can best be defended in Czechoslovakia. This question concerns not only Czechoslovakia itself but your neighbors and allies, and the entire world communist movement'. He appealed to his Czechoslovak listeners to 'find within yourselves the necessary unity, courage, and will power' to overcome the 'dangerous phenomena' in the country. At this stage, Brezhnev still appears to have believed that Dubček and his colleagues could sort out the mess on their own, but he darkly hinted that 'we are ready to offer our support'. In his various harangues, the Soviet leader also unwittingly exposed the insidious conspiratorial mindset that pervaded the Kremlin's outlook. It was either 'underground' elements, or '1.5 million former members of the once-disbanded fascist and bourgeois parties', or this or that political 'club' or writer, who were 'organizing' and 'calling for the overthrow' of the party leadership, and all were 'directed by forces linked to the West'.[46] It was almost impossible for the Czechoslovaks to defend themselves convincingly against such misdirected and exaggerated claims. However, for a short time after the May Moscow summit Dubček and other centrist reformers did attempt to rein in the media and vowed to 'mobilize all means' to 'suppress' any 'anti-communist counter-revolutionary platform'. By recognising the existence of such 'rightist forces', the Dubčekites were 'committed to doing something about them',[47] but could not go as far as the Soviets wanted without completely undercutting the logic of 'socialism with a human face'.

In June and July, large-scale Warsaw Pact manoeuvres were undertaken on Czechoslovak soil. They were clearly intended as a psychological, as well as a military, lever to pressure Prague further to crack down on the 'counter-revolutionaries'. The war games were accompanied by a Soviet press and telegram campaign which reached fever pitch following the publication of Vaculík's 'Two Thousand Words Manifesto'.[48] On 14–15 July, towards the end of the manoeuvres, a highly significant conference of the leaders of the 'Warsaw Five' – the USSR, Poland, East Germany, Hungary and Bulgaria – was held in the Polish capital.[49] The Czechoslovaks pointedly refused to attend, preferring a bilateral meeting with their Soviet counterparts. The outcome of the conference, the famous 'Warsaw Letter' addressed to the Central Committee of the KSČ, represented in effect an ultimatum and rationale for the forthcoming military intervention. The warning signs were more or less explicit: 'the reactionaries' offensive, supported by imperialism, against your party and...social system...threatens to push your country off the path of socialism and, consequently, imperils the interests of the entire socialist system. In this struggle [against reaction] you may count on the solidarity and comprehensive assistance of the fraternal socialist countries'. Four conditions were categorically laid down 'for the preservation of the socialist system in Czechoslovakia': 'a resolute and bold offensive against rightist and antisocialist forces'; 'a cessation of the activities of all political organizations that oppose socialism'; 'the party's assumption of control over the news mass media'; and 'solidarity in the ranks of the party itself on the fundamental basis of

Marxism–Leninism [including] steadfast observance of the principles of democratic centralism'.[50]

Regardless of the Czechoslovaks' indignant response to the accusations in the Warsaw Letter, which included a barbed reminder to Moscow about mutual non-interference in the internal affairs of 'fraternal' countries, the Soviet Politburo, while 'proceeding with all the steps needed to send troops into Czechoslovakia', agreed to one last ditch attempt at a political solution to the crisis.[51] This was the bilateral meeting of Soviet and Czechoslovak Politburo members at Čierná nad Tisou, a small railway community on the Slovak–Ukrainian border, and the subsequent joint gathering of East European leaders in Bratislava. The talks in Čierná, which lasted from 29 July to 1 August, were extremely tense. Kosygin came straight to the crux with the revealing and hurtful words: 'we can assure you that if we wanted to, we could occupy your entire country in the course of twenty four hours'. Later in the proceedings Dubček was literally reduced to tears by the vitriolic diatribes of Shelest, who reportedly launched an anti-Semitic outburst against Kriegel, that 'Galician Jew'.[52] According to Williams, the main result of the 'negotiations' was 'six oral promises' made by Dubček and three other top Czechoslovak reformers to their Soviet counterparts. Although Dubček always denied their existence, Williams insists that there is 'overwhelming evidence' for the promises, the most important of which were to uphold the party's 'leading role'; regain control of the media; ban KAN, K-231 and the Social Democrats; prevent damaging reforms in the security services; and remove the three radicals, Pelikán, Kriegel and Císař.[53] The Soviets were adamant about these 'promises', but it is a moot point whether their fulfilment would have averted the invasion – in all likelihood not.

Another outcome of the Čierná talks was the decision to convene a multilateral meeting in Bratislava for 3 August. This conclave of leaders of the 'Warsaw Five' and Czechoslovakia injected a slightly hopeful note by agreeing a joint public statement which averred that 'each fraternal party takes into account national characteristics and conditions…based on the principles of equality, respect for sovereignty and national independence, [and] territorial integrity'. This wording represented something of a victory for the beleaguered Czechoslovaks, but was more than counter-balanced by the insistence that 'it is the common international duty of all socialist countries to support, strengthen and defend' the historic achievements of socialism.[54] Since the opening of the archives, however, the Bratislava meeting is best remembered for the infamous 'Letter of Invitation', which five hard-line Czechoslovak communist leaders wrote to Brezhnev requesting Soviet 'intervention and all-round assistance'. One of the quintet, Bil'ak, clandestinely handed the short missive to Shelest in the gentlemen's lavatory during a break in the proceedings![55] This appeal gave the Soviets' greater 'freedom of action' and, as far as Moscow was concerned, committed 'the signatories to seize power when allied military units entered Czechoslovakia'.[56]

Preparations for such 'fraternal assistance' were in their final stages when Brezhnev, alarmed by secret reports from ambassador Chervonenko that Dubček was still 'not ready' for a 'decisive struggle with the rightist forces', decided to telephone the Czechoslovak leader on 9 and 13 August.[57] In the first call Brezhnev adopted an ostensibly fatherly tone, urging 'Sasha' (Dubček) to implement the 'commitments' made at Čierná and to unite with the 'healthy forces' in the KSČ 'in the fight against the Right'. The second conversation was far more strident. An exasperated Brezhnev accused a defensive Dubček of 'deceiving us' by his prevarication and lame excuses for delaying the overdue crack down in Prague, to which Dubček abjectly responded: 'if you believe we are deceiving you, then take the measures you regard as appropriate...by all means go ahead'. He even offered his resignation as First Secretary, but ended with the words: 'I promise you, Cde. Brezhnev, that I'll do everything necessary to fulfill our agreement'.[58] It was not enough. Indeed, by then:

> the majority of the [Soviet] leadership could not but arrive at the conclusion that the KSČ had not only lost all control over the media and was in the process of losing control over the organs of power, but that it had entirely lost its ability to act and to hold the party together.[59]

Thus, on 17 August the Soviet Politburo voted 'unanimously' to 'provide armed assistance and support to the Communist Party and people of Czechoslovakia'.[60] The next day this decision was relayed to the other participants in the intervention, East Germany, Poland, Bulgaria and Hungary. 'Operation Danube', the largest mobilisation of troops and weaponry in Europe since World War II, was about to be launched.

All commentators agree that the Soviet-led invasion was militarily competent, but politically misjudged. It was undoubtedly a tragedy for the vast majority of Czechs and Slovaks, including most of the party leadership. In retrospect, it is hard to understand how Dubček and his colleagues failed to 'read the signs' of the impending intervention and even harder to accept that they had no contingency plans for such an eventuality. The warning signals were pretty obvious as early as the 'Warsaw Letter', but Dubček always claimed that he was shocked by the entry of Soviet troops into his country. On the night of 20–21 August, 165,000 soldiers and 4,600 tanks crossed the Czechoslovak borders and within a week their respective numbers had risen to around half a million and 6,000.[61] As for the timing, it is almost certainly the case that the Soviet Politburo wished to pre-empt the convocation of the Fourteenth Extraordinary Congress of the KSČ, scheduled for 9 September, which would have formally ratified the reformist course undertaken since January and likely removed many of the last conservative stalwarts from the party's leading national and regional bodies. As it turned out, the congress convened clandestinely at a factory in the Prague working-class district of Vysočany on 22 August with the delegates adopting a fiercely anti-invasion tone.[62] The Soviet commanders of the operation were in no mood for mercy: early in the morning of 21 August, the Minister of Defence, Grechko, delivered this blunt message to his Czechoslovak counterpart: 'tell Dzúr that if they fire just one shot, I'll hang him on the nearest aspen!'[63] The admonition was heeded. Dzúr, President Svoboda and the KSČ Presidium instructed the Czechoslovak army to remain in their barracks and the population to stay calm. Thus, there was no organised armed opposition. Nevertheless, by the end of the year the deaths of 108 citizens had been recorded – the invasion was not bloodless.[64] Brave civil resistance was put up, but it was a grossly unequal contest and within days the country was pacified and under Soviet military control.

Politically, the Warsaw Pact's 'fraternal assistance to the Czechoslovak people' quickly degenerated into disarray. The plan was that on the night of the military intervention, the hard-liners Bil'ak, Kolder, Indra and others would isolate the 'right-wing counter-revolutionaries' in the KSČ Presidium, establish a pro-Moscow 'worker and peasant revolutionary government' and rapidly begin to restore order once the population's acquiescence had been secured, an outcome which, remarkably, the Soviet leaders appeared to anticipate. It was a political miscalculation of staggering proportions. In the event the conservatives were outmanoeuvred in the Presidium, which in the early hours of 21 August voted by seven to four to condemn the invasion. Thereafter, according to one Soviet eyewitness, the 'healthy forces' went 'a bit haywire' and 'were unable to recover from the shock'.[65] One got drunk, another went to the safety of his country home, two others fled to the Soviet embassy.

In this unexpected impasse, Brezhnev was forced to deal with Dubček and the rest of the Czechoslovak reformist leadership, most of whom had been arrested in their offices. They were flown to Moscow and from 23–26 August they 'negotiated' with the Soviet Politburo in the Kremlin.[66] A distraught and ill Dubček together with his intimidated colleagues were in no position to withstand the verbal battering that was inflicted on them, Černík later describing Boris Ponomarev's attitude as 'hateful, superpower, cavalier'.[67] Eventually, all save Kriegel agreed to sign the secret 'Moscow Protocol', a document more or less dictated by the Soviets. Under its terms, foreign troops were to be stationed in Czechoslovakia until 'the threat to socialism' had passed, key personnel changes would be made, party control of the media rapidly restored, 'anti-socialist' organisations would be banned, and the Vysočany congress declared null and void. These and other issues were to form the basis of the 'normalisation' that was to come. But two important concessions had been wrung from the Soviets: Dubček and the majority of the reformers would remain in office, at least for the time being, and the post-January course was not entirely repudiated.

In conclusion to this section, we must address the pivotal question: why did the Soviets invade? In his monumental work published in 1976, H. Gordon Skilling identified three core elements in Moscow's decision: first, military-strategic considerations; second, the perceived threat to the Soviet model of socialism in Czechoslovakia; and third, the 'spillover' effect of reform to other East European states, including the Soviet Union. A crucial factor was security, both of the USSR and the East European bloc as a whole. Skilling declines to prioritise these various inputs, but concludes that 'perhaps the final Soviet judgment...was that only an invasion could consolidate Soviet hegemony and avert the danger of eventual loss of control of the Communist Party and of its policy in Czechoslovakia, and, ultimately, over the entire area of Eastern Europe'. It would appear, too, that the Soviet leaders did not so much fear the collapse of socialism and a return to capitalism in Czechoslovakia, as a thoroughly reformed socialist system based on democratic norms, cultural freedom and popular participation.[68] In short, the Kremlin leadership operated on the basis of 'the primacy of politics' and the threat to Soviet bloc security, arrogantly abrogating to itself the right to define 'socialism' and the duty to defend it by any means whenever it was believed to be under threat.

In his assessment, Williams, with the benefit of declassified archival sources, emphasised the 'subjective' aspect of interpersonal relations and the attenuation of what Brezhnev termed 'political love' between the Czechoslovak and Soviet Politburos. Williams focused on the role of cognitive frameworks, such as images, ideas and beliefs, in the interaction between the two antagonists, notably Brezhnev and Dubček, and claimed that the Soviets had stereotypical images of their 'partners' in Eastern Europe. The Czechoslovak reformers stood accused of breaking the Soviet 'operational code' of correct political behaviour in three ways: they were reluctant to meet their Soviet counterparts; they did not clearly indicate whether they allied themselves to the pro-Moscow faction in the KSČ; and finally they failed to carry out their promises to reassert control over the direction of reform. Hence, the signals emanating from Prague were mixed and were interpreted in the Kremlin as indications of 'dangerous dithering, if not outright deceit'. The Czechoslovaks were perceived as unpredictable, unreliable and insincere in their dealings with Moscow. By August 1968 the Soviet Politburo had come to the decision that the Dubček leadership's reluctance to fulfil its obligations to restore 'order' in Czechoslovakia represented a 'betrayal of fraternal relations [and a] betrayal of friendship with the USSR'. For Williams, it was this erosion of trust that drove the Kremlin to use military force.[69]

From Invasion to 'Normalisation'

Unprecedented national unity spontaneously erupted on 21 August and the days thereafter in condemnation of the invasion, defence of Czechoslovak state sovereignty, support for the arrested reformist leaders, rejection of the collaborationist 'traitors', and demands for the withdrawal of the Warsaw Pact forces. From Prague to Brno to Bratislava, in towns and villages throughout the republic, Czechs, Slovaks and ethnic minorities of all social backgrounds and generations were one in opposition to the occupation of their country. Paradoxically, a profound sense of freedom pervaded in the midst of military subjugation. National defiance was expressed in multiple ways: 'graffiti, placards, petitions, jokes, songs, and poems, the composition of which was often coordinated at local "slogan centres" staffed by students, educators, artists, and actors'.[70] As ever, humour played its role: 'Lenin! Wake up! Brezhnev's gone mad!'[71] Many ordinary people, well versed in the Russian language thanks to compulsory teaching in schools since 1948, remonstrated with the bewildered Soviet tank crews, asking them why they had invaded when clearly no 'counter-revolution' was taking place. Underground radio and television broadcasts and the independent press encouraged the defacement or removal of all motorway, street and building signs. Water and food was commonly denied the invaders by sullen citizens who did their best to shun the foreign troops. Three brief general strikes on 21, 22 and 23 August brought the country to a standstill. There were also several brave examples of non-armed resistance carried out by members of the Czechoslovak army, secret and civil police, and departments of the ministry of interior. Official party, government, parliamentary and trade union bodies, despite operating in extraordinarily difficult conditions, lent their weight to the popular non-violent campaign. Even after the conclusion of the Moscow negotiations, the KSČ Central Committee reiterated that 'socialism with a human face...remains the mission of our nations'.[72]

Ultimately, however, this impressive display of civil resistance and national unity came to naught. While oppositional acts continued to be perpetrated, the early signs of creeping capitulation became evident. The basis for this tragic outcome was the Moscow Protocol and its insistence on an ill-defined 'normalisation'. On their return from the Soviet capital in the early hours of 27 August, the Czechoslovak leaders hastened to inform the nation about the main 'agreements', though none dared to mention the existence of the secret protocol. Dubček's tearful radio address, in which he promised the continuation of the reforms once 'order' and 'consolidation' had been achieved, went a long way in calming the tense situation. With the benefit of hindsight, it can be said that there was much wishful thinking and self-delusion in the belief, both among many politicians and the population at large, that Soviet troops could be withdrawn relatively quickly and that the principal post-January reforms could be salvaged. One by one, with the sole exception of federalisation, these innovations were reneged on in the following months. One by one, the leading reformers resigned or were forced out. Although Dubček tried hard to chart a middle course, balancing attacks on 'anti-socialist elements' with repeated assurances that the reforms could be protected, it was impossible to reconcile Soviet demands with popular aspirations.[73] Post-invasion development, then, was an unedifying spectacle of piecemeal retreat and compromise which disarmed, disoriented and dismayed the vast majority of Czechs and Slovaks. 'Realism' – an acceptance that Moscow's demands had to be met if worse was not to befall the country – gradually prevailed in the face of continued 'resistance' and Husák, no doubt with his personal power goals in mind, emerged as the prime advocate of this position. But even he, soon to be the Soviets' chosen successor to Dubček, reportedly intoned on the day of the invasion: 'now you can see what a mess that idiot Brezhnev has made!'[74] If he did indeed utter these words, Husák had forgotten them by the autumn as he began his astute campaign of giving 'clear leadership' and a 'unified line' to society. And he was not alone – other conservatives and luke-warm reformers entered the fray driven either by conviction, inertia or careerism.

Between September 1968 and spring 1969, Czechoslovak political life was in limbo as intense inner-party conflict and crisis paralysed stable governance. Public opinion surveys carried out from 6 to 13 December revealed 'pessimistic sentiments of oppression, pow-erlessness, uncertainty and non-information, of disillusionment and betrayal'. Only 4 per cent of respondents in the Czech lands and 7 per cent in Slovakia expressed 'faith and hope' in the future.[75] In an attempt to rally support for the beleaguered reform programme and its diminishing adherents, students held sit-ins, the metalworkers' union 'KOVO' threatened a general strike, workers' councils were formed in over one hundred enterprises and the creative unions began to speak out against the return of censorship and 'closed politics'. The most famous act of defiance was the self-immolation of Jan Palach, a Charles University student, on 16 January 1969 in protest against the reimposition of censorship and the post-August political retrenchment. He died three days later. His sacrifice was fol-lowed by several other, less celebrated, youthful suicides.[76] Although Palach's funeral turned into an outpouring of grief and anger and caused temporary panic in government circles, his death had the unintended consequence of deepening the divisions in the KSČ elite and convincing 'many centrist liberalizers that the country would only continue to lurch from crisis to crisis unless a new style of party lead-ership were adopted'.[77] In this atmosphere, actively encouraged by insistent Soviet pressure, an anti-Dubček coalition gathered strength in the party hierarchy. Likewise, many citizens began to lose faith in his protestations of reformist zeal and to lament his concessions to the Kremlin.

The perfect pretext to remove Dubček came in late March 1969. The unlikely occasion was the world ice hockey championships in Stockholm where the highly motivated Czechoslovak team defeated the Soviets twice in the space of a week.[78] The country was thrown into an orgy of celebration bordering on chaos. On 28 March, half a million people demonstrated in 69 towns and cities. Nine Soviet garrisons were attacked and the offices of the Soviet airline, Aeroflot, were ransacked in central Prague by a throng estimated at 3,000 to 4,000 people. Unsubstantiated rumours have circulated ever since that the dirty work was in fact perpetrated by the Czech secret police. Whatever the case, the Soviet leaders were furious, blaming reformers, particularly Smrkovský, for 'unleashing counter-revolutionary, anti-Soviet actions'. Not only the ambitious Husák, ranting against 'petty-bourgeois elements' and 'enemy forces', but also erstwhile reformers like Černík and Svoboda, then rounded on Dubček, who was effectively isolated and broken. On 17 April, the KSČ Presidium voted almost unanimously to accept Dubček's resignation and to replace him with Husák as First Secretary. In the Central Committee later in the day, only 22 members out of 182 voted against these momentous personnel changes.[79] Husák's great attribute was that he was seen as a firm leader, who had been persecuted in the 1950s and who could bring cohesion to a party and country that yearned for stability after months of 'crisis fatigue'. He had also become 'Moscow's man'.

Dubček's demise elicited scarcely a negative murmur in the wider party and among students, workers and intellectuals. Regardless of the new leader's pronouncements that the reforms would continue within reasonable limits – 'who wants to give up post-January policies, comrades?' – the concept of 'socialism with a human face' was definitively dead and buried and the era of 'normalisation' was about to take shape. The harsh meaning of this became plain in August 1969 on the first anniversary of the invasion. Huge demonstrations in Prague, Brno and other cities were violently suppressed by the Czechoslovak security forces resulting in a number of fatalities. The disturbing reality is that the drift to 'normalisation' was as much conditioned by domestic pressures and power rivalries as by external interference from the Kremlin.

What was the longer-term significance of the brutal crushing of the short-lived Prague Spring? In Czechoslovakia, the military intervention engendered a profound transformation in the political culture of the population. Historic Russophile sentiment was wiped from the face of the nation almost overnight and any hope the Soviet leaders may have had of friendship between the two peoples rapidly faded. During the 1970s and 1980s, the whole notion of 'reform communism' came to be regarded with cynicism, many oppositional activists and citizens becoming convinced that the Soviet model could not be renewed or rejuvenated. Some felt betrayed by the reform communists', albeit reluctant, acceptance of the Soviet occupation. More than this, a deep apathy towards 'politics' in general appeared to envelop society by the early 1970s. All 'isms' and master narratives became suspect as many Czechs and Slovaks retreated into their private worlds and 'socialist consumerism'. As we shall see in the next chapter, such attitudes may have been exaggerated in the historiography, yet their existence not only posed major problems for the new pro-Muscovite rulers of Czechoslovakia, but also for their Soviet overlords.

In the arena of international politics and intra-bloc relations, the so-called 'Brezhnev Doctrine' was propounded by Soviet theorists as a means of justifying the invasion. The doctrine, first enunciated in *Pravda* in September 1968 and formally in operation through to the Gorbachev era, restricted the sovereignty of communist states by asserting the duty of the USSR to intervene in any socialist country if events there threatened the existing order or the common interests of the Soviet bloc as a whole. In a truly disingenuous feat of sophistry, it was denied that this 'limited sovereignty' contradicted the concept of national self-determination. By promulgating the doctrine, the Brezhnev leadership made it abundantly clear that in the final resort the Soviet Politburo reserved the exclusive right to decide when socialism was in danger and to overcome that danger by armed force if necessary. It was not a happy omen for the peoples of Eastern Europe. Further afield, the crushing of the Prague Spring accentuated the shift to 'polycentrism' in the international communist movement which had originated with the Sino-Soviet split in the early 1960s. Among many West European communist parties, the Italian, Spanish and French in particular, the Czechoslovak reforms and their untimely demise underlay the emergence of 'Euro-communism'. This important trend of the 1970s and 1980s sought to define the theoretical and practical grounds for a transition to socialism more in tune with indigenous conditions and less beholden to the Soviet model. Like communism in general, 'Euro-communism' and the parties that advocated it fell victim to the collapse of Marxism–Leninism in 1989–91.

Chapter 6: Everyday Normalisation, 1969–88

Following Dubček's replacement as party leader by the pro-Moscow Husák in April 1969, the process of 'normalisation' (*normalizace*) began in earnest. The term has two connotations: it was applied at the time to denote the shorter-term goal of restoring order after the upheavals of the Czechoslovak Spring, but it is also used by scholars to define the entire existence of the Husák regime, 1969–89. Leaving aside the issue of what constitutes a 'normal' communist system, the original aim of 'normalisation' was essentially to reconstruct the status quo ante, which demanded above all the dismissal of reformists from the party, state, economic and cultural apparatuses. This purge was achieved relatively smoothly, but the new 'consolidated' system, despite moderate economic achievements in the 1970s, suffered from a looming crisis of legitimacy – the majority of Czechs and Slovaks, especially the young and the educated, accepted neither the premises of normalisation nor the regime's ultimate dependence on Soviet armed might. Eventually, many became indifferent to it and tried to ignore its strictures, even its very 'being'. The long process of the decay of communism, not only in Czechoslovakia but throughout Eastern Europe, can be dated fairly accurately from this time. The normalisers' renunciation of the reform programme and the reimposition of an authoritarian Soviet model elicited opposition in the shape of independent counter-cultures, self-publishing ventures and various human rights initiatives, the most significant of which was Charter 77. A potent combination of embryonic civic activism, economic stagnation, internal implosion within the party-state structures and the 'Gorbachev phenomenon' in the USSR gradually eroded the ostensibly impregnable foundations of the 'post-totalitarian' edifice,

152

and in November–December 1989 the so-called 'Velvet Revolution' peaceably shunted the despised communist 'dinosaurs' from power and installed a multi-party democracy.

Among the questions we shall address in this chapter are: what did normalisation signify, what were its aims and how was it implemented in post-invasion Czechoslovakia? Why did most Czechs and Slovaks acquiesce in the rigours of normalisation? How did the party attempt to gain legitimacy in the eyes of a sullen and alienated population? To what extent did an implicit 'social contract' exist between state and society that swapped 'socialist consumerism' for public political conformity? How far did conditions differ in Slovakia from the Czech lands? And what role did 'dissident' intellectuals play in the undermining of the Husák regime? It is vital to remember, however, that for the vast bulk of people daily existence beyond politics continued in the 1970s and 1980s. What was 'everyday life' under normalisation and what opportunities opened up for citizens to adapt, negotiate and subvert the system? Who benefitted and who lost? Finally, and from a broader perspective, how far was normalised Czechoslovak society affected by the vast modernising changes that were sweeping through Europe and beyond in the 1970s and 1980s – rampant consumerism, mass communications, youth sub-cultures and social diversification?

The Politics of Normalisation

The Seven Wonders of Czechoslovakia
Everybody has a job.
Although everybody has a job, nobody works.
Although nobody works, the Plan is fulfilled up to 105 per cent.
Although the Plan is fulfilled up to 105 per cent, there's nothing
    in the shops.
Although there's nothing in the shops, we've got enough of
    everything.
Although we've got enough of everything, everybody steals.
Although everybody steals, nothing ever goes missing anywhere.
And the Eighth Wonder of the World is that it has been working
    for forty-one years.
(Revolutionary slogan, Brno, November 1989)[1]

This epigram from the late 1980s conveniently symbolises the political, economic and ethical crises engendered by Husák's normalised regime, and its numbing effects have recently been reiterated by a leading Czech historian: 'the frustration of hopes and plans; the many thousands of destroyed careers in the arts and sciences; the tens of thousands of exiles; the breaking of people's moral backbone; the rule of the mundane; the lie, the indifference, and incompetence; years of hopelessness, dull pressure, and universal decline'.[2] Indeed, the recurring themes that punctuate the historiography of normalised Czechoslovakia provide an unrelentingly grim picture: alienation, apathy, careerism, collaboration, corruption, disillusionment, informing, manipulation, opportunism, passivity, stagnation, 'inner emigration', 'civilised violence', a 'timeless' era of monotony and ritualised conformity. Precisely because this negative discourse is almost entirely hegemonic in the existing literature and, more to the point, is in many ways historically accurate, it is extremely difficult to penetrate beyond this 'reality' in order to understand the nuances, subtleties and compromises of daily life under normalisation. Before attempting this, however, we must define 'normalisation' and assess its key political features.

The Essence of Normalisation

The concept was aptly elucidated in early September 1968 by the Soviet party daily, *Pravda*, as 'the full exposure and suppression of subversive activity by rightist, anti-socialist forces, the elimination of their influence over part of the population and particularly the young, and the decisive strengthening of the Communist Party's leading role in the work of state agencies, in the ideological and public spheres'.[3] Thus, normalisation was perpetually, though increasingly implicitly, filtered through the prism of the Prague Spring and its prime political goal was to prevent another outbreak of reformist zeal. This sacrosanct aim was clearly enshrined in a turgid mass-circulated document *The Lessons of the Crisis Development in the Party and Society after the 13th Congress of the KSČ* ratified by the Central Committee in December 1970.[4] In concrete terms, normalisation – or the various euphemisms employed by the normalisers such as 'consolidation' or 'differentiation' – signified the removal of the leading Dubčekite reformers and their supporters (the 'anti-socialist forces'), the repeal of virtually all innovations associated with 'socialism with a human face', the rapid reimposition of censorship of the media and culture, a return to a tight centrally planned economy and a strict recentralisation of the party's authority over the security services and the armed forces. Crucially, beyond its overtly repressive and anti-reformist thrust, normalisation also meant the restoration of order, stability and certainty in all aspects of the lives of Czechoslovak citizens, a vital part of which was economic regeneration.

This state of affairs came to be known as 'real existing socialism', a polity that was to be unchanging and unchangeable. The outward signs of this immutable predictability and uniformity were legion: the ubiquitous flags and slogans on walls and in shop windows – 'With the Soviet Union for All Time!'; the carefully staged 'spontaneous' mass rallies and celebrations of the same anniversaries every year; the same photo of the 'leader' in all public offices; the never-changing editorials in the newspapers, which unfailingly contrasted successes at home with decline abroad; the recurrent political rituals of comradely bear-hugs, flowers and wreath laying. As far as the party leadership was concerned, the perfect normalised system was a world where all outcomes were intended, desirable and certain, where fundamental items of policy and ideology were non-contested and where the 'quiet life' – a key notion for Husák – was guaranteed for all. To this extent, normalisation was an unrealisable myth, a charade, almost a theatre in which scarcely anyone, ruler or ruled, truly believed. It also signified, as the famous novelist Milan Kundera and Timothy Garton Ash have suggested in their different ways, a monumental act of 'forgetting': anything or anyone from the recent past that reminded Czechs and Slovaks of a more democratic and humane road of development was swept under the carpet, a taboo subject.[5]

Who initiated and implemented normalisation? It is clear that Soviet pressure, particularly in the early months after the invasion, was ultimately paramount – the very presence of tens of thousands of Red Army troops made any meaningful 'resistance' on the part of Czechoslovak politicians and citizens a potentially dangerous matter. Moreover, on many occasions Moscow intervened directly in the political process in Prague through a variety of channels. Hence, the Kremlin provided the general guidelines for normalisation, but the actual detail was generally left in the hands of Czechoslovak communists, an outcome that Kieran Williams calls 'auto-normalisation'. This was carried out by four groups of KSČ leaders in the period August 1968 to 1971: initially, 'centrists', such as Dubček, who wished to preserve reform but unwittingly undermined it; 'realists', those moderate reformers like the enigmatic Husák, who repudiated liberalisation soon after the invasion in the name of 'order' and 'consolidation'; 'neo-conservatives', who initially supported elements of reform, but by August were keen adherents of Soviet intervention; and, finally, the so-called 'super-normalisers', who had staunchly opposed any reform after January 1968.[6]

The dominant group was the 'realists', often middle-aged party members who for various reasons adapted to the highly proscribed conditions laid down by the Soviets after August 1968 and astutely presented themselves as the only alternative to dreamy liberals and stuck-in-the-mud Stalinists. This was particularly true of Husák, who emerged as the Soviets' favourite to succeed Dubček, but who had his opponents among the other 'normalisers' and had to fight assiduously to maintain his authority. However, the 'centrists' played a major role in the early stages of normalisation. They were undoubtedly in an invidious situation, but many of them, including Dubček and especially his Prime Minister Černík, were prepared to renounce much of the reformist programme and their former colleagues in the name of 'political realism' and 'the lesser evil'. Indeed, the abject behaviour of the post-August Dubček executive demoralised and disoriented the population, severely, and probably permanently, undermining the legitimacy of reform communism and in the opinion of several experts greatly facilitating public acquiescence in the 'normalised' regime.[7] Among the first priorities of the new Husák leadership after Dubček's ouster was to purge the party of 'counter-revolutionary rightists', both at the top and at the grassroots. The latter turned out to be a complex and time-consuming operation stretching into 1970 and 1971.

Rooting Out Reform

The purge started with party and state elites and percolated down to mass 'screenings' (*prověrky*) of all KSČ members in 1970. It is possible that both phases were initiated and directed by domestic normalisers, but behind-the-scenes and fairly blunt Soviet pressure was undoubtedly applied. Already before Husák's ascendancy several outspoken reformers had resigned their offices or had been forced out – Kriegel, Mlynář, Šik and Smrkovský among others. Over 20,000 rank-and-file members voluntarily quit the party in the first half of 1969 and tens of thousands more, many of them industrial workers, followed in the ensuing months.[8] After his demotion in April 1969, Dubček retained his seat in the Presidium until September, but in December was unceremoniously despatched to Ankara as Czechoslovak ambassador to Turkey, a post he occupied until May 1970. In the next month he was expelled from the party, becoming a minor official in the West Slovak state forestry commission where he stayed until 1985. Černík was dismissed as Prime Minister in January 1970 to be replaced by

Lubomír Štrougal, an emerging force among the 'realists'. By this time no eminent reformer of 1968 remained in the Presidium. Inserted into the new leadership were hard-line conservatives such as Bil'ak, Miloš Jakeš and Indra, the first two of whom played prominent roles in organising and implementing the mass purge of party members which began in January 1970 and was to last the entire year.

The prime aim was to cleanse the KSČ of all committed reformists, or at least of all those who disagreed with the Soviet 'fraternal assistance' of August 1968 and the subsequent 'consolidation' drives. Husák had insisted, however, against the resolute demands of the 'super-normalisers' that there would be no return to the dark days of Stalinist repression and he does appear to have successfully opposed the arrest of the leading figures of the Prague Spring. Instead he and his colleagues opted for a more mundane 'exchange of party cards' as the best method of weeding out uncompromising opponents. This major exercise was to be carried out by so-called 'screening commissions', 70,217 of which were created in the course of 1970, composed of 235,270 trusted party veterans.[9] Their daunting task was to interview every member of the party and judge whether they exhibited the 'correct' attitude to post-August developments. According to archival figures, 1,508,326 people were screened, of whom 326,817 (21.7 per cent) were excluded from the party, 67,147 being 'expelled' outright.[10] The percentages were higher in the Czech lands than in Slovakia.

But what did it mean to lose one's party card? There were two categories of dismissal: the 'cancellation of membership' (zrušení členství) and 'expulsion' (vyloučení). The latter was worse: virtually all those expelled lost their jobs and had to take up more menial positions. Often the most independent-minded and idealistic, some of these disillusioned and angry 'former communists' were to play an active role in the opposition to Husák's regime. The post-purge KSČ was still a mass party, but it was an overwhelmingly docile organisation composed largely of malleable careerists and compromised opportunists.[11] Only 26.4 per cent were manual workers, the traditional social base of the party, demonstrating that the purge had failed in one of its main goals: to bolster proletarian membership.[12] Many experienced skilled officials and economic managers had been replaced by time-serving dilettantes, a phenomenon which did little to boost the efficiency and professionalism of the Czechoslovak political, economic and cultural apparatuses. A strict nomenklatura system was established, which meant that all responsible jobs and functions had to be occupied by trusted communists, and it is estimated that by 1980 there were approximately

550,000 such positions.[13] However, unlike in the first two decades of communist rule, the vast majority of party members in the 1970s and 1980s almost certainly retained very little, if any, faith in Marxism–Leninism, itself a damning reflection of the 'crisis of ideology' that afflicted the regime and country after 1968.

The purge, however, went deeper than the party: whole professions and institutions were affected and thousands of non-communists were removed from their fields of expertise, creating an entire cohort of 'second-class citizens'. The mass media were particularly badly hit. Several radical newspapers and periodicals were proscribed, the Union of Journalists lost nearly half of its 4,000 membership and even *Rudé právo* suffered the dismissal of 45 of its 80 editors.[14] Universities, especially social science and humanities faculties, were far from immune – of 16,000 university lecturers, over 600 were either sacked or emigrated. Students, school teachers and educational administrators fared better proportionally, but several hundred were still subject to expulsions and recriminations. In the autumn of 1970, a new centralised Socialist Union of Youth (*Socialistický svaz mládeže* – SSM) was established, purged of 'progressives'. The trade unions and their affiliated workers' councils, which had proved highly troublesome during the months after the Soviet invasion and into 1969, were fairly rapidly brought to heel, approximately 20 per cent of union functionaries being removed by 1970–71.[15]

The cultural world was singled out for special harassment and scapegoating. Many famous writers, including Havel, Klíma, Kohout, Kundera and Vaculík were blacklisted, their work banned and withdrawn from shops and libraries. Artistic associations and unions were disbanded and replaced by domesticated hack organisations. Job demotion or enforced foreign exile were the most common forms of punishment for these irreconcilables – philosophers became taxi-drivers, novelists became stokers, playwrights became brewers, historians became window cleaners.[16] Some were compelled to swap Prague for Vienna. Their sons and daughters were barred from university and college. A debilitating 'brain-drain' sapped the country of talent – many tens of thousands chose to emigrate illegally – and travel to the West for those who remained was severely restricted. In the opinion of most observers the sad outcome was that, regardless of the occasional critical film or semi-censored article, Czechoslovakia became a 'cultural desert' largely divorced from global trends and innovations.

The scale of the purges and persecutions suggests that resistance was futile. Indeed, after the demonstrations of August 1969 there were no further acts of mass opposition to normalisation and resistance 'was broken down incrementally through enticements, threats, and appeals to "reason"'. Thus, the majority of Czechs and Slovaks, demoralised by the sordid political compromises of their erstwhile leaders, were reluctant to confront the regime and withdrew into morose and superficial consent.[17] Nevertheless, in the early 1970s isolated groups of opponents, or in some instances individuals, dared to break the enforced conformity and demand a restoration of civil and political rights. They were met with a series of mini-show trials. Among the most celebrated cases were those of the historians Jan Tesař and Milan Hübl, the latter an ex-friend of Husák; Jaroslav Šabata, former party secretary in Brno; Rudolf Battěk, a leading KAN activist in 1968; and Luděk Pachman, an international chess grandmaster. The sentences were stiff: Hübl and Šabata, for example, received six and a half years imprisonment while Pachman got two years. According to archival sources, in the years 1969 to 1974 a total of 3,078 people were tried in civilian courts for politically motivated 'actions against the republic', almost 80 per cent in the Czech lands.[18] By the mid-1970s, it was precisely these groups of persecuted people – intellectuals, academics, journalists, former reform communists – who were to form the backbone of what became known in the West as the 'dissident movement'.

From 'Social Contract' to 'Privatised Citizenship'

The purge and selective coercive sanctions notwithstanding, it is important to recognise that the instillation of fear was just one means by which the country was normalised. One measure, often overlooked in the historiography, which engendered a degree of voluntary compliance was the Nationalities Law of October 1968. This enactment was intended to defend the rights, particularly language and cultural provision, of the four minority nationalities in Czechoslovakia – Hungarian, German, Polish and Ukrainian (Ruthenian), around three-quarters of a million inhabitants (Roma were excluded). As such it was generally welcomed by their representatives, notably the Magyars, but resolutely opposed by many Slovaks. There were several other social measures and policies which helped to bind the regime and sectors of Czechoslovak society. Maternity leave and family allowances, direct assistance to single parents and disabled or orphaned children, subsidies for nurseries, school meals and children's clothing, and low interest loans for newly-weds to assist with accommodation and furniture all improved markedly in the first years of normalisation. Even the émigré scholar, Vladimir Kusin, who was no friend of the Husák establishment, argued that the amount of financial support given from public funds to children, mothers and families 'can be the envy of every country in the world'.[19] There was virtually full employment, meaning very few Czechoslovaks lived below the poverty line. What is more, women's job prospects increased – by 1974 they comprised almost 48 per cent of the total labour force, although on average they continued to be paid lower wages than men and were over-represented in traditional fields of employment. The same was the case in higher education, where women were concentrated in pedagogy and the humanities.[20] The perennial and dire housing shortage was partly alleviated by the construction of thousands of *paneláky*, mass-produced prefabricated blocks of flats hastily erected on the outskirts of all major cities. Although these buildings were hardly aesthetically pleasing and became the locus of many social problems such as alcoholism, drug abuse, juvenile delinquency and a perceived decline in sexual morality, for hitherto under-privileged people they did represent an equivocal step into modernity.[21]

More broadly, commentators have invariably explained the acquiescence of the Czechs and Slovaks to the imposition of the stultifying normalisation system by a tacit 'social contract' between rulers and ruled that is said to have emerged in the early 1970s as the economy showed indications of tentative amelioration. The unwritten 'deal' was that the state would deliver reasonable economic growth, full employment, relatively high standards of living and free health and educational services in return for which the populace would pay public obeisance to the regime and desist from overt acts of opposition.[22] It is an interpretation not shared by all experts and for most people everyday life remained hard throughout the period. But until the late 1970s the authorities' wager on rational consumerism and the 'quiet life' did appear to pay certain dividends. Unpublished public opinion surveys undertaken in these years demonstrate that while consumers had real concerns over both the quantity and quality of goods, they were largely satisfied with the supply of basic commodities, held hopes for a 'better life' in the future and regarded prices as essentially stable.[23] For most of the 1970s inflation was virtually non-existent (characteristically, beer prices never rose!), the Czechoslovak economy functioned moderately well, thousands of upwardly mobile careerists and mediocrities stepped into the shoes of the purged, and, unlike in Poland, there were no visible signs of mass discontent or 'dissident' intellectual–worker cooperation. Indeed, according to H. Gordon

Skilling the contract 'created a kind of web of social relationships with a life of its own and gave many people a real stake in the continuance of the system in its existing form'.[24] Why rock the boat when the consequences were unpredictable and potentially dangerous?

The most recent research, however, has suggested that the Husák regime found other, more mutually affirming, means of forging a modicum of legitimacy beyond economic concessions and social trade-offs. Paulina Bren has argued that the party offered citizens the prospect of 'self-realisation' through a 'socialist way of life' as an alternative to unregulated capitalist consumerism. The underlying premise is that both the regime and the majority of Czechs and Slovaks shared the view that the public sphere of political engagement and civic action, which had proven so volatile in 1968–69, should be forsaken in favour of the calmer domesticated spheres of the family and social and friendship networks, a phenomenon Bren calls 'privatised citizenship'. In this private sphere women were to play the dominant role as mothers, producers and improvers of '"interhuman" social relations' following the upheavals of the Prague Spring, and the archetypal site of this social healing project was the kitchen and the ever-burgeoning country cottage. The theory was that as the nuclear 'socialist family' was nurtured, so the larger 'national family' would be maintained and consolidated. This gendered task was, it seems, successfully propagandised in the 1970s and 1980s through a number of highly popular television serials in which women acted as influential role models. For Bren, 'official culture ceased to promote a nation of eager, publicly active communists; rather, it sought to create a nation of private persons joined in their mutual quest for the good life, which, the regime insisted, could best be had under communism'.[25]

The significance of this undertaking is twofold. First, it was a crucial component of the wider aim of the 'depoliticisation' of society, which lay at the heart of normalisation: there was no room for collective political activity under Husák, even from erstwhile 'communists'. In this sense, the fundamentals of normalised politics were 'antipolitics', and it worked for almost 20 years. Marxist ideology, or at least terminology, was never eschewed – indeed, women were lauded for their dual roles as homemakers and productive workers and 'socialism' continued to be propagated as the best means of realising human potential and creativity. But ideological references became ritualised, a source of popular indifference, mockery, lampoon, even contempt. It might also be noted that depoliticisation was not restricted to communist polities. It was the Czechoslovak variant of global developments after the crises of the 1960s and 1970s that witnessed the relative decline of welfare states, the emasculation of trade unions and the growth of individualisation, privatisation and personalised consumption.[26]

Second, the striving for a 'privatised citizenship' reflected the social mood after 1968, which was broadly desirous of 'normality' and the 'quiet life', and thus describes a different, more complex social reality than the 'cynical' contract between party and population, or the even more simplistic 'state versus citizen' binary. This does not mean that critical political perspectives entirely disappeared from public opinion, as witnessed, for instance, by citizens' letters to Czechoslovak Television and Radio.[27] But the strong implication is that a measure of complicity existed between state and society on basic social conventions and cultural mores rooted in shared socio-economic aspirations, improved welfare provision and wary attitudes to unruly 'intellectuals'. An extreme case would be 'the collaborative part played by locals' inhabiting the peripheries of the country in the 'patriotic' duty of guarding the state borders against Western subversion.[28] Yet at the same time, many citizens paid lip service to the state's version of 'normality', constantly transgressed the boundaries between the 'official' and 'unofficial' and often sought to live beyond the confines of sanctioned practices and ideas. Thus, it seems reasonable to conclude that popular reactions to the normalised regime could be best characterised as 'disengaged collusion'; that is, the vast majority of people were neither convinced 'oppositionists' nor staunch 'conformists', but inhabited an intermediate contradictory 'grey zone' where they lived both within and beyond the 'system'. Such incongruities and dissonances of the normalisation regime were evident in the specific conditions of Slovakia.

Normalisation in Slovakia

A recurrent theme of this book is that perceptions and attitudes were often markedly different in Slovakia from those in the Czech lands, resulting in mutual misapprehension, mistrust and occasionally overt suspicion. In important ways this trend continued into the 1970s and 1980s. As a generalisation, the Slovak experience of normalisation was more ambivalent than the Czech, to an extent even constructive. Indeed, powerful myths arose. In the myopic view of some Czechs, 'traitorous' Slovaks, notably Husák and Bil'ak, dominated the higher echelons of power in Prague permitting Slovakia to be cushioned by a so-called 'soft version' of normalisation. This was far from the full story, but undoubtedly Slovakia did gain certain concessions. How to account for the differing perceptions among Czechs and Slovaks? The federalisation of the state goes part way in answering this question. The federalisation bill, passed somewhat hastily by the National Assembly on 27 October 1968 and operative from 1 January 1969, was the sole major reform of the Prague Spring that the Soviet leaders were prepared to tolerate. No doubt they were well aware of its potential to 'divide and rule' in the tense atmosphere of post-invasion Czechoslovakia and it is surely the case that some, perhaps many, Slovaks were 'bought off' by the federalisation law and were thus less averse to normalisation than the depressed and demoralised Czechs. Under its provisions, deeply held Slovak aspirations for self-determination and access to responsible positions were partially fulfilled, softening the blow of the renunciation of the other Dubčekite reforms. Peaceable federalisation of a hitherto centralised state was a major, indeed historically unique, constitutional achievement.[29] It formally recognised a voluntary union of equal national states whose two constituent republics, the Czech and Slovak, would hold authority via their respective National Councils over a wide range of issues: education, culture, justice, health and trade among others. Further enactments were ratified that restricted the possibility of *majorizácia*, the Slovak fear of being out-voted by the more numerous Czechs. Federal bodies, based in Prague, were to retain competency over relatively few key areas such as foreign policy and defence, and Slovaks were to be permitted greater access to federal posts and sinecures. However, contrary to Slovak expectations, many 'common affairs' were designated, including industry, agriculture, planning, finance and social welfare, which increasingly came under the federal prerogative, in effect recentralising the economy. Moreover, the prospective creation of a Czech Communist Party as a balance to the Slovak party never materialised, largely because it was viewed as a potential hotbed of 'right-wing counter-revolution'. In the event, the KSČ remained the real power-broker in line with Husák's, and the Soviets', insistence on a unified defederalised party.

Paradoxically, the normalisers' attempt, conscious or otherwise, to 'pacify' the Slovaks with the accoutrements of self-autonomy was a dangerous political game in that it revived the distinctly un-Marxist spectre of 'bourgeois nationalism'. To be sure, communist leaders and theoreticians had always harboured an ambivalent attitude towards nationalism – it could never be allowed to supplant class, although it could be used to bolster the flagging legitimacy of fragile regimes, as in Gomułka's Poland or Ceauşescu's Romania. But according to Pavel

Kolář, 'anxieties about "Prago-centrism" and Slovak particularism grew in the 1970s and 1980s among the ruling bureaucracy'.[30] A constant fear seemingly pervaded the KSČ elite that nationalist senti-ment, especially among the Slovak intelligentsia, might be induced by federalisation and its inconsistencies. In the opinion of one expert, by the mid-1970s these official concerns over potential 'bourgeois nationalism' had engendered 'a renewed emphasis on international-ism and socialist patriotism', a process one oppositionist termed the 'Sovietisation' of Slovak academia.[31] This is not to say that expressions of nationalist rhetoric were endemic in normalised Slovakia, but the ultimate worry was that nationally inclined malcontents could infil-trate the KSS, and Slovak culture in general, as was perceived to be the case in the 1960s under Dubček's secretaryship. After all, Husák himself had first-hand knowledge of such incursions.

The fundamental dichotomy of federalisation, however, not only in the fraught conditions of autumn 1968 but throughout the era of normalisation, was that it 'was to be initiated not as a component of democratisation, as originally anticipated, but within a political system in which the basic elements of democracy were lacking'.[32] Indeed, the authoritarian Husák regime took concrete steps in late 1970 and early 1971 to strengthen federal organs and erode many of the residual rights of the republican bodies, notably the Slovak. So much so that one respected Czech commentator later insisted that Czechoslovakia 'was from the beginning of normalization a federation in name only', and that the entire undertaking represented a manoeuvre which scarcely impinged on the Czech collective consciousness except as yet another bitter example of Slovak 'perfidy' at a time of national crisis.[33] Regardless of the historical accuracy of this notion, the Czechs' embed-ded resentment of Slovak 'opportunism', combined with the Slovaks' sense of moral triumph, which even the watered down federalisation could not erase, and the creation of self-confident administrative and business elites in Slovakia in the course of the 1970s and 1980s, helped prepare the ground for the *coup de grâce* 20 years later: the splitting of the country into two independent sovereign states.

There were many other factors, however, that explain the relative stability of the normalisation regime in Slovakia. Federalisation fos-tered a growing bureaucratisation in Bratislava and elsewhere, which meant avenues of upward social mobility and influence for many tens of thousands of young and ambitious Slovaks. The Slovak economy, enjoying fairly buoyant levels of state investment, underwent a modernisation programme which benefitted industrial workers and their families. Urbanisation expanded, educational facilities, social

welfare and pensions improved and the gap in the standard of living between Czechs and Slovaks significantly narrowed. The purge
in the KSS and overall levels of persecution were less vindictive and
cultural life less restricted than in Bohemia and Moravia. In light
of these developments, Slovaks, in retrospect at least, have tended
to regard the normalisation era more benignly than Czechs. For
instance, opinion polls conducted in the post-communist period
revealed that surprisingly high numbers of Slovaks looked back positively on the achievements of the years 1969–89, some even regarding it as the most successful period of the entire twentieth century.[34]

Normalisation as a Way of Life

A pivotal question on the normalisation era is: why was the regime
apparently so stable? Why was this repressive, inhumane and banal
system capable of reproducing itself with so few signs of overt opposition? An important way of addressing this conundrum is to try to
understand the patterns of everyday life under normalisation, the
strategies of survival deployed by citizens and the complex web of
mutual compromises and diverse loyalties engendered by the pressures of 'normalised' existence. Between the two extremes of joining
the power holders or fleeing the country, actively 'conforming' or
becoming an outcast 'dissident', there were a plethora of intermediate
hybrid positions and attitudes that most citizens adopted. The bottom
line is that very few, if any, people genuinely identified with the goals
of the regime, scarcely anyone – party members included – believed
the hollow slogans and ritualised Marxist–Leninist teachings, and to
this extent there was an underlying crisis of ideology at the heart of the
system, a recognition that 'real existing socialism' was at, or coming
to, a dead-end. This in turn meant that ultimately the party suffered
from a debilitating lack of popular political legitimacy, a reality grossly
exposed in the autumn of 1989. But the 'normalised' system lasted
for 20 years and was able to integrate, or co-opt, most citizens into its
structures and patterns of behaviour. This needs to be explained.

Fear, Surveillance and 'Civilised Violence'

The conventional explanation is that 'conformity' was the product of
the inculcation of fear and the intimidation of doubters and oppositionists by the seemingly omnipotent security services, the StB.[35]

This facet of the normalised regime should never be overlooked. Indeed, it was axiomatic in Prague in the 1980s that any pub could be inhabited by a plainclothes police agent straining to overhear conversations – one could never be sure, so better to be a bit careful. 'Special branches' (*zvláštní pobočka*) affiliated to the StB operated in major enterprises, universities and other workplaces. Minor, and not so minor, acts of repression littered everyday life under Husák, affecting large numbers of 'ordinary' people, not just a handful of 'dissidents'. Although long-term detention or imprisonment was rarely necessary, partly because the shock waves of an individual's demotion or dismissal from work would affect all employees and lessons were easily learnt, low-level persecution was endemic and typically impacted on people's livelihood, not physical existence. The unofficial sociologist, Jiřina Šiklová, provides a telling example. In spring 1988, a respected small-town secondary school teacher, Mrs Hana Jüptnerová, delivered an emotional eulogy at the funeral of a local 'dissident', Pavel Wonka, who had died suspiciously in police custody. In response 'the school board immediately terminated her employment contract, and ever since she has been washing dishes in a confectionary shop'.[36] Or take the case of a student-functionary in the Socialist Union of Youth who was expelled from that body for organising a punk festival in August 1984.[37] Or the experience, no doubt replicated in numerous instances across the country, of a bright youngster who had great difficulties enrolling first at a local grammar school and later at the English Department of Brno University because of her 'bourgeois' social background; that is, her father and uncle were well-known shop-owners. Class, evidently, still mattered in normalised Czechoslovakia. In the end, and this is instructive, it was personal connections that ensured her eventual success: being acquainted with, or consciously cultivating, the 'right' person often proved crucial.[38]

Nevertheless, a feeling of fear, it appears, was not all-pervasive and probably afflicted the intellectual strata – even, ironically, the political leaders – far more than manual labourers and office workers.[39] But it surfaced if citizens for whatever reason came into contact with the StB. A friend related her discovery of 'fear': 'was I afraid then [in the 1970s]? I do not think so, I was still too young...We were mostly defiantly laughing at possible tapping devices used by the secret police'. However, in 1979 she found herself at the StB precinct in Brno and was confronted by a fat file on her 'activities'. The police agent, who she vaguely recognised, offered her the extremely rare opportunity of travelling to Britain as part of a university group on condition that she spy on her student co-travellers. She courteously declined the 'invitation'. 'After that episode, I lived in fear.' Why? Because 'the level of detail they possessed indicated that people from my very close entourage must have given them the information'.[40] And from that moment on she could trust no one. The sense of constant surveillance was unnerving, psychologically crippling and ultimately, combined with multiple everyday frustrations, humiliations and indignities, forced her to emigrate illegally in the early 1980s. This kind of treatment is what Milan Šimečka, the renowned dissident-chronicler of normalisation, described as 'civilized violence'.[41] Gone were the days of leather-clad thugs and physical intimidation. Secret police officers now dressed in suits, had degrees in history, called suspects in for interview during normal working hours and politely shook their hand after an amicable two-hour chat over a cup of coffee.[42] But they could still ruin your life.

Chatas, *Hustlers and Stolen Breeze Blocks*

Another more prosaic, but nonetheless compelling, reason for normalisation's relative longevity is that in material terms most Czechs and Slovaks had 'never had it so good'. As we have seen, the tacit 'social contract' between the state – the virtual sole provider of employment, goods, services and 'gifts' – and society promised a decent standard of living in exchange for public political compliance. But more than this, as several re-emigrants to the country emphasised after disappointing sojourns in the West in the late 1960s and early 1970s, socialist Czechoslovakia offered 'a less demanding work environment, cheap entertainment and leisure, state-funded health care and...a "more spiritually mature nation than that in America"'.[43] The message was clear: 'normalised' citizens could live tolerably well and get paid solid money without having to work hard (sometimes scarcely at all), with no threat of unemployment and with affordable social and recreational activities essentially guaranteed. And, as an added bonus, they could salvage their consciences for compromising with the hated regime by convincing themselves that they inhabited a state that valued European 'culture' and 'heritage' over crass and shallow American consumerism.

This message, in the collective memory at least, appears to have got through. According to the anthropologist David Altshuler, normalisation is 'remembered by Czechs for the offer of unprecedented possibilities for material accumulation', not only of consumer goods, but 'widespread financial and logistical support for do-it-yourself family house construction projects'.[44] Indeed, by the early 1980s many citizens were able to erect their own homes providing they had obtained, sometimes using an inventive combination of fair means and foul, the necessary 'building licence' (*stavební povolení*) from the relevant municipal and architectural authorities. Moreover, the archetypal example of the socialist 'good life' was the craze for the country cottage (*chata*) that swept the country in the 1970s and 1980s. In order to escape the stultifying rigours of normalisation, many people sought refuge in building or buying their own space in the peace and quiet of the countryside where they were free of the long arm of party propaganda and the secret police. Official statistics show that the number of such abodes in the Czech lands grew from 128,000 in 1969 to 225,000 by 1981.[45] The result was that on Friday afternoons the main cities became denuded as tens of thousands of Czechs (the phenomenon was far less developed in Slovakia) flocked to their *chata* with crates of beer and sausages in tow. Often returning on Monday morning, it meant that many Czechs were effectively working a three or four-day week by the 1980s. Nevertheless, the authorities colluded in this private, non-collectivist, ostensibly petit-bourgeois activity because ultimately it served to fulfil that key goal of the normalised regime: the creation of a 'de-politicised' and partly de-urbanised population engaging in 'government-mediated' pursuits and more motivated by 'things' than ideas.[46]

In addition, Czechs and Slovaks, living in an economy of shortages, learnt to cope by becoming masterfully adept at bending the rules in myriad ways: moonlighting, bartering, bribery, hoarding, speculating, pilfering and smuggling.[47] Paradoxically, in this sense 'normalised' existence was anything but dull and uniform – it was, rather, remarkably and inexplicably 'free' and liberating. Many citizens circumvented the dire paucity of reliable media coverage of domestic and foreign events by tuning into German or Austrian television or listening to Radio Free Europe and the BBC World Service. Even scarce Western goods became fairly widely available through the network of state-sponsored Tuzex outlets. These were shops, first established in 1957, which sold all manner of 'luxury' products up to and including cars (a Chrysler cost $5,000 in 1977), apartments and land, but only for Western currency or *bony* – special coupons purchased either legally from the national bank or, increasingly common under normalisation, illegally from shady get-rich-quick 'hustlers' (*veksláci*).[48] A veritable 'black economy' took shape in the 1970s and 1980s based on semi-private, semi-legal petty entrepreneurship which saw many a mechanic knock off early from his official work in a state-run garage in order to carry out his 'second' job of mending a friend's car, who, as a butcher, pays him with a kilo of choice meat. Or take the example of one of my acquaintances in Prague in the early 1980s whose car wing-mirror was stolen. I was more than a little surprised when, in response to my naïve statement that he would have to buy an expensive new one, he said: 'You must be joking! You can't get them anywhere. I'll just have to steal one from someone else.'

There was little ethically uplifting about this style of living, which fostered corruption, low-level theft and a kind of spiritual vacuum, encapsulated in the ubiquitous saying: 'we pretend to work and you pretend to pay us!' But it did mean that consumer desires were partly gratified and citizens learnt to 'play the system' as best they could. And what is more, these 'shadow' activities were effectively endorsed by the authorities because they either helped oil the not-so-smooth wheels of the economy, services and supply of goods, or were a precious source of much-needed *valuta* – foreign currency, especially dollars. The warped and cynical moral universe of normalisation appears to have penetrated the supposed guardian of law, order and traditional values: the judiciary. In the mid-1980s, a civics teacher in central Moravia took his class of teenage students to the local courthouse to witness socialist justice at first hand. It was an all-too-common case of 'theft of socialist property', in this instance building materials. The presiding judge reprimanded the defendant with the words: 'that you stole the breeze blocks, I can understand – there's a shortage of them on the market. But the bricks, too?! You could have bought them!'[49]

Young people found their own way of navigating the system. By the mid-1980s, a few radicals attempted to 'opt out' as best they could by living 'as if' – 'as if' the system did not exist. Others, such as Miloslav Nevrlý and his friends, sought to escape the frustrating restrictions on foreign travel by regularly visiting the wildernesses and myths of rural Romania. His 1981 book, *Carpathian Games* (*Karpatské hry*), gained something of a cult following among many Czechs and Slovaks.[50] But invariably the youthful rebellion entailed an embrace of an 'imagined West' (*Západ*) in the form of rock music, fashion, beards and badges, although this did not necessarily imply a politicised rejection of 'socialism' and an espousal of 'capitalism'.[51] The regime looked askance at this uncritical adoption of 'bourgeois values', most demonstrable in its heavy-handed treatment of bands such as The Plastic People of the Universe, which will be discussed below. But the authorities were prepared at times partially to accommodate potentially 'subversive' or 'alternative' sub-cultures in an attempt to engender a modicum of support or more likely as a safety valve for pent-up youth frustrations.

A good case in point is the story of the Jazz Section of the Czech Musicians' Union, 'one of the most remarkable cultural institutions in "normalized" Czechoslovakia'.[52] Formed somewhat incongruously at the height of normalised repression in 1971, disbanded in 1984 and its leaders arrested in 1986, the Section arranged numerous semi-illicit jazz and rock concerts and festivals and published 'for internal use only' a multitude of ideologically risqué books and journals, a few even by semi-censored authors such as Bohumil Hrabal. This inevitably brought the Section into conflict with the authorities, who more than once in the late 1970s and early 1980s attempted to dissolve the organisation. But in their protracted struggles with the regime, the Section's leaders, sometimes with the backing of sympathetic judges and cultural officials, doggedly operated on the basis of 'legal resistance' and, while they 'persistently refused to subordinate their activities to Communist control', they were 'careful not to appear as oppositional or associate themselves openly with any dissident groups'.

Hence, until the mid-1980s the Section managed to retain a precarious semi-independent existence and in so doing influenced many tens of thousands of mainly younger people in the Czech lands, as well as in Slovakia. The very fact of its longevity in the face of official persecution says something salient about normalisation. First, as Peter Bugge suggests in his study of the Jazz Section, the regime recognised certain limits of the law and wished to be seen to uphold 'socialist legality', blunting the repressive edge of the state. Second, and most significant, the authorities were not monolithic in their approach to the Section or to cultural life in general. This ambivalence fostered a 'curious twilight zone where the rule of law half existed' and where 'space' was created 'for various forms of independent activism "from below"'. Finally, by the mid-to-late 1980s these semi-tolerated activities and bodies had spawned a measure of self-confidence and fortitude among a 'third generation' of students and other young people, who, unlike their parents and grandparents, were largely untainted by notions of 'Stalinism', 'neo-Stalinism' and 'reform socialism', and were beginning to conquer their fear and break loose of the sordid compromises of normalisation. These attributes became palpable in the heady days of the 'Velvet Revolution'.

'Co-Responsibility' in the 'Grey Zone'

Understandably, nowadays most older Czechs and Slovaks do not wish to be reminded of their complicity in the establishment and preservation of the despised normalised regime. But this notion of 'co-responsibility' in many ways strikes at the heart of the matter and in essence it is an all-too-human story of adaptation, co-optation, survival and 'making the best of a bad job'. To this extent, it has universal implications well beyond so-called specific Czech characteristics of passivity, indifference and buffoonery. To borrow Alexei Yurchak's terminology on 'late socialism' in the USSR, many Czechs and Slovaks lived 'outside' (*vne*), but not disconnected from, the system.[53] This was a symbiotic state of being whereby a person could respect 'law and order, stability, and the enforcement of [socialist] morals' and even agree that 'dissidents...were dangerously rocking the boat', but simultaneously might 'like jeans, have long hair, and listen to the Beatles'.[54]

   A recent influential case study of the normalisation process in the Philosophical Faculty of Charles University, Prague, has stressed the impact of 'co-responsibility' on the part of academic staff and students for the 'consolidation' of the faculty after the events of 1968. Asking the key question – how was it possible that the very same intellectuals who had upheld the ideas of reformed socialism assumed a stance of loyalty towards the renewed faculty in the 1970s and 1980s? – the authors describe a complex combination of surveillance from above and relative autonomy from below that went beyond fear and intimidation. The latter, to be sure, were present at all times, but never absolute. The first step was to convince enough academics that they 'might play a constructive role in creating the new consensus', which included identifying opportunities, perks and sources of personal advancement. This was then internalised as a form of 'auto-suggestion', whereby staff persuaded themselves that they were partly responsible for the new developments, while doing their utmost to construct an 'ideologically harmless profile'. This sentiment was enhanced by the existence of 'a highly stratified society' in the university micro-environment by which 'it was... possible to teach at a leading ideological faculty while being or not being a Marxist, being or not being a party member, collaborating or not collaborating with the Secret Police'. As the normalisation of the faculty proceeded, many members of staff became controllers and supervisors, who were themselves in turn controlled and supervised from above. The authors argue that 'it was this effective distribution of responsibilities amongst a huge number of people which made...

COMMUNIST CZECHOSLOVAKIA, 1945–89

the new dictatorship bearable and, from the perspective of the system, functional'. Hence, their controversial conclusion is that:

> Normalisation...did not establish itself as a prefabricated plan to subjugate society. The involvement of the masses did not go according to the script...To make the system genuinely viable, it needed to be embraced and created by the people themselves. Therefore, one of the typical features of Normalisation was surprisingly a certain level of openness, naturally within the boundaries set by the basic ideological framework and power hierarchy.[55]

This phenomenon was more broadly noticeable in the so-called 'grey zone', a term first used in the late 1980s by unofficial historians to denote those scholars who worked in the official structures and institutions, but who also kept in contact with persecuted and harassed colleagues, thus inhabiting a kind of no-man's-land, or 'grey zone', between consent and opposition.[56] The concept then broadened to include large numbers of qualified hard-working professionals in many fields, who 'reluctantly...cooperated with the establishment...and accepted certain benefits in exchange for their relative conformity' while remaining essentially sympathetic to 'dissident' views. What is the significance of this notion? First, in the opinion of a leading Czech sociologist, the people of the 'grey zone', as expert workers, were crucial for the functioning and maintenance of the regime, but at the same time they were well aware of the incompetency and absurdity of the system and thus inclined towards the 'opposition'. Second, although occupants of the 'grey zone' lacked the personal courage of the 'dissidents' and were ever-fearful that their 'collaboration' would be held against them, they increasingly became advocates of economic reform and human rights. Finally, the battle for the hearts and minds of the 'grey zone' between the regime and the 'opposition', a battle which by the late 1980s was being won by the latter, became pivotal for the future of the country both before and after the collapse of communism.

The Challenge of 'Dissidence'

In a seminal essay 'The Power of the Powerless', written at the height of normalisation in 1978, the playwright turned human rights activist Václav Havel attempted to dissect the nature of power, conformity and dissent under normalisation and in so doing theorised many of the attributes of 'co-responsibility' and the 'grey zone' outlined above.[57]

Distinguishing between the 'post-totalitarianism system' in operation since the Prague Spring and the 'classical dictatorship' of the Stalinist period, he re-examined the contemporary interrelationship between state and society and, rather than holding the Soviets or the Husák clique solely accountable for the sorry plight of normalised Czechoslovakia, Havel penetratingly and disturbingly exposed the involuntary popular pillars of the regime. The lines of conflict in post-totalitarianism were not drawn according to social class (rulers against ruled), but ran through each person, 'for everyone in his or her own way is both a victim and a supporter of the system'. Hence, overt terror was no longer the defining feature of the communist state since the methods of repression had become internalised, 'naturalised' for every citizen. This was one of Havel's cardinal revelations. He asked the seemingly innocuous question: why does the humble manager of a Prague fruit and vegetable shop display the slogan 'Workers of the World, Unite!' among his onions and carrots? Because he genuinely believes in international worker solidarity and feels compelled to communicate this enthusiasm to his customers? Almost certainly not. The slogan, Havel conjectured, was a sign and carried a definite meaning: 'I, the greengrocer XY, live here and know what I must do. I behave in the manner expected of me... am beyond reproach...and therefore have the right to be left in peace'. Or more prosaically: 'I am afraid and therefore unquestioningly obedient'. The slogan was thus rooted in the greengrocer's vital self-interests. He declared his loyalty by accepting the state-prescribed ritual and the pseudo-reality of all-embracing hypocrisy and lies. But in fulfilling this role of self-deception, and this was key for Havel, the greengrocer denies his own individuality and becomes a player in the political game, reinforcing the state 'lie' and thus *perpetuating the system.*

This amoral mutual dependency between rulers and ruled, what Havel termed 'the principle of social *auto-totality*', reflected the compulsion of the post-totalitarian system to draw everyone into its sphere of power, 'not so they may realize themselves as human beings, but so they may surrender their human identity in favour of the identity of the system, that is, so they may become agents of the system's general automatism and servants of its self-determined goals'. The alternative to this existential degradation and moral corruption, according to Havel, was for citizens to 'live within the truth' as part of a wider attempt to form a measure of civic solidarity. He exhorted his fellow Czechs and Slovaks not to acquiesce in communist rituals and lies, to overcome their fear and to rediscover their suppressed identities, dignity and self-respect. This was possible and necessary, because no one, not even communist officials, believed any longer in the mobilising capacities of

Marxist–Leninist ideology. Paradoxically, ideology was both omnipotent and irrelevant. If the people refused to abide by the rules of the game – not simply by dramatic gestures like striking, demonstrating and rioting, but by everyday actions like speaking openly at a public meeting, organising a private rock or jazz concert, declining to mouth meaningless phrases and slogans, practising their religion, neglecting to vote in farcical elections – the apparently monolithic power structure would be revealed in all its nakedness and feebleness. Precisely here was the 'power of the powerless', because 'living in truth' represented the most fundamental threat to a system which depended on mass compliance to the 'lie'. In sum, Havel's sublime message was more moralistic than political, but its prime significance lay in its insistence that 'opposition' was 'a way of life accessible to anyone' not just to groups of brave 'professional dissidents'.[58]

However, at many levels this optimistic scenario remained wishful thinking. The majority of Czechs and particularly Slovaks were left scarcely touched by the often abstract theories and ideals of the intellectual oppositionists, or at least were rarely prepared to break their stance of 'disengaged collusion' with the system. The onus of the struggle therefore did indeed fall on those who were to become 'professional dissidents', even though they baulked at the notion of an elitist core potentially divorced from the 'people'. The most influential of these various oppositional currents was Charter 77. The Charter was a loose association of ideologically highly disparate activists, intellectuals, former politicians and those who listed their occupation as 'worker', ranging from revolutionary Trotskyists and reform communists on the left to independent socialists and centrist liberal democrats, to Catholic clergy and Protestant thinkers on the right. But political labels did not interest them. What did unite them was the firm belief that fundamental human and civil rights – freedom of expression, freedom from fear, freedom of religious confession, the right to education, freedom of association – had to be actively and publicly defended and fought for. These and other inalienable rights were formally enshrined in the Czechoslovak constitution and had been reinforced in the summer of 1975 by the Helsinki Final Act signed by all European countries, together with the USA and Canada.

The Myths and Realities of Charter 77

The basic principles and goals of the Charter were laid down in a short founding Declaration issued on 1 January 1977, which was distributed with great difficulty at home and abroad and thus immediately vilified in the official media. Written in a deliberately conventional and legalistic style, the document combined a critique of the existing ruling party apparatus for its curtailment of human rights and enforcement of a power monopoly with a broad appeal for the maintenance of civic rights, defined as the responsibility not just of the state authorities but of 'everyone'. The signatories, of whom there were initially a mere 243 rising to around 1,500 by the late 1980s, denied that the Charter was a formal organisation or, somewhat disingenuously, that it sought to engage in oppositional political activity. Indeed, implicitly, it aimed to pursue a dialogue with the powers-that-be and to hold them to account for the defence of constitutional rights and freedoms. The proclamation concluded with the words: 'We believe that Charter 77 will help to enable all citizens of Czechoslovakia to work and live as free human beings'. Three spokespeople were named to represent the Charter in any future dealings with state bodies: Jan Patočka, an eminent philosopher, Jiří Hájek, who had been Foreign Minister in 1968, and Havel.[59] Among the other leading Chartists were Mlynář, Vaculík, Kohout, Petr Pithart, an ex-journalist and lecturer, and Petr Uhl, a radical non-communist leftist and former political prisoner.

We might well ask: why has Charter 77, basically an inchoate community of a few hundred Prague (and Brno) intellectuals, gone down in history as the most celebrated opposition movement in Czechoslovakia, and possibly the whole of Eastern Europe? What did the Chartists actually do, and what was their relevance in the dark days of normalisation? One of the Chartists' prime activities was issuing numbered documents in defence of universal rights and victimised colleagues, and raising public awareness of a range of political, social, economic, cultural and environmental problems. They were passionate about the indivisibility of freedom and human rights for all and about keeping alive the flame of an independent, pluralistic and humanistic Czech culture and academia. Hence, they strove to organise a kind of 'alternative culture' consisting of unofficial private lectures and seminars, literary readings, theatrical and musical performances, and artistic 'happenings'. Havel and his co-workers also attempted to collaborate with like-minded activists in Poland and Hungary, but such ventures were regularly disrupted by the police. Importantly, the Chartists brought the plight of persecuted Czechoslovak citizens, including 'ordinary' workers, to the attention of various international bodies and dignitaries, and, as quintessentially writers, they laboriously produced *samizdat* (self-published) books, articles, essays and feuilletons which were distributed in small numbers and furtively passed from hand to hand.[60] In this manner, their works reached a limited domestic audience, although in all likelihood their impact on the majority of the population was minimal.

As part of an emergent oppositional trend in Eastern Europe and the USSR, the Chartists caught the imagination of Western journalists and politicians as 'heroic anti-communists' at precisely the moment at the end of the 1970s and early 1980s – the years of Reagan's 'Evil Empire' and the 'new' Cold War – when the West needed to invent and name a 'dissident' movement in the Soviet bloc. For this, the Chartists, like the independent 'Solidarity' trade union in Poland, fitted the bill perfectly regardless of their apolitical, even anti-political, inclinations. It did not matter that in many ways the 'anti-communist' label was wide of the mark in that large numbers of these 'dissidents' were Marxists, ex-communists or broadly socialist in orientation. Hence, one or two 'celebrities' – Havel in Czechoslovakia, Lech Wałęsa in Poland – gained almost mythical status as bold 'freedom fighters', while many no less dedicated critics remained totally unknown in the West. The bravery and steadfastness of East European human rights activists should never be doubted: they suffered for their beliefs and those of us who, mercifully, have never been thrust into their predicament must display due humility. But they were neither lone heroes nor revered prophets consciously and deftly plotting the downfall of communism. Like all Czechs and Slovaks, they were forced to make messy compromises with the regime, were bedevilled by grave vacillations and uncertainties, were never sure of the way ahead and struggled to combine the public and private spheres of life.

The Chartists' resonance, as H. Gordon Skilling has noted, lies more in the slim measure of hope for an alternative better future that they offered their compatriots:

> Charter 77 was 'a challenge to full and active citizenship', calling on others to defend their rights as citizens…It was an act of 'civic courage', defying the coercive power of the state and accepting the penalties for such action. It also confronted the pervasive apathy and silence, appealing to people to conquer their despair, to entertain hopes and to act on them. It expressed a determination not to wait for change to come from above or from outside, but to do something now, on one's own, to bring it about…It was not a mere expression of discontent by isolated individuals, but 'a collective public protest'…[As such] Charter 77…struck at the very foundations of real socialism.[61]

The nigh-on hysterical reaction of the authorities to the publication of the Charter is proof of Skilling's last assertion. The party Presidium hastened to categorise it as an 'anti-state, counter-revolutionary document...prepared in collusion with foreign countries' with the aim of creating a 'bourgeois party'. *Rudé právo* lambasted the signatories as 'failures and usurpers' (*ztroskotanci a samosvanci*), an 'anti-Charter' statement was rapidly produced and workers, officials and artists were induced to denounce the real one even though no one had read it! What is more, the regime's legal experts deemed Charter 77 an 'illegal organisation' that sought to 'damage the republic's interests' both at home and abroad. Its members, therefore, could be subject to criminal prosecution. This was no idle threat. Leading Chartists were routinely followed by the secret police and repeatedly hauled in for interrogations, their offspring were denied access to higher education, their houses were bugged and searched, they were blackmailed, and all visitors, especially foreigners, were monitored. Some activists were arrested, charged and sentenced to long prison terms. For example, in October 1979 Havel received a six-year term and four of his colleagues in VONS (the Committee for the Defence of the Unjustly Prosecuted set up in April 1978) were also imprisoned for lengthy spells. Neither were the police above overt violence and beatings, even against women, or inciting anti-Semitism in a crude populist attempt to discredit the Chartists. Yet, interestingly, on occasion the heavy hand of the state was tempered. Havel and Kohout were allowed to keep their well-appointed apartments and country abodes. In addition, pensions, disability grants and foreign earnings were often permitted to other banned writers and intellectuals, at least until the mid-to-late 1970s. Hence, it has been concluded, in line with Bugge's assessment outlined above, that 'there was...a complex dialectic, evolving over time, between the increasing abilities of the state to harass opponents...and its fluctuating desire to do so'.[62]

There is a danger here though. Given the over-exposure of the Charter in the West, it has often been overlooked that the Czechoslovak oppositional movement comprised diverse elements, not simply persecuted Prague writers and defrocked reform communists. Indeed, there was no one 'movement' or 'dissident community'. Independent clandestine Christian groups were established in Slovakia, mobilising relatively large numbers of people, and by the mid-to-late 1980s the activism of various student, environmental and peace networks was beginning to displace the Chartists' more moralistic and legalistic approach. Crucially, the Chartists did not invent 'dissent'. They learned from, built on and uneasily co-existed with other anti-conformist associations and currents, some of which avoided the Charter altogether.[63] The most noteworthy was the musical underground which had been active since the early 1970s and which was generally more radical and nihilistic than the 'old-guard' intellectuals. The impact of the experimental band The Plastic People of the Universe is legendary. Arrested in a police crackdown in March 1976 for 'disturbing the peace' and depicted by the regime as drug-crazed obscene hooligans, the saxophonist Vratislav Brabenec and the group's artistic director and *spiritus movens* Ivan Jirous (alias Magor, or 'madman') were put on trial in Prague with two other young musicians in September and sentenced to eight and eighteen months respectively. The story has it that Havel and other oppositionists, galvanised by the authentic creativity of the Plastics, their craving for artistic freedom and the state's draconian response, packed the courthouse corridors and for the first time aged former communist officials-cum-dissidents, young long-haired musicians, staid Protestant ministers and Catholic intellectuals, fiery anti-establishment underground critics and veteran secular novelists who knew little or nothing about rock music all co-mingled and in some odd way psychologically bonded. And out of this intoxicating brew emerged the idea of founding Charter 77. As Jonathan Bolton admirably shows, the process was far more complex than that, but undoubtedly the practical dynamism, quixotic ethos and sheer elan of the musical underground helped to inspire many dissidents who coalesced around the Charter.[64]

The Dilemmas of Dissidence

Havel's brilliant treatise 'The Power of the Powerless' was notable, too, because it hinted at the crucial dilemmas of the intellectual dissident community throughout the late 1970s and 1980s: what should be its relationship to the eponymous greengrocer, that is, the broader public? And how should it disseminate its views and convictions to a wider audience? Should it openly oppose the regime, or should it seek some form of dialogue with the communist authorities? Should it attempt to politicise and institutionalise its activities by forging 'parallel structures' to existing official organisations or at least by cooperating with sympathisers within those bodies, or should it prioritise moral appeals in the hope of inspiring individuals' self-consciousness and self-activation? How to prevent its 'ghettoisation' into an isolated band of 'right-thinking' and high-minded intellectuals? And at a purely existential human level, how to avoid being wiped out by the secret police? Other issues, apparent with the benefit of hindsight, have exercised many scholars: given the patriarchal nature of Czechoslovak society, what role did women play in the dissident movement? Why was the Charter almost exclusively a Czech, even Pragocentric, phenomenon with scant appeal in Slovakia? How far did the Chartists' critiques of 'consumer society' as a potentially damaging attribute of Western civilisation cut them off from the 'inadequate' and 'materialistic' masses? How could meaningful links with oppositionists in the rest of Eastern Europe be forged? These painful, and in many ways ultimately unresolvable, questions resounded throughout the existence of Charter 77 and engendered fairly profound divisions and disagreements among its adherents.

Let us take the example of what might be termed 'morality' versus 'practice'. One of the first clashes of opinion among the Chartists occurred in 1978 following the *samizdat* publication of an essay entitled 'The Parallel Polis' by the Catholic philosopher and mathematician, Václav Benda. In this influential tract, Benda asserted that the apolitical ethical platform hitherto pursued by the Charter under Patočka and Havel's patronage was admirable, but was leading nowhere. His more activist politicised solution was basically to ignore existing state institutions and form alternative 'parallel' social, political, economic and cultural structures, which would gradually expand the realm of liberty already partially achieved by *samizdat* and the musical underground. He believed that eventually under 'constant pressure, the apparatus of the state would little by little give up'.[65] It was not a completely new idea – Jirous had previously talked of a 'second culture'. But despite its rather vague formulations, which were subject in turn to criticism by several other Chartists, including Havel, Benda's notion of a 'parallel polis' struck a chord both at home and throughout East Central Europe largely because it became entwined with the resurgence of the concept of 'civil society'.

Civil society is a nebulous phenomenon, not easily definable by historians, political scientists or sociologists. This is partly because it represents inter alia a set of abstract values – tolerance, trust, mutual respect and dialogue. In the East European context, civil society denoted the emergence of unofficial counter-cultures, such as the revival of religious belief, environmental concerns, youth and feminist movements, independent theatrical and artistic performances and 'happenings'. More specifically, civil society referred to the aggregate of precisely those networks, associations and institutions which Benda wished to create independently of, and diametrically opposed to, the state. Hence, it became a powerful explanatory tool for many Western scholars seeking to understand the rapid collapse of communism in the late 1980s. It was widely argued that this unexpected event occurred because the brave 'dissidents' had created a 'civil society', which increasingly undermined and paralysed the communist state from within.[66] The proposition is attractive, but often over-played. The reality was that, regardless of the best intentions of the Chartists, the selective repression unleashed by Husák's normalised regime, unlike the more restrained stance of the Polish and Hungarian authorities, combined with the relative acquiescence of most citizens, made it almost impossible for a broadly based independent civil society to develop in Czechoslovakia.

How best, then, to assess Charter 77 and the dissident movement's legacy? In essence, the Chartists desperately struggled to keep alive 'an alternative [vision of society] that was tolerant, open, and committed to nonviolent change and spirited debate' in the face of constant police surveillance and harassment and, it must be said, a fair degree of popular apathy and estrangement. The Chartists' ultimate achievement, according to one recent expert, was to create an aura of 'moral authority' which by 1989 permitted them to 'guide the energies of massive crowds of demonstrators, and to shape the revolutions as nonviolent debates about the structure of a tolerant, liberal democracy'.[67] It has also been persuasively argued that, while dissident ideas had limited social impact in the 1980s, 'dissident practice had a profound influence on civic organization in 1989 by virtue of the fact that Civic Forum and Public against Violence [popular citizens' initiatives in the Czech lands and Slovakia respectively] were modeled on Charter 77'.[68] There is no need to inflate artificially the historic import of the Chartists to recognise that they helped to create the conditions for a remarkable civic solidarity and community in the heady days of November and December 1989.

The portrayal of the 'normalisation' regime from 1969 to 1989 has been almost entirely negative in both Western and post-communist Czech and Slovak historiography. The same can be said of popular memory, and for good reason. Following the turmoil of the Prague Spring and the Warsaw Pact invasion, the new leadership under Husák did its best to stifle all critical political, social and cultural currents. The KSČ was purged of reformists from top to bottom; the media was rapidly tamed and harsh censorship reintroduced; those independent-minded writers, journalists and academics who refused to recant the principles of 1968 were silenced, their works banned; potentially rebellious organisations or unions were emasculated and brought under strict party control; committed malcontents and 'dissidents' were dealt with by the reinvigorated security services; and by the early 1970s any residual mass discontent was effectively bought off by a tacit 'social contract' between state and populace which exchanged 'socialist consumerism' for ritualised public expressions of political loyalty. 'Normalised' life appeared dull, uniform and, above all, unchangeable. Most citizens adapted relatively easily to this state of affairs, some, perhaps many, benefitted to varying degrees. As such, the regime, cocooned by the presence of thousands of Soviet troops, boasted of its stability and permanence in an era of 'real existing socialism'. But increasingly this myth of normalisation became exposed in the 1980s, victim of a plethora of internal and external pressures, large and small. These tensions, bordering on crisis proportions by the end of the decade, culminated in the so-called 'Velvet Revolution' of November–December 1989 which confined the communist system to the dustbin of history.

Chapter 7: 1989 – The Demise of Communism

Over a quarter of a century has passed since the pivotal events of late 1989 that marked the end of the communist experiment in Eastern Europe and, more broadly, of the 'short twentieth century'.[1] Even so, scholars are still wrestling with many intractable questions that arise from the revolutions of 1989: why did the seemingly impregnable fortresses of communism disintegrate in a matter of weeks in the autumn of that year? With the notable exception of Romania, why was this historic transformation achieved so peacefully? To what extent were these 'revolutions' in the classical sense of the term, or were they rather, in Timothy Garton Ash's famous compound, 'refolutions', a potent mixture of reform 'from above' and revolution 'from below'?[2] Were internal or external developments the main motor of change? What role did 'the people' play in the overthrow of communism, or, conversely, did the machinations of leading actors account for the extraordinary occurrences? How far do political, economic or socio-cultural processes explain the demise? More specifically for our purposes, why by the late 1980s were growing numbers of Czechs and Slovaks beginning to shake off their apathy, fear and sullen conformity and participate in public acts of defiance and opposition? What was the meaning of the Czechoslovak revolution? Was it organised and consciously led? Or was it a spontaneous outpouring of popular anger, creativity and community with little or no central direction? Or was the collapse of communism largely the result of the implosion of the KSČ and the inability of the leadership to control its subordinates; that is, did the party *lose* power rather than the people *win* it? To what extent can the events of November and December 1989 be represented as a 'multiplicity of revolutions' – Czech, Slovak, regional, urban, rural, youth, intellectual, worker? And, most intriguingly perhaps, what were the varying ideological motivations of the revolutionaries? These issues form the hub of my final chapter.

Why Did Communism Collapse?

It goes without saying that the sudden and unexpected breakdown of an entire political system is a highly complex and multifaceted phenomenon with deep-seated structural and shorter-term contingent origins. Revolutions are the product of interrelated indigenous and exogenous crisis conjunctures, the actions (and non-actions) of powerful individual agents, the dynamic strivings and moods of whole populations and the conscious manipulation of symbols, myths, language and images. In Czechoslovakia's case, and this holds for most other East European countries, by the late 1970s and into the 1980s four factors were beginning to shatter the illusion of immutability and stability of the normalised regime. First, the centrally planned economy was showing distinct signs of strain and the standard of living was slowly deteriorating, even in comparison with other socialist states such as Hungary. Hidden inflation, shortages and poor quality of goods, low worker morale and productivity, a lack of material incentives, over investment in out-dated uncompetitive industries to the detriment of modern technologies, and the burden of huge state subsidies for public services and failing enterprises were making it increasingly difficult for the government to fulfil its part of the 'social contract'. This in turn engendered social discontent and frustration, compounded by the popular image of affluent neighbouring capitalist states: why can't we live like the Viennese? Despite a slight improvement in the mid-1980s, nagging and unresolved economic problems continued to demand the urgent attention of party bosses.

Second, as we saw in the previous chapter, the emergence, consolidation and diffusion of what the West called the 'dissident movement' undermined the legitimacy of the Husák regime and kept alive the fragile hopes for a more democratic pluralistic alternative. Third, by the mid-to-late 1980s the Communist Party was almost imperceptibly losing its internal cohesion and sense of unity and purpose as creeping tensions began to appear not only among the leaders themselves, but also between the central executive in Prague and regional officials and rank-and-file members. Cracks were starting to appear in the hitherto impenetrable wall of communism, emboldening a society which was gradually shedding its fear and conformity. These subtle changes were intimately interwoven with the fourth, and arguably most significant, factor – the 'Gorbachev phenomenon'. From March 1985, the new Soviet leader's reformist policies of *perestroika* (economic reconstruction) and later *glasnost* (public 'openness' bordering on free expression), though largely unwelcome for most East European communist leaders, could not be totally ignored in Prague, Warsaw, Budapest and East Berlin. The distasteful and dangerous element for the Czechoslovak normalisers was that many of Gorbachev's innovations bore uncanny resemblances to Dubček's 'socialism with a human face' and thus implicitly undermined the entire legitimacy of the regime.[3] By the autumn of 1989 the ramifications of this were truly historic. Before addressing these themes in greater detail, I will set the scene by outlining the main developments of the crucial years 1988–89.

1988–89: A Narrative Overview

By the late 1980s, there were a few tentative signs that change was in the offing. In December 1987, Miloš Jakeš replaced Husák as First Secretary of the KSČ, although the latter retained the basically ceremonial position of President of the Republic. It was hardly a promising move – Jakeš's reputation was as a dull-witted hard-line 'normaliser'. However, subsequent leading personnel shuffles represented a modest nod in the direction of *perestroika* (*přestavba* in Czech). In December 1988, two despised arch-conservatives, Bil'ak and Josef Kempný, were removed from the Presidium and several younger officials were promoted, some of whom were more detached from Husákite policies and less fearful of change.[4] Measured *přestavba* reforms were introduced in the economy and indications of innerparty tension and conflict began to surface, even in public. Sensing a lack of purpose and self-confidence among the party elites and increasingly inspired by Gorbachev's *glasnost*, Czechoslovak society gradually became more animated, often spearheaded by student activists. In the years 1987–89, numerically small, but diverse oppositional groupings began to spring up and citizens showed themselves more prepared to mobilise and raise their voice. Cumulative actions – street demonstrations, ubiquitous *samizdat* publications, protest letters and petitions, artistic 'happenings', unofficial lectures, seminars, musical and theatrical performances – served to test the limits of the leadership's tolerance and commitment to Soviet-style *perestroika*.

The youthful members of the loose organisations who arranged these 'events' were rarely explicitly political or overtly confrontational, but they were deemed so by the authorities and hence often became radicalised and more prone to direct action than their 'dissident' elders, most of whom remained wedded to 'traditional' forms of dialogue and the power of the word. As Padraic Kenney has suggested, 'peace, ecology, conscientious objection, human rights, and self-government' – to which we might add religious engagement and women's rights activism – 'were all part of a shared opposition to the regime'.[5] Thus, a plethora of societies such as the Czechoslovak Helsinki Committee, the Democratic Initiative, the Movement for Civil Freedom, the Society of T. G. Masaryk, the Czech Children, the Independent Peace Association, the John Lennon Peace Club, the Society of Friends of the USA, the autonomous student body STUHA and the playfully titled Society for a Merrier Present, were founded, several of which mocked the communists as much as critiqued their policies.[6]

Ecological concerns, pollution and poor air quality, greatly exacerbated by the Chernobyl nuclear disaster in Ukraine in April 1986, became sources of genuine public disaffection, and not just among 'dissidents' and restless youth. Increasingly, 'ordinary' citizens – often mothers of young children – petitioned local authorities to improve the environmental quality of life as the industrial 'gigantomania' so beloved of communist planners impelled people to challenge the regime stoically and to stand up for their rights. Green issues were promoted by groups like Brontosaurus, the Slovak Union of the Protectors of Nature and the Land and, most aggressively, by 'Bratislava Aloud' (*Bratislava/nahlas*), a document described by one scholar as 'perhaps the most comprehensive condemnation of developed socialism published anywhere in Central Europe'.[7] In Slovakia and southern Moravia, there was a marked resurgence of religious activity with some Catholic pilgrimages attracting tens of thousands of participants of all ages. Embryonic ethnic issues were being raised; for example, a network representing the interests of the Magyar minority in Slovakia was formed. Ex-reform communists founded Rebirth – the Club of Socialist Reconstruction (*Obroda*), which, precisely because it was supportive of Gorbachev's liberalising policies, aroused anxiety in official circles. Even the Socialist and People's Parties, hitherto quiescent collaborators with the communists, were beginning to show real signs of independent activity.

The very existence and proliferation of these unauthorised and informal associations, though as yet involving a small minority of the population, often operating in isolation from each other and lacking any clear leadership or common programme, is important for at least three reasons. First, intellectuals around Charter 77 were no longer the prime organisers of such initiatives. Rather, it was students, young people, even blue-collar workers with no previous connections to the opposition movement who were participating in, and shaping, independent actions, suggesting that 'the gap between the activities of the dissidents and the concerns of ordinary citizens was narrowing'.[8] The students at the forefront of the demonstrations of 1988–89 had no personal knowledge of Stalinism or of the traumatic experiences of 1968–69. They had matured under normalisation and, to a certain extent buoyed by Gorbachev's *perestroika*, were not as fearful and intimidated as their elders. For them, 'communism was no longer an obstacle so much as an irrelevance'.[9] Crucially, they were more optimistic about the prospects for change than their disillusioned and dispirited parents and grandparents. Second, new forms of electronic media – PCs and, above all, videos – were beginning to challenge the regime's monopoly of control over communication and information. This was particularly evident at the time of the 17 November 1989 events, when home-made videos of the police violence against peaceful students proved vital in galvanising public support. Already in 1988, the government had stopped jamming Radio Free Europe and other Western radio and television stations and even the widely available Soviet news media, enlivened by the commitment to *glasnost*, were more informative than their Czechoslovak counterparts. Only by late November 1989 was there more accurate and objective reporting by domestic journalists and broadcasters. Finally, the gradual accretion of oppositional mobilisation indicated that the party leadership, effectively straitjacketed by Moscow's reformist agenda, was 'helpless to counteract the growing popularity of dissident groupings, underground activities and religious life'.[10]

This inability to stifle popular activism was also displayed by an unprecedented series of unofficial public demonstrations. On 21 August 1988, the occasion of the twentieth anniversary of the Warsaw Pact invasion, on 28 October, Czechoslovak Independence Day, and on 10 December, the fortieth anniversary of the Universal Declaration of Human Rights, many thousands, mainly students and young people, took to the streets to protest against the incumbent regime. The pressure was stepped up in January 1989, when students and other activists organised a so-called 'Palach Week' to commemorate the self-immolation of Jan Palach in January 1969. The disproportionate police response, including the use of tear gas and water cannon against peaceful protestors and even curious bystanders, aroused widespread public indignation and did much to discredit the authorities, as did the arrest and sentencing of Havel and other leading Chartists. Petitions and open letters demanding their release were signed by over 3,000 people, culminating in June 1989 with the circulation of 'Several Sentences' (*Několik vět*). This was a short declaration, endorsed by 40,000 citizen-signatories, which inter alia appealed to the government to free all political prisoners, restore fundamental civil and human rights and permit a public discussion of the 1950s, the Prague Spring and normalisation.[11] It was in this tense atmosphere, heightened by dramatic developments in Hungary, Poland and the GDR, not least the exodus of thousands of East Germans to Prague and the dismantling of the Berlin Wall, that the decisive events of 17 November 1989 took place in Czechoslovakia.

On that day, students from several faculties of Charles University had organised an officially approved march through the city marking the fiftieth anniversary of the death of Jan Opletal, a student-hero shot by the Nazis. A massive and unprecedented 50,000 to 55,000 protestors took part, many bearing banners such as 'Democracy and Law', 'Genuine Perestroika', 'Free Elections' and 'We Don't Want Violence'. As the procession reached National Avenue (*Národní třída*), a rump of around 5,000 students crying 'We Have Empty Hands' were severely and indiscriminately beaten by a phalanx of 1,500 special riot police causing nigh-on 600 casualties.[12] This unprovoked violent assault on flower-carrying law-abiding youths proved to be the death-knell for the old regime. Disgusted by the fact that the police had 'laid hands on our children' (*sáhly nám na děti*), in the days that followed hundreds of thousands of citizens took to the streets, more or less occupied the huge Wenceslas Square in central Prague and roared their acclamation as Havel, Dubček and other long-silenced dissentients addressed the crowds. These mass demonstrations were almost entirely peaceful, which became a defining characteristic of what was soon to be called the 'Velvet Revolution'. Above all, there was a real sense of solidarity, emotion and, it must be said, of freedom as millions of disbelieving and euphoric Czechs and Slovaks suddenly realised that the repressive leviathan was losing its will to fight back. It was indeed a heady and intoxicating brew.

Within two days of the student march, Chartists and other diverse oppositionists created Civic Forum (*Občanské fórum* – OF) as an umbrella body to orchestrate the popular movement and negotiate with the collapsing, but tenacious, communist authorities. As such, the

Coordinating Centre of OF fairly swiftly transformed itself into a kind of shadow cabinet and Havel, somewhat reluctantly, found himself a political figurehead and 'leader' of a fast emerging revolution. In the absence of objective media reporting, students travelled widely to outlying towns and villages to spread the word of what was happening in the capital. After several days of fraught talks, fierce disagreements over the composition of a new cabinet and a two-hour general strike on 27 November, a 'Government of National Understanding' was sworn in on 10 December by President Husák, who thereafter immediately resigned to be replaced by Havel later in the month. Dubček was elected Chair of the Federal Assembly.[13] It is essential to recognise, however, that while the world focused on the unfolding drama in Prague, largely spontaneous local and regional revolutions were occurring throughout the republic, notably in Bratislava where on 19 November Slovak activists and students created Public Against Violence (*Verejnost' proti násiliu* – VPN), the Slovak equivalent of Civic Forum.[14] Faced with this systemic crisis of legitimacy, the turmoil in neighbouring socialist states and Gorbachev's continued insistence on Soviet non-intervention, the 41-year-old Czechoslovak communist regime capitulated with startling rapidity in the space of two or three weeks.

Implosion of the Party

This cataclysmic and totally unforeseen development was greatly facilitated by creeping fissures in the communist edifice. The insistence on 'monolithic' party unity did much to paper over these breaches and even today it is difficult to adduce conclusive evidence of overt divisions among elite cadres. But hints there were. It is often argued that the Prime Minister, Štrougal, represented a nascent and cautious 'Gorbachevite' reformist wing in the KSČ executive until his forced resignation in late 1988, and that the party was rent along neo-moderate, conservative and arch-normaliser lines. There can be no doubt, however, that Gorbachev's policies utterly disoriented the Czechoslovak leaders, exposing to one and all their incompetence, impotence, lack of direction, endemic corruption and fear of change that paralysed the party as a whole. No one epitomised these deficiencies more than the new KSČ boss, Jakeš, who was universally ridiculed for his inarticulate ungrammatical ramblings.[15] At the same time, he and other party elders remained confident that they could see off the internal opposition, a classic case of under-estimating the enemy.[16]

Because virtually every comrade could agree that *glasnost*-inspired critical debate about the past, present and future was taboo, the main bone of contention throughout the party was *přestavba*, or economic reconstruction, which was formally launched by the party in March 1986. By the spring and autumn of 1987 limited legislation had been ratified designed to encourage greater efficiency and a measured de-centralisation of the strictly centralised planned economy, but many experts, such as Valtr Komárek, and enterprise managers wished to go further. In general, however, the economic initiatives were tardy and inadequate, the prime reason being that the KSČ elites were deeply concerned that the untouchable Leninist shibboleth – 'the leading role of the party' – would be definitively undermined if decentralisation was pursued to its logical conclusion. Nevertheless, as Michal Pullmann has convincingly argued, the new language of *perestroika/přestavba* and economic liberalisation imported from Moscow seriously undermined the ideological unity of the party and debilitated the fragile social consensus of late socialism. For Pullmann, *perestroika* 'did not *cause* the collapse of state socialism in Czechoslovakia', but by uncovering the hollowness of the normalised regime's claims to 'boost stability, general order, or well-being', it threatened the party apparatchiks' authority and presaged a crisis of official discourse and ideology. Pullmann's interpretation of the revolution thus emphasises the internal implosion of the communist regime, privileges the role of 'alternative elites' in the 'grey zone' and murky semi-official strata, and attenuates what he calls the 'minimal' impact of the dissidents.[17]

The most recent research on the Communist Party in the late normalisation period has built on Pullmann's path-breaking work by focusing on the deleterious effects of *přestavba* on the broader relationship between the party leadership, regional and local organisations and society as a whole. David Green has argued that historians have underestimated the scope and impact of *přestavba* and its sister initiative *demokratizace* (democratisation) on the party at all levels – and on the revolution itself. Green's essential argument is that in the years 1988–89:

> although the KSČ did not advocate change through popular protest, its policies of *přestavba*...and *demokratizace*...inspired and encouraged others...to do so. During the revolution, the tensions which *přestavba* stoked among the Communist Party leadership, its functionaries and membership led to the Party's loss of its 'leading role' in society.

Crucially, in the tense and confusing situation of November and December 1989, when the KSČ executive was roundly condemned for its vacillation, lack of vision and inability to issue concrete information and directives, the bulk of the party membership repudiated the leadership's severely restricted conception of reform. This withdrawal of support 'resulted in the Presidium quickly losing authority [which]...ultimately led to the wholesale rejection, by a majority in the Czechoslovak Communist Party, of the former Presidium, *přestavba*, and much of what the Party had stood for in the late 1980s'. This in turn 'enabled the revolution to proceed smoothly and seemingly unopposed, leading to notions of a "Velvet" revolution'.[18]

Green also demonstrates how the process of reform permitted subterranean divisions and fragmentations at the sub-elite level among official bodies, such as the Socialist Union of Youth, which effectively gave institutional cover to 'alternative' forums like the independent student associations, peace groupings and ecological initiatives.[19] To the extent that lower-ranking party and state functionaries, 'official' professionals and cultural and academic figures in the 'grey zone' and grassroots party members belonged to urban social strata and came into contact with 'public opinion', they may have shared, or at least sympathised with, certain aspects of popular cultural and ideological trends. Indeed, according to James Krapfl, 'opinion leaders' in 1989 'were frequently members of the "grey zone"', some of whom were communists.[20] Hence, the great divide between rulers and ruled, between the power brokers and the powerless, was arguably not quite so stark in Czechoslovakia (and elsewhere in Eastern Europe) as is generally believed. As such, this degree of interaction between the middle and lower layers of the 'party-state' apparatus and an embryonic 'civil society' helps us to understand the revolutions of 1989 in that the internal cohesion, unity and sense of purpose of the communist authorities had been eroded by long-term association with alternative discourses and value systems. In short, communist parties were far from monolithic entities and were vulnerable to change from within and without. By late 1989 there were even indications that the security forces, the coercive backbone of the communist state, were becoming resigned and dispirited, unsure of how to react to largely peaceful crowds.[21] If the regime was not exactly crumbling from within, the vacillation, indecision and perception of drift were palpable to ever-growing numbers of people. Citizens were beginning to lose their fear.

The 'Gorbachev Phenomenon' in Eastern Europe

There is almost universal consensus that while internal factors partially account for the transformations in Eastern Europe in the second half of the 1980s, Gorbachev's reformist policies in the USSR were absolutely crucial. Debate still rumbles on, however, about the precise nature of his role in the demise of East European communism. Perspectives differ depending on methodological approach. If the emphasis is on high-level political, diplomatic and military decision-making, then the Soviet leader occupies a central, even determining, space. If, however, the focus shifts to social movements and mass participation 'from below' in the overthrow of communism, Gorbachev's input becomes more opaque and ambiguous, though hardly invisible as shown by his often rapturous receptions during state visits (he toured Czechoslovakia in April 1987). He was rarely a radical reformer, at least before 1988–89, did not consciously seek to undermine incumbent conservative rulers and stuck, almost to a fault, to his principled stance of non-interference in the internal affairs of East European countries. That said, no scholar can seriously doubt Gorbachev's decisive agency on developments in the period 1985–90. Nowhere was Gorbachev's centrality more graphically illustrated than in his rejection of the 'Brezhnev Doctrine', a rejection which unravelled over time from an implied distaste for Soviet military intervention to uphold shaky communist regimes to a far more explicit repudiation of that possibility in the last 12 months before the autumn of 1989.[22] By then the days of armed Soviet 'fraternal assistance' were over, and hence the invasion of August 1968 was, tacitly at least, repudiated.

It is hard to summarise Gorbachev's evolving policies towards his East European allies, not least because they tended to be confused, improvised, contradictory and hesitant, regularly subordinated and subject to more pressing concerns both at home and abroad. Neither should it be forgotten that he was faced with an unenviable dilemma: how to initiate meaningful reform in Eastern Europe without destabilising the entire region? But one thing is certain: he had absolutely no intention of provoking the precipitous and definitive collapse of socialism and of the Soviet bloc, hitherto regarded by successive Kremlin leaders as the historic and inviolable product of the Red Army's victory in World War II. To this extent, the revolutions of 1989 were very much unpremeditated and unforeseen outcomes. The General Secretary's broad goal was to 'turn "little Brezhnevs" in Eastern Europe into "little Gorbachevs"'.[23] That is, he sought, albeit gradually and vicariously, to extend his domestic policies of *perestroika* and *glasnost* to his erstwhile 'friends' in the Soviet bloc. In the end, he was out-manoeuvred and out-paced by millions of citizens who had essentially discarded 'reform socialism'.

A Multiplicity of Revolutions?

It would be misleading, however, to construe the revolutionary moment of 1989 as a single united 'people' pitted against a single despised 'enemy'. As Krapfl prudently reminds us, 'Czechoslovakia in 1989 consisted simultaneously of one nation and two, of one community and many, and an accurate investigation of the policies and culture of the revolution must acknowledge this sometimes tense, often complicated, but always concurrent unity and multiplicity'. The events and meanings of 1989 were not infrequently interpreted differently by Czechs and Slovaks, and differently again by the Slovak Magyar minority. The experience of Prague, Bratislava, Brno and other big cities was 'more exceptional than emblematic' and bore little relation to developments in rural communities.[24] How was the revolution understood by diverse social classes and sub-classes: intellectual 'dissidents', students, industrial workers, farmers? Was it simply an anti-communist uprising in the name of liberal democracy and market freedoms? What motivated a heterogeneous population to go out on the streets in massive numbers? What united them, if anything? Did Czech and Slovak women put forward any gender-related demands? What were the variable responses of local and regional authorities to the mass actions of November and December 1989? And given that there is evidence that life did not change that much in smaller towns and villages after 1989, we might even ask to what extent a 'revolution' actually occurred.[25] In these important ways, it can be persuasively argued that there was more than one 'Velvet Revolution'. I will take two prime examples: the specificities of the Slovak revolution and the multiple, sometimes competing, ideological motivations of the 'people-revolutionaries'.

The Slovak Revolution

Given that one of the most significant outcomes of the revolution was the so-called 'Velvet Divorce' of 1992–93 and the creation of independent Czech and Slovak republics, it would appear logical to conclude that ethnically based nationalism lay at the core of Slovak concerns in 1989. But this would be largely inaccurate. For, regardless of the mutually reinforcing recriminations, mistrust and misperceptions that have sullied Czech–Slovak relations throughout the twentieth century, the notion of Slovak separatism was weak in the revolutionary euphoria of November and December 1989. According to Krapfl:

> the revolution of 1989 was first and foremost the genesis of trans-cendent solidarity. The emergence of a new sense of community was chronologically primary in the experiences of revolutionary protagonists, and initially terms such as *nation* and *people* were used to describe the community without thinking too carefully about their implications.[26]

Surprisingly, in the early days and weeks of the revolution many Slovaks, especially in central and eastern parts, chose to establish autonomous branches of the Czech Civic Forum (OF) rather than affiliate to the firmly Bratislava-based Public Against Violence (VPN). Outside of the Slovak capital there was a good deal of local and regional cooperation in Slovakia between OF and VPN associations. At this stage, Prague and Bratislava had little direct input into what were overwhelmingly spontaneous and localised citizens' initiatives. Important implications of the initial coexistence of influential OF and VPN branches in Slovakia are that the eventual bifurcation of the civic movement along 'national' lines was not inevitable, that internal federation and 'an integrated symbiosis was possible', and that asser-tive nationally inclined impulses in Slovakia were not immediately paramount. Indeed, the word 'nation' was as yet invariably used in the singular by both Czech and Slovak representatives. Nevertheless, the VPN leadership in Bratislava sought 'a thoroughly democratic federation of Czechs and Slovaks and legal arrangements guarantee-ing the rights and standing of nationalities according to the principle of full and real equality'.

The dizzying, largely uncontrollable, events on the ground in the first weeks of the revolution were gradually institutionalised and sys-tematised by a complex process of 'empire-building' in which com-peting towns, localities, regions and eventually the 'centre' – Prague and Bratislava – struggled to stamp their authority on developments. Out of this hectic amalgam of local and regional patriotisms came the first signs of an ethnic, as opposed to civic, understanding of nationhood. In Slovakia's case, this emerged from the desire of the

VPN Coordinating Committee in Bratislava 'to speak on behalf of the entire Slovak public and to maintain independence vis-à-vis OF in Prague'. It also had something to do with the interventions of various Slovak émigrés, the more extreme of whom warned of a 'Prague-engineered genocide of Slovaks' and called for outright independence by 10 January 1990. Though these 'crackpots' were scorned by VPN activists and Bratislava students, they did have growing influence in parts of north and central Slovakia. For example, the first appeal to put an end to the joint Czechoslovak state originated in the northern Slovak town of Dolný Kubín on 12 December. It nonetheless fell on deaf ears as throughout November, December and well into January 'expressions of Czechoslovak identity remained much more the norm in Slovakia than any emphasis on an exclusively Slovak community'. Even the legacy of Tomáš Garrigue Masaryk, whose concept of 'Czechoslovakism' had alienated many Slovaks in the interwar period, was to a certain extent reappropriated at this time.

The catalyst that changed this essentially inclusive and unitary sense of nationhood both in the Czechs lands and Slovakia was the so-called 'hyphen debate' that reverberated through the republic from late January 1990. It was sparked by President Havel's ostensibly consensual motion to remove the word 'socialist' from the official name of the state. Not content with this formulation, several Slovak communist delegates in the Federal Assembly proposed hyphenating the title, a counter-demand that 'riveted public attention on the national question' for the next three months. It was a highly contentious stratagem laden with divisive historical associations, particularly for Czechs – 'Czecho-Slovakia' had been used during the short-lived Second Republic after the Munich 'tragedy'. For most Slovaks, however, it was simply a matter of equality and Slovak visibility. The eventual compromise was the somewhat cumbersome 'Czech and Slovak Federative Republic'. The unpalatable outcome of the hyphen war was an increasingly strident and radicalised nationalist discourse on all sides, typified by the creation of extremist groupings such as the Club for the Defence of the Czech Nation and the National Council for the Liberation of Slovakia. Even in Moravia, regionalist demands and anti-Prague sentiment became fairly widespread. The well-known denouement, largely the work of two ambitious nationalist-populist politicians Václav Klaus and Vladimír Mečiar, was the division of the unitary state into the Czech and Slovak republics on 1 January 1993. It was a formal split that had relatively few active adherents among the respective peoples, but was graphic testimony to mutual indifference and a distinct lack of commitment to continued coexistence.

Meanings of the Revolution

Even as the revolutionary upheavals in Eastern Europe were in motion, Western analysts and reporters had arrived at two fundamental assumptions about the meaning of the events, both of which deserve careful consideration. The first was that the communist regimes were doomed to collapse and the 'revolutionaries' would inevitably 'win' the contest for power. The second, and more controversial, commonplace was that the mobilised citizenry was firmly united in its desire for a parliamentary democracy based on a capitalist market. Famously, before the year was out the American scholar Francis Fukuyama presumptuously trumpeted 'The End of History' and the universalisation of Western liberal democracy as the final form of human government.[27] It was not long before President George Bush Snr and Prime Minister Margaret Thatcher were being hailed for definitively 'winning' the Cold War and defeating Soviet 'totalitarianism' once and for all. In reality, the ideological influences and strivings of Czech and Slovak citizens in late 1989 were multiple, complex and fluid, and emerged as much from immediate revolutionary experience as from paradigmatic pre-revolutionary discourses.

As Carol Skalnik Leff has argued, the 'aura of inevitability' of the demise of Czechoslovak communism appears far more obvious with the benefit of hindsight than it did at the time.[28] It is true that soon after coming to power Gorbachev let it be known to his East European allies that the Red Army would no longer automatically bail out fragile unpopular governments. But this did not mean that those same 'dinosaurs' – Husák, Honecker, Ceauşescu – would not be tempted by the Tiananmen 'solution' of June 1989, when the Chinese military viciously, and successfully, crushed the student pro-democracy campaign in Beijing. In the event, only the Romanian dictator followed this violent path, but the Czechoslovak army was placed on alert and on 22 November 4,000 armed members of the People's Militia were stationed in Prague. Aside from the possibility of armed suppression, there was no guarantee for the students and dissidents who led the revolution that the 'masses' would support them. Popular attitudes in the 1980s towards the Chartists, for example, were hardly positive and no-one knew whether industrial and white-collar workers would be shaken out of their apathy and conformity to add crucial weight to an 'intellectual' revolution. Hence, the students, actors and other 'educated' revolutionaries who initiated the mass actions in the early days after 17 November faced a palpable double danger: they could be violently dispersed by the coercive might of the state and left isolated and vulnerable by a resigned public. As a Brno theatre director candidly said: 'the inescapable fact is that every one of us will have to decide for himself. Take a risk and believe that everything will work out, and if it doesn't, then reconcile yourself to the fact that you are in for it'.[29] The last five words are instructive: if the 'revolution' failed, the participants would be punished by a resurgent communist regime. This, after all, was the not-so-distant lesson of normalisation after 1969.

One of the most unexpected, and revealing, recent discoveries about the ideological underpinnings of the 'Velvet Revolution', and one that has been overlooked by most scholars, is that many citizens from a variety of social backgrounds retained broadly social-ist values and ideals and were not simply motivated by the lure of capitalist liberal democracy, not least because very few had any clear notion of 'capitalism'. It is also true that socialism was the subject of fierce contestation, popular understandings of it were often vague and it enjoyed far from universal support, notably in the main urban centres. But as Krapfl succinctly argues: 'Czechs and Slovaks did not reject the Communist regime because it was socialist but because it was unresponsively bureaucratic and "inhumane"'. Indeed, the archives are replete with 'appraisals of socialism that were overwhelmingly positive, calling for its preservation and renewal, not its dismantling'.[30] Public opinion surveys from 23–24 November and 9–12 December 1989 indicate that 45 and 41 per cent of respondents respectively maintained that 'Czechoslovakia should follow a socialist path', while a mere 3 per cent favoured 'a capitalist path'. In addi-tion, 47 and 52 per cent sought 'something in-between', presum-ably a kind of 'third way'. Moreover, 73 per cent disagreed with the re-privatisation of industry and 83 per cent with the privatisation of collectivised agriculture.[31] Other longer-term surveys are less unequiv-ocal, admittedly, and almost 80 per cent rejected the leading role of the KSČ, but if the November–December sample of over 1,800 people is to be believed, a majority of Czechs and Slovaks supported a leftist form of governance.[32]

Other evidence backs up this claim. Many posters and slogans harked back to 'socialism with a human face', Bratislava students maintaining that 'the historical foundation for the solution of our problems is to resume in a positive way the process of reconstruction… which our society began to undertake in the 1960s'.[33] Students in Olomouc and Banská Bystrica likewise adopted pro-socialist stances, as did Bratislava railway workers. Others sought a 'renewal' of social-ism, collective farmers in eastern Slovakia calling 'for a new, modern face of socialism'. Furthermore, 'many Czechs and Slovaks in 1989 drew as much inspiration from the contemporary Soviet example as they did from their own past', and, paradoxically, the language and methods of Marxism, ubiquitously propagandised by the state, 'to a significant extent…made it possible to "think" the revolution'. Civic Forum and Public Against Violence spokespeople had to tread carefully when broaching the prospect of jettisoning socialism for fear of popular criticism. Hence, one VPN representative insisted in a television debate that 'the dispute in our society today is not for or against socialism, but about the form of socialism…Socialism is after all not the heritage of [party] functionaries…[it] is the heritage of the citizens of this country'. Even Havel in his early revolutionary orations did not feel able to dismiss the entire 40 years of communist misrule, referring only to the last 'twenty years of silence'. As Krapfl suggests, this implied that '1968 could serve as a starting point for a new departure'.

For many working people, socialist ideals were intimately interwoven with a thorough democratisation of enterprises, collective farms and trade union structures. This primarily involved removing or recalling figures of authority who had lost the employees' confidence. By March 1990, almost one-fifth of company directors and many managers had been replaced largely because they were viewed by their workforces either as incompetent or as political appointees, or both. In the unions, hitherto totally subordinate to the KSČ, the main complaint was that party-appointed functionaries did not properly defend their members' interests. Thus, soon after 17 November the first free democratic elections were held and new grassroots strike committees and coordinating centres began to spring up at the local and regional levels. The pace of change was extraordinary and within four months, despite resistance by incumbent hierarchies, 95 per cent of union organisations had been either completely or partially reconstructed from below. In the universities too, student activists played a leading role not only in enforcing staff dismissals in faculties and departments, but also in winning far-reaching representation on governing bodies and in pushing through important policy innovations. For example, a ban was initiated on the detested, but compulsory Marxism–Leninism courses and male students were exempted from weekly military training. Municipal administration was likewise democratised with many communist officials resigning, voluntarily or involuntarily, though it is noteworthy that in the early days of the revolution communist-era institutions such as the National Committees, initially established in 1945, were broadly recognised and accepted.[34]

My emphasis on a putative 'socialist spirit' of 1989 is not to contend, of course, that it represented the driving force of the revolution. Far from it. In his exhaustive study, Krapfl has vividly and conclusively shown that the principal 'ideals of November' emerging from what he calls the 'collective effervescence' of the street protests were non-violence, self-organisation, freedom, democracy, fairness and, above all, 'humanness'.[35] Non-violence was a conscious goal of the revolutionaries counterpoised against the violence that was widely seen as inherent in the communist system. It was deemed 'a way of life', not just a political programme and aspiration, and was epitomised in the very name of the Slovak civic movement, Public Against Violence. Students in particular did their best to prevent any form of violence by the populace, which also had the practical aim of forestalling any state backlash. 'Self-organisation', perceived as the opposite of excessive management and bureaucracy, was evident in the first public demonstrations after 17 November, the majority of which took place spontaneously. Hundreds of thousands of people simply showed up to express their pent-up anger at a regime that was almost universally regarded as callous, incompetent and out-dated. The fundamental principle of 'freedom' was taken for granted, but rarely explicitly defined, or even voiced. 'Democracy' was closely equated with the ubiquitous demand for free elections, and with pluralism and dialogue. Elections to strike committees in late November and involvement in the General Strike were formative for 'citizens [who] grew accustomed to participating directly in the government of their affairs'. This right for citizens to be consulted, to voice their opinion, was applicable to everyone without exception.[36] This was the basic meaning of democracy in 1989: no longer should decisions be made 'about us without us'. The desire for 'fairness' reflected the embedded value of social levelling and the wholesale distaste, often manifest in humorous ditties and sayings, of the 'comrades' hypocritical and ill-gotten perks and privileges: 'Long live the Central Committee! But with laborers' pensions!'[37]

According to Krapfl, however, the revolution of 1989 is 'incomprehensible' without an appreciation of the 'central ideal' of 'humanness' (*lidskost/l'udskost*), or humanity (*humanita*), 'to which all others were logically subordinate…The desired new society was to be a society for people, not for parties, machines, systems, or bureaucracies'. The 'Velvet Revolution', like other East European transformations in 1989, was thus historically unique in placing 'the sanctity of the human being' above that of ideologies and political practices.[38] That the fine principles of 'the dignity of human life' and popular unity inevitably dissipated into internecine political struggles in post-communist Czechoslovakia, as elsewhere, does not detract from the transcendent ideals that galvanised hundreds of thousands of people in the autumn of 1989.

In summary, we are left with the notion that the moral bankruptcy of communism was the prime cause of popular alienation from the Czechoslovak regime and the main reason for its desperate lack of political legitimacy. At this level, the revolution was epitomised by the search for human dignity, public ethics and at bottom 'freedom' and 'truth', nebulous, contentious, but universal and transcendent values that temporarily united the 'nation'. Economic and material concerns were undoubtedly evident, but in my estimation were far from decisive. Indeed, such issues as shortages, price rises and poor quality consumer goods tell us little about the timing of the revolution – Czechs and Slovaks had suffered these multiple frustrations for decades and the economic situation was probably slightly better in the late 1980s than the earlier part of the decade. Social class may be relevant here; that is, blue-collar workers may have been more agitated by low living standards and the hope for improvement than idealistic students and intellectuals, but with the important proviso that many workers and collective farmers echoed the ethical strivings of their 'middle class' co-revolutionaries.

The question of the timing of the 'Velvet Revolution' is best explained by contemporaneous developments in neighbouring socialist states, particularly the symbolic breach in the Iron Curtain on the Austro-Hungarian border, the election of a non-communist Prime Minister in Poland and the tearing down of the Berlin Wall and accompanying mass demonstrations in the GDR. Clearly, there can be no monocausal explanation for revolutionary situations and state crises, but in the case of the 1989 revolutions it was ultimately the changing moral and political climate, combined with a coterminous debilitating implosion of the Communist Party, that destroyed communism in Czechoslovakia and Eastern Europe as a whole.

Chapter 8:   Conclusion – Into the
               Dustbin of History?

Post-communist parliamentarians in the newly formed Czech Republic were unequivocal about their immediate past and the calamitous legacy of communism:

> The Communist Party of Czechoslovakia, its leaders and its members, are responsible for the ways our land was governed in the years 1948–1989 and in particular for the systematic destruction of the traditional values of European civilization, for the conscious violation of human rights and freedoms, for the moral and economic decline accompanied by judicial crimes and terror against dissenters, for substituting a command economy for a market one, for the destruction of the traditional principles of the laws of ownership, for the misuse of education, training, science and culture for political and ideological goals, for the reckless destruction of nature…[Therefore] the regime based on Communist ideology…was criminal, illegitimate and deserves condemnation.[1]

In his memoirs the famous Czech author, Ivan Klíma, who suffered under both Nazism and communism, concurred with this judgement, calling the communist movement 'a criminal conspiracy against democracy'.[2] It is a view officially expounded by the Institute for the Study of Totalitarian Regimes, a Czech government funded organisation that is expressly concerned with impugning the communist past. Indeed, at an extraordinary congress in December 1989, chastened KSČ leaders had themselves remorsefully spoken of the party's 'unjustified repressions' and 'faults, mistakes and deformations against humanity and democracy'.[3] Given this ostensibly genuine, though

200

limited, mea culpa, should historians dare to infer that these damning assessments do not fully encapsulate the 41-year-old experience of Czechoslovak communist rule?

Communist Czechoslovakia: A Balance Sheet

Still today, many Czechs and Slovaks (and other Central and East Europeans) would no doubt endorse the idea that their country had endured four decades of illegal totalitarian misrule, state-sponsored violence and socio-economic, cultural, moral and ecological devastation. And as we have seen throughout this book on many counts they are quite right to do so. The Czechoslovak communist regime was vindictive, hypocritical, arrogant, wasteful, corrupt, nepotistic, incompetent and either massively or selectively repressive, in its Stalinist guise claiming hundreds of lives. Even if we accept that Cold War conflicts and domestic tensions impacted on the state's reactive backlash against 'the enemy within', it is undeniable that hundreds of thousands of citizens suffered in ways short of the ultimate sanction in an indefensible assault on civil society. Politically, communism was, in essence, an undemocratic and increasingly spiritually bankrupt system. Socioeconomically, in comparison to affluent capitalist states, it largely failed to satisfy the material and consumer demands of its citizens, sometimes at a basic level.[4] Too often party leaders appealed to the baser instincts of human nature, pitting sections of society against each other. Too often they lay supine before their Kremlin masters, almost slavishly following the Soviet model, unable or unwilling to defend national interests. Too often their sanctimonious ideological goals or crass power lust determined their policy decisions, clouding independent rational judgement. The negative balance sheet is plentiful and perhaps we should simply agree with the parliamentarians and dump the 'forty lost years' in Czechoslovakia into the dustbin of history.[5]

However, a key task of the historian is to challenge popular stereotypes and complicate received wisdom. As such, it seems to me that there are several important shortcomings and oversights with the dominant 'anti-communist' paradigm perpetuated by sections of the media and not a few rightist politicians. First, it is unidimensional and unduly restrictive in its fixation with history 'from above' and state repression. The lived experiences of Czechoslovak citizens under communism were far more complex, diverse and dynamic than this interpretation would have it, and these micro-trajectories need to be strictly contextualised and historicised. For example, many of the grandfathers and grandmothers of those young Czech and Slovak 'revolutionaries' who gleefully overthrew the despised 'dinosaurs' in November 1989 voted communist in the free elections of May 1946 and their fathers and mothers enthusiastically approved Dubček's 'socialism with a human face' in 1968. Moreover, the 'criminal conspiracy' view draws too sharp a binary dividing line between the evil 'them' – the minoritarian communists and their few fellow travellers – and the benign 'us' – the mass of downtrodden, suppressed and powerless citizens. It is as if 'the party' was composed solely of megalomaniac 'totalitarian' leaders who at all times 'imposed' their views on an atomised society and never interacted with it; as if the latter never influenced the policy makers; as if Czechs and Slovaks actively, consistently and 'inevitably' opposed the authorities, or at least passively rejected their socialist principles.

Evidence I have presented in this volume suggests this was not always the case. Most citizens learnt to 'live' the system, adapt to its strictures, and negotiate or subvert some of its harsher features. What is more, they interacted with municipal and local party-state authorities, and some, perhaps many, identified with certain official values and even benefitted from state policies in various ways. In short, as I surmised in Chapter 4 they took up a stance of 'critical loyalty' towards the party and its guiding ideology. Essentially, this is a position adopted by historians of other Soviet-style state socialist systems. For example, Corey Ross in his fascinating exploration of the East German dictatorship has convincingly argued that:

> although the SED [communist] regime managed to abolish the autonomy of social organizations, its representatives at the grass-roots...nonetheless depended on a degree of popular cooperation in order to carry out orders from above...Coercion and indoctrination alone were hardly suitable for encouraging people to become an honorary union representative, a member of an arbitration committee, a police assistant or a National Front local representative...Thus ordinary people played a part in the construction of East German socialism, and indeed one that was more than merely reactive [and they] could frequently use the structures at hand in their own interests, adapting and changing them in the process.[6]

This was, to be sure, a decidedly asymmetrical power relationship, but one that scholars of the state–society nexus under communism ignore at their peril.

Second, in my understanding communism was a project 'in the making'; it did not emerge ready made from a blueprint whose six points could be ticked off by party leaders.[7] Day-to-day policies had to be forged and reforged, were generally the result of intense debate and disagreement among powerful vested interests and routinely suffered from unforeseen outcomes. Like all politicians, communist bosses, no matter their intentions, could not regulate everything in their domains and were subject to external pressures and constraints. This is not to say that Gottwald and Husák were 'just like' Clement Attlee and Tony Blair. They were clearly not democratic parliamentarians who must assiduously court public opinion, but neither were they omnipotent, omnipresent or omniscient. And even less so were their numerous bureaucratic subordinates in the mushrooming ministries and offices. Neither were party apparatchiks entirely divorced from society and its fluctuating and diverse political and social currents. Put in colloquial terms, the KSČ was composed of concrete fallible human beings, who at the lower and shop-floor layers were part and parcel of Czechoslovak society, its structures and networks, but who at the higher levels tended to scrabble around pretending to be in control over processes that were often beyond them. And, significantly, there evolved a debilitating division between the *apparat* and rank-and-file party members, meaning that in an important sense the communist party was never a single homogeneous body based on 'iron' Leninist discipline. Indeed, by the late 1980s distinct signs of internal implosion had become apparent.[8]

Third, communist Czechoslovakia, at least in the 1960s, can claim to have given birth to two ideological and cultural phenomena of global significance: 'socialism with a human face' and the 'New Wave'. The former represented an ambitious attempt to 'make the communist project more resonant with rapidly modernizing societies'.[9] In its quest to marry democracy and socialism, which in the context of Cold War Europe was an extremely arduous task, it inspired a generation of leftists and 'Euro-communists' to seek an alternative path to modernity between capitalist democracy and Moscow-style socialism. More relevant, it informed Gorbachev's reformist *glasnost* and *perestroika* in the 1980s, which transformed Soviet politics and international relations and in the process made the world a safer place.[10] As for culture, in comparison to the rather torpid state of literary and artistic production in today's Czech and Slovak republics, the 'New Wave' of the mid-1960s, the technical and design artefacts on display at the Brussels World Fair in 1958 and even some of the works of the normalisation period of the 1970s and 1980s demonstrated that creativity, innovation and experimentation, qualities rarely associated with communist polities, were not entirely anathema to the party-state guardians of culture. The avant-garde films of the mid-to-late 1960s, in particular, continue to influence world cinematography, but more than this the art of Czechoslovakia and other East European communist states offered 'new testimony about mankind' and the human spirit beyond the pillorying of 'this or that political regime'.[11]

Fourth, communism in Czechoslovakia, as elsewhere, cannot be dismissed as a 'preordained failure'. As Pavel Kolář has rightly recommended, 'we [should] give up the conception of Eastern European communism as a "deviation" from an ultimately triumphant direction of historical development...[because it] was not an aberration from "modernity" but a different form of "modernity"'.[12] If we shift our gaze away from state coercion, anti-democratic politics and gross megalomania, we may come up with slightly different perspectives on communism's historical legacy. For example, did it in any way bridge the gap between the 'advanced' West and the 'backward' East? Did it in any shape or form create a distinct 'socialist modernity'? Did communism raise the living, educational and cultural standards of hitherto disadvantages sections of the population? Did it achieve social justice in any substantive sense? Did it help to modernise Slovakia and thereby forge the foundations of a vibrant national identity capable of independent existence after 1993? Did it emancipate women in any meaningful way? Did it find new non-exploitative means of realising human potential? To what extent were the notions of egalitarianism, self-sacrifice, collective responsibility and the 'dignity of labour', which lay at the heart of communist ideology, broadly appealing as a moral code of righteous behaviour? I am acutely aware that contemporary Czech communists often defend the actions of their predecessors along these lines and I have no wish to be seen as an apologist for a discredited system. Neither, of course, can we answer these difficult questions with an unequivocal 'yes': the results were patchy at best, reactionary at worst, but at all times profoundly contradictory. My contention is that analysts, in their rush to revile the political thuggery of the Stalinist years and the 'civilised violence' of normalisation, should not overlook the more positive and inclusive attributes of socialist ideology, attributes which genuinely motivated and mobilised large numbers of Czechs and Slovaks across the social spectrum, and to a limited extent continued to do so right through to the 'Velvet Revolution' as we saw in the previous chapter.

Finally, how can we account for the post-1989 phenomenon of 'ostalgia' – the hankering for the 'lost world of communism'? It is most applicable to the former GDR, but there is also evidence that in the contemporary Czech Republic the popular memory of normalisation is one of 'peaceful' everyday life free of the threat of unemployment, interminable personalised political intrigues and crass corruption. There is, then, a certain nostalgia for the state socialist order, for the 'quiet life', for decent living standards, for friendly 'uncomplicated' local communities and for extended social networks, all of which contrast markedly with the seemingly rampant disintegration of social life, rising crime levels and egocentrism characteristic of the post-1989 period. The same goes for 'socialist' popular culture. For example, normalisation TV series and pop music are still regarded very fondly, particularly by older members of society.[13] All this assuredly does not mean that citizens today want to turn the clock back – they don't. For the younger generation communism is but a bizarre curiosity. But, together with the polls of Slovak citizens which indicate that a surprisingly high percentage regard the socialist years as a time of progress epitomised by federalisation and modernisation, it does imply that the communist experience for many Czech and Slovaks was not totally negative and cannot be simply reduced to 'a criminal conspiracy against democracy'. Indeed, as Muriel Blaive has controversially suggested: the 'communist epoch…undoubtedly produced more social consensus than it is comfortable to admit'.[14]

In sum, if my interpretation is anywhere near persuasive the balance sheet of Czechoslovak communism is less categorically pejorative than is commonly perceived by many contemporary Czech and Slovak politicians, journalists, scholars and 'ordinary' citizens. Although the coercive and interventionist essence of the dictatorship must retain centre stage in any general account, this 'traditionalist' viewpoint needs to be refined by a more complex, differentiated and nuanced understanding of the key question of state–society interrelations. Indeed, a younger cohort of Czech and Slovak historians is already articulating this historiographical and theoretical shift, moving beyond the limited and self-fulfilling 'totalitarian' perspectives of the 1990s and early 2000s. It is to be hoped that this process will continue and that this book contributes to the on-going debate about the history and meaning of communism in Czechoslovakia and, more broadly, Eastern Europe.

Notes

Chapter 1: Introduction – Communist Czechoslovakia in Historical Perspective

1. A. Sayle, *Stalin Ate My Homework* (London, 2011), pp. 49–52.
2. This is fundamentally the experience of the father of one of my best Czech friends. The People's Militia was composed of armed communist workers, whose main aim was to ensure security in and around industrial enterprises.
3. I use the terms 'state socialism', 'socialist dictatorship' and 'communist dictatorship' more or less interchangeably in this book. I realise there are important theoretical distinctions between them, but the finer nuances of political theory are not my main concern.
4. A. Orzoff, *Battle for the Castle: The Myth of Czechoslovakia in Europe, 1914–1948* (New York, 2009), pp. 11–13.
5. The word 'German' signifies the dominant German-speaking Austrians in the Habsburg Empire, around three million of whom had lived in Bohemia and Moravia for several centuries. A much smaller number inhabited parts of Slovakia.
6. For exact figures, see V. L. Beneš, 'Czechoslovak Democracy and its Problems, 1918–1920', in V. S. Mamatey and R. Luža (eds), *A History of the Czechoslovak Republic, 1918–1948* (Princeton, 1973), p. 40. The census did not differentiate between Czechs and Slovaks, of whom there were over two million.
7. On the *Pětka* and *Hrad*, see Orzoff, *Battle for the Castle*, pp. 9, 12, 16–17, 63–6.
8. P. Bugge, 'Czech Democracy 1918–1938: Paragon or Parody?', *Bohemia*, vol. 47, no. 1 (2006–07), pp. 19–20, 26.
9. M. Feinberg, *Elusive Equality: Gender, Citizenship, and the Limits of Democracy in Czechoslovakia, 1918–1950* (Pittsburgh, 2006), p. 9.
10. For details, see G. Capoccia, 'Legislative Responses against Extremism: The "Protection of Democracy" in the First Czechoslovak Republic (1920–1938)', *East European Politics and Societies*, vol. 16, no. 3 (2002), pp. 691–738.

11. For a biting critique of Czech hegemony in the First Republic and of Czech nationalists' indifference to a multi-ethnic conception of the state, see M. Heimann, *Czechoslovakia: The State that Failed* (New Haven, 2009), pp. 48–9, 65–70.
12. H. Kieval, *Languages of Community: The Jewish Experience in the Czech Lands* (Berkeley, 2000), pp. 198, 206, 213–16.
13. This is essentially the view of J. W. Bruegel, 'The Germans in Pre-war Czechoslovakia', in Mamatey and Luža (eds), *A History of the Czechoslovak Republic*, pp. 167–87.
14. J. Mlynárik, 'The Nationality Question in Czechoslovakia and the 1938 Munich Agreement', in N. Stone and E. Strouhal (eds), *Czechoslovakia: Crossroads and Crises* (London, 1989), p. 93. See also Heimann, *Czechoslovakia*, pp. 55–7, 60.
15. Orzoff, *Battle for the Castle*, pp. 208–9.
16. On the long-term significance of these painful debates, see K. Bartošek, 'Could We Have Fought? The "Munich Complex" in Czech Policies and Thinking', in Stone and Strouhal (eds), *Czechoslovakia*, pp. 101–19.
17. Heimann, *Czechoslovakia*, p. 87.
18. On the Protectorate, see C. Bryant, *Prague in Black: Nazi Rule and Czech Nationalism* (Cambridge: MA, 2007). The most recent monograph on the Slovak Republic is J. Mace Ward, *Priest, Politician, Collaborator: Jozef Tiso and the Making of Fascist Slovakia* (Ithaca, 2013).
19. K. Gottwald, *Spisy*, vol. 1 (Prague, 1951), p. 322.
20. Cited in Heimann, *Czechoslovakia*, p. 83.
21. See Z. Suda, *Zealots and Rebels: A History of the Ruling Communist Party of Czechoslovakia* (Stanford, 1980), pp. 148–56; I. Lukes, *Czechoslovakia between Stalin and Hitler: The Diplomacy of Edvard Beneš in the 1930s* (Oxford, 1996), pp. 253–8. Under the terms of the 1935 pact, the USSR would render military aid to Czechoslovakia if such support was also forthcoming from the French. Clearly this was not the case in September 1938.
22. See F. I. Firsov et al., *Secret Cables of the Comintern, 1933–1943* (New Haven, 2014), pp. 160–2.
23. This paragraph is based on M. R. Myant, *Socialism and Democracy in Czechoslovakia, 1945–1948* (Cambridge, 1981), pp. 25–46, quotation at 34.
24. J. Rupnik, 'The Roots of Czech Stalinism', in R. Samuel and G. Stedman Jones (eds), *Culture, Ideology and Politics: Essays for Eric Hobsbawm* (London, 1982), p. 306.
25. For a critique of this interpretation, see M. Blaive, 'Internationalism, Patriotism, Dictatorship and Democracy: The Czechoslovak Communist Party and the Exercise of Power, 1945–1968', *Journal of European Integration History*, vol. 13, no. 2 (2007), pp. 55–68.
26. The idea of the 'rootedness' of Czech communism is in part derived from B. F. Abrams, *The Struggle for the Soul of the Nation: Czech Culture and the Rise of Communism* (Lanham, 2004); and M. Blaive, 'The Czechs and their Communism, Past and Present', in D. Gard et al. (eds), *Inquiries into Past and Present* (Vienna, 2005), available at www.iwm.at/index.php?option=com_content&task=view&id=259&Itemid=286.

27. P. Kenney, review of A. Kemp-Welch, *Poland under Communism: A Cold War History* (Cambridge, 2008), in *International Review of Social History*, vol. 54, no. 1 (2009), p. 121.
28. See, for example, the various declarations of Czechoslovak anti-communist exiles cited in F. D. Raška, *Fighting Communism from Afar: The Council of Free Czechoslovakia* (Boulder, 2008), pp. 3–4, 6, 23–5.
29. See, for instance, J. Belda, 'Some Problems Regarding the Czechoslovak Road to Socialism', *History of Socialism Yearbook 1968* (Prague, 1969), pp. 113–54. For Western scholars who gave ample coverage to domestic factors, see J. Bloomfield, *Passive Revolution: Politics and the Czechoslovak Working Class, 1945–1948* (London, 1979); and Myant, *Socialism and Democracy in Czechoslovakia*.
30. I am indebted to Vítězslav Sommer for this formulation.
31. On 'muddling through', see L. Holy, *The Little Czech and the Great Czech Nation* (Cambridge, 1996), p. 16.
32. The concept of 'totalitarianism', first espoused by Italian fascist theorists (and their opponents) in the 1920s, was popularised in the 1950s and 1960s essentially by American political scientists who applied it not only to Mussolini's Italy, but more centrally to Nazi Germany and the Soviet Union. It found its clearest rendition in the famous 'six-point syndrome' elaborated by Carl J. Friedrich and Zbigniew Brzezinski, *Totalitarian Dictatorship and Autocracy* (Cambridge: MA, 1956; 2nd edn New York, 1966). The six traits were: a single official ideology; a single mass party typically led by a dictator; a system of party and secret police terror; state control over the means of mass communication; a state monopoly of armed coercion; and central direction of the entire economy. Starting in the late 1960s, this model came under concerted challenge by historians, political scientists and other experts and today it has been largely superseded by a new cohort of scholars. See M. Geyer and S. Fitzpatrick (eds), *Beyond Totalitarianism: Stalinism and Nazism Compared* (New York, 2009). For an eloquent reaffirmation of the continued relevance of totalitarianism, see P. Grieder, 'In Defence of Totalitarianism Theory as a Tool of Historical Scholarship', *Totalitarian Movements and Political Religions*, vol. 8, nos 3–4 (2007), pp. 563–89.
33. See, for example, M. Pullmann, 'Sociální dějiny a totalitněhistorické vyprávění', *Soudobé dějiny*, nos 3–4 (2008), pp. 703–17.

Chapter 2   Communism on the Road to Power, 1945–48

1. Abrams, *The Struggle for the Soul of the Nation*, p. 10. Much of my discussion on the impact of war is based on Abrams's excellent chapter 1, pp. 9–38.
2. Statistics calculated from H. Krejčová, 'Český a slovenský antisemitismus 1945–1948', in K. Jech (ed.), *Stránkami soudobých dějin: Sborník statí k pětašedesátinám historika Karla Kaplana* (Prague, 1993), pp. 159, 165.
3. Abrams, *The Struggle for the Soul of the Nation*, p. 18.
4. J. T. Gross, 'Themes for a Social History of War Experience and Collaboration', in I. Deák et al. (eds), *The Politics of Retribution in Europe: World War II and Its Aftermath* (Princeton, 2000), p. 23.

NOTES 209

5. R. Okey, *Eastern Europe 1740–1985: Feudalism to Communism*, 2nd edn (London, 1986), p. 191.
6. John Lampe cited in Gross, 'Themes for a Social History', p. 20.
7. Abrams, *The Struggle for the Soul of the Nation*, pp. 31–2.
8. C. Brennerová, 'Cesta k únoru 1948: Teze k výzkumu soudobých dějin', *Dějiny, theorie, kritika*, no. 2 (2006), p. 219.
9. Gross, 'Themes for a Social History', pp. 21, 23 (emphasis in the original).
10. Abrams, *The Struggle for the Soul of the Nation*, p. 25.
11. The US army liberated western parts of Bohemia, but General Eisenhower chose not to continue the push to Prague, fearing large losses.
12. On the Fučík cult, see P. Steiner, *Making a Czech Hero: Julius Fučík through his Writings*, The Carl Beck Papers, no. 1501 (Pittsburgh, 2000).
13. Statistics from Suda, *Zealots and Rebels*, p. 165; and Abrams, *The Struggle for the Soul of the Nation*, pp. 34–5.
14. V. Mastny, 'The Beneš–Stalin–Molotov Conversations in December 1943: New Documents', *Jahrbücher für Geschichte Osteuropas*, (1972), p. 380.
15. Abrams, *The Struggle for the Soul of the Nation*, p. 33.
16. A. J. Liehm, *The Politics of Culture* (New York, 1973), pp. 47–8.
17. Abrams, *The Struggle for the Soul of the Nation*, pp. 10, 14.
18. A. J. Rieber, 'Popular Democracy: An Illusion?', in V. Tismaneanu (ed.), *Stalinism Revisited: The Establishment of Communist Regimes in East-Central Europe* (Budapest, 2010), p. 104.
19. I am indebted to Professor Alfred Rieber for this interpretation.
20. Cited in K. Kaplan, *Nekrvavá revoluce* (Prague, 1993), p. 23.
21. Cited in V. V. Marjinová, 'Od důvěry k podezíravosti. Sovětští a českoslovenští komunisté v letech 1945–48', *Soudobé dějiny*, nos 3–4 (1997), p. 452.
22. My discussion draws heavily on Rieber, 'Popular Democracy', pp. 103–28; and Myant, *Socialism and Democracy in Czechoslovakia*, pp. 36–40.
23. For examples of these reports, see T. V. Volokitina et al. (eds), *Vostochnaia Evropa v dokumentakh rossiiskikh arkhivov 1944–1953 gg.*, vol. 1 (Moscow, 1997), pp. 201–2, 229–33, 381–4, 393–9, 649–55, 661–4.
24. For details, see K. Kaplan, *The Short March: The Communist Takeover in Czechoslovakia, 1945–1948* (London, 1987), pp. 12–14, 24, 31.
25. Cited in C. Kennedy-Pipe, *Stalin's Cold War: Soviet Strategies in Europe, 1943 to 1956* (Manchester, 1995), pp. 108–9.
26. My account is based on K. Krátký, 'Czechoslovakia, the Soviet Union and the Marshall Plan', in O. A. Westad et al. (eds), *The Soviet Union in Eastern Europe, 1945–89* (Basingstoke, 1994), pp. 9–25, quotations at 12, 13, 17.
27. The Soviet minutes of this meeting can be found in Volokitina et al. (eds), *Vostochnaia Evropa*, pp. 672–5.
28. Cited in J. Korbel, *The Communist Subversion of Czechoslovakia, 1938–1948: The Failure of Coexistence* (Princeton, 1959), p. 183.
29. Krátký, 'Czechoslovakia', p. 22.
30. Volokitina et al. (eds), *Vostochnaia Evropa*, pp. 649–55.
31. For highly critical secret Soviet reports from September and December 1947, see A. Di Biagio, 'The Establishment of the Cominform', in G. Procacci et al. (eds), *The Cominform: Minutes of the Three Conferences 1947/1948/1949* (Milan, 1994), pp. 19–20; and T. V. Volokitina et al. (eds), *Sovetskii faktor v vostochnoi Evrope 1944–1953: Dokumenty, tom 1 1944–1948* (Moscow, 1999), pp. 514–23.

32. Č. Adamec et al., *What's Your Opinion? A Year's Survey of Public Opinion in Czechoslovakia* (Prague, 1947), pp. 14–15.
33. Kaplan, *The Short March*, pp. 14–15, 45.
34. The Czech émigré Josef Korbel spoke of the communists' 'operation grand deceit'. See his *The Communist Subversion of Czechoslovakia*, p. 142.
35. K. Gottwald, *Spisy*, XII (Prague, 1955), p. 253.
36. Abrams, *The Struggle for the Soul of the Nation*, pp. 179, 326 fn. 3.
37. K. Gottwald, *Spisy*, XIII (Prague, 1957), pp. 230–1.
38. Cited in Belda, 'Some Problems', p. 123.
39. Bloomfield, *Passive Revolution*, p. 120.
40. Belda, 'Some Problems', pp. 113–30.
41. My discussion is based on Abrams, *The Struggle for the Soul of the Nation*, pp. 89–103. The communists were less successful in winning the hearts and minds of the Slovak people.
42. Cited in Abrams, *The Struggle for the Soul of the Nation*, p. 94.
43. Cited in Abrams, *The Struggle for the Soul of the Nation*, pp. 95, 97–8. Jan Hus was a religious reformer burnt at the stake for heresy in 1415, subsequently becoming a national hero.
44. Brennerová, 'Cesta k únoru 1948', pp. 218–21.
45. J. Dobeš, 'Socialismus v politické teorii a praxi let 1945–1948', in Z. Kokošková et al. (eds), *Československo na rozhraní dvou epoch nesvobody* (Prague, 2005), pp. 276–86, 414.
46. See V. Prečan, 'The Czech Twentieth Century?', *Czech Journal of Contemporary History*, vol. 1 (2013), p. 13.
47. Kaplan, *Nekrvavá revoluce*, p. 54.
48. For details, see I. Lukes, *On the Edge of the Cold War: American Diplomats and Spies in Postwar Prague* (New York, 2012); and V. Smetana, 'Concessions or Conviction? Czechoslovakia's Road to the Cold War and the Soviet Bloc', in M. Kramer and V. Smetana (eds), *Imposing, Maintaining, and Tearing Open the Iron Curtain: The Cold War and East-Central Europe, 1945–1989* (Lanham, 2014), pp. 55–85.
49. R. M. Douglas, *Orderly and Humane: The Expulsion of the Germans after the Second World War* (New Haven, 2012), p. 96.
50. Security Services Archive (ABS - Prague), fond (f.) 310-24-6, listy (ll.) 1, 1b, 33.
51. D. Gerlach, 'Beyond Expulsion: The Emergence of "Unwanted Elements" in the Postwar Czech Borderlands, 1945–1950', *East European Politics and Societies*, vol. 24, no. 2 (2010), p. 273; M. Spurný, 'Political Authority and Popular Opinion: Czechoslovakia's German Population 1948–60', *Social History*, vol. 37, no. 4 (2012), p. 452. The number of murders is taken from B. Frommer, *National Cleansing: Retribution against Nazi Collaborators in Postwar Czechoslovakia* (Cambridge, 2004), p. 34.
52. C. S. Leff, *National Conflict in Czechoslovakia: The Making and Remaking of a State, 1918–1987* (Princeton, 1988), p. 93.
53. B. Frommer, 'Expulsion or Integration: Unmixing Interethnic Marriage in Postwar Czechoslovakia', *East European Politics and Societies*, vol. 14, no. 2 (2000), p. 381.
54. Cited in E. Glassheim, 'Ethnic Cleansing, Communism, and Environmental Devastation in Czechoslovakia's Borderlands, 1945–1989', *Journal of Modern History*, vol. 78, no. 1 (2006), p. 74.

55. J. Křen, *Konfliktní společenství. Češi a Němci 1780–1918* (Toronto, 1989).
56. Figures from Frommer, *National Cleansing*, p. 91.
57. L. Kalinová, *Společenské proměny v čase socialistického experimentu. K sociálním dějinám v letech 1945–1969* (Prague, 2007), p. 104; Glassheim, 'Ethnic Cleansing', pp. 79–80 fn. 64.
58. Glassheim, 'Ethnic Cleansing', pp. 73–81, quotations at 78, 80.
59. J. R. Felak, *After Hitler, Before Stalin: Catholics, Communists, and Democrats in Slovakia, 1945–1948* (Pittsburgh, 2009), pp. 2–3.
60. This paragraph is based on Bloomfield, *Passive Revolution*, pp. 91–105; K. Kovanda, 'Works Councils in Czechoslovakia, 1945–47', *Soviet Studies*, vol. 29, no. 2 (1977), pp. 255–69; and D. Státník, 'Závodní rady – iluze a skutečnost', in Kokošková et al. (eds), *Československo*, pp. 374–86.
61. On communist activism in Plzeň, see J. Šlouf, 'KSČ na Plzeňsku v letech 1945–1948', MA thesis, Charles University, Prague (2008).
62. Kalinová, *Společenské proměny*, p. 103.
63. Kaplan, *Nekrvavá revoluce*, p. 400.
64. Myant, *Socialism and Democracy in Czechoslovakia*, p. 107.
65. G. Wightman and A. H. Brown, 'Changes in the Levels of Membership and Social Composition of the Communist Party of Czechoslovakia, 1945–73', *Soviet Studies*, vol. 27, no. 3 (1975), p. 402.
66. This paragraph is based on Feinberg, *Elusive Equality*, pp. 195–205; D. Musilová, 'Ženské hnutí 1945–1948: naděje a zklamání', in Kokošková et al. (eds), *Československo*, pp. 339–45; and D. Nečasová, *Buduj vlast – posílíš mír! Ženské hnutí v českých zemích 1945–1955* (Brno, 2011).
67. This paragraph is based on Myant, *Socialism and Democracy in Czechoslovakia*, pp. 135, 137–42, quotation at 141.
68. The most detailed work on these crises and on the February events is K. Kaplan, *Pět kapitol o únoru* (Brno, 1997).
69. M. Myant, 'New Research on February 1948 in Czechoslovakia', *Europe-Asia Studies*, vol. 60, no. 10 (2008), pp. 1707–8.
70. Extracts of cabinet discussions can be found in Kaplan, *The Short March*, pp. 155–71.
71. On the Zorin visit, see V. Murašková, 'Únorová krize roku 1948 v Československu a sovětské politické vedení', *Soudobé dějiny*, no. 2–3 (1998), pp. 314–17.

Chapter 3:   Stalinism Reigns, 1948–53

1. For a recent overview, see K. McDermott and M. Stibbe (eds), *Stalinist Terror in Eastern Europe: Elite Purges and Mass Repression* (Manchester, 2010).
2. See I. Halfin, *Terror in my Soul: Communist Autobiographies on Trial* (Cambridge: MA, 2003).
3. Cited in A. Oxley et al. (eds), *Czechoslovakia: The Party and the People* (London, 1973), p. 88.
4. K. Kaplan, *Political Persecution in Czechoslovakia 1948–1972* (Cologne, 1983), pp. 7–11; Myant, *Socialism and Democracy in Czechoslovakia*, pp. 219–26.

212 NOTES

5. Statistics from M. Hauner, 'Crime and Punishment in Communist
Czechoslovakia: The Case of General Heliodor Píka and his Prosecutor
Karel Vaš', *Totalitarian Movements and Political Religions*, vol. 9, no.
2–3 (2008), pp. 343–4; figures for Slovakia are from J. Pešek, 'The
Establishment of Totalitarianism in Slovakia after the February Coup of
1948 and the Culmination of Mass Persecution, 1948–1953', in M. Teich
et al. (eds), *Slovakia in History* (Cambridge, 2011), pp. 293–4.
6. Statistics from J. Pelikán (ed.), *The Czechoslovak Political Trials, 1950–1954:
The Suppressed Report of the Dubček Government's Commission of Inquiry*, 1968
(London, 1971), pp. 56–7; J. Foitzik, 'Souvislosti politických procesů ve
střední a východní Evropě', in J. Pernes and J. Foitzik (eds), *Politické procesy v Československu po roce 1945 a 'případ Slánský'* (Brno, 2005), pp. 11, 13,
15–16; K. Kaplan and J. Váchová (eds), *Zemřelí ve věznicích a tresty smrti,
1948–1956: Seznamy* (Prague, 1992), pp. 53–60 and non-paginated adden-
dum. For details on judicial executions, see O. Liška and coll., *Tresty smrti
vykonané v Československu v letech 1918–1989* (Prague, 2006)
7. Pelikán (ed.), *The Czechoslovak Political Trials*, pp. 130–2, 246–54, 260–77,
quotations at 131, 246, 261.
8. Kaplan, *Political Persecution*, pp. 16–17; for a detailed case study, see
O. Vojtěchovský, *Z Prahy proti Titovi! Jugoslávská prosovětská emigrace v
Československu* (Prague, 2012), pp. 436–505.
9. Pelikán (ed.), *The Czechoslovak Political Trials*, p. 136.
10. K. Kaplan, *Sovětští poradci v Československu 1949–1956* (Prague, 1993);
K. Kaplan, *Nebezpečná bezpečnost: Státní bezpečnost 1948–1956* (Brno, 1999),
pp. 25–33.
11. Pelikán (ed.), *The Czechoslovak Political Trials*, pp. 131, 138; Kaplan,
Political Persecution, pp. 17–18.
12. K. Kaplan and J. Váchová (eds), *Akce B – vystěhování 'státně nespolehlivých
osob' z Prahy, Bratislavy a dalších měst, 1952–1953* (Prague, 1992), pp. 5–7,
121, 176.
13. K. Jech (ed.), *Vystěhování selských rodin v Akci K ('kulaci') 1951–1953:
Seznamy a vybranné dokumenty* (Prague, 1992), pp. 6–7, 105.
14. Kaplan, *Political Persecution*, pp. 11–15.
15. Kaplan, *Political Persecution*, pp. 15–16.
16. This paragraph is based on Kaplan, *Political Persecution*, pp. 16, 19–23.
17. For details, see K. McDermott, 'A "Polyphony of Voices"? Czech Popular
Opinion and the Slánský Affair', *Slavic Review*, vol. 67, no. 4 (2008), pp.
840–65.
18. National Archive of the Czech Republic (NA), Archive of the Central
Committee of the KSČ (AÚV KSČ), f. komise 1, sv. 2, a.j. 13, ll. 6-7.
19. For details, see K. Kaplan, *Report on the Murder of the General Secretary*
(London, 1990); I. Lukes, 'Rudolf Slansky: His Trials and Trial', Cold War
International History Project, Working Paper No. 50 (Washington DC,
2006).
20. NA, f. 014/2, sv. 9, a.j. 71, l. 2; NA, f. nezpracovaný fond and f. rezoluce
Slánský, nezpracovaná čast fondu.
21. NA, f. 05/1, sv. 416, a.j. 2460, l. 2; f. 014/12, sv. 8, a.j. 64, l. 7; f. 014/12, sv.
8, a.j. 61, ll. 8-9; f. 01, sv. 18, a.j. 29(3), ll. 272-3; and ABS, fonds 310-114-6,
7, 9, 11, 13, 16 (unpaginated).
22. ABS, fonds 310-114-6, 7, 9, 11, 12, 13, 16; NA, f. 014/12, sv. 8, a.j. 61, l. 21.

23. NA, f. 014/12, sv. 8, a.j. 64, l. 3; f. 19/13, a.j. 122 (2), l. 118; ABS, f. 310-111-3, l. 9; NA, f. 12, jedn. 59, l. 57.
24. NA, f. 014/12, sv. 8, a.j. 61, ll. 8, 19, 24; f. 014/12, sv. 8, a.j. 64, ll. 3, 6; f. 014/2, sv. 9, a.j. 71, ll. 4, 12-13; ABS, f. 310-114-6.
25. ABS, f. 310-114-6; NA, f. 19/13, a.j. 122 (2), l. 127.
26. Heimann, *Czechoslovakia*, p. 178.
27. J. Connelly, 'Students, Workers, and Social Change: The Limits of Czech Stalinism', *Slavic Review*, vol. 56, no. 2 (1997), p. 312.
28. Material in this and the next paragraph is based on R. K. Evanson, 'The Czechoslovak Road to Socialism in 1948', *East European Quarterly*, vol. 19, no. 4 (1985), pp. 469–92, quotations at 469, 473, 474, 479.
29. E. Taborsky, *Communism in Czechoslovakia 1948–1960* (Princeton, 1961), pp. 167, 176.
30. Evanson, 'The Czechoslovak Road', p. 480.
31. For details, see T. Inglot, *Welfare States in East Central Europe, 1919–2004* (Cambridge, 2008), pp. 72–8.
32. Spurný, 'Political authority and popular opinion', pp. 452–76, quotations at 455, 456, 460, 461, 462, 463.
33. This paragraph is based on Connelly, 'Students, Workers, and Social Change', pp. 307–35, statistics and quotations at pp. 310, 331, 335.
34. S. Clybor, 'Laughter and Hatred are Neighbors: Adolf Hoffmeister and E. F. Burian in Stalinist Czechoslovakia, 1948–1956', *East European Politics and Societies*, vol. 26, no. 3 (2012), p. 590.
35. M. Drápala, 'A Life of Illusion: The Politics of Vítězslav Nezval', in *The Prague Yearbook of Contemporary History 1998* (Prague, 1999), pp. 178, 207, 210.
36. Clybor, 'Laughter and Hatred', p. 590.
37. Clybor, 'Laughter and Hatred', pp. 592–4, quotations at 592.
38. Liehm, *The Politics of Culture*, pp. 54, 58–9.
39. P. Kolář, 'Communism in Eastern Europe', in S. Smith (ed.), *The Oxford Handbook of the History of Communism* (Oxford, 2014), p. 214.
40. Leff, *National Conflict in Czechoslovakia*, p. 99.
41. For a balanced assessment of Slovakia's economic performance under communism, see A. Capek and G. W. Sazama, 'Czech and Slovak Economic Relations', *Europe-Asia Studies*, vol. 45, no. 2 (1993), pp. 214–8; see also J. Rychlík, *Češi a Slováci ve 20. století. Spolupráce a konflikty 1914–1992* (Prague, 2012).
42. Leff, *National Conflict in Czechoslovakia*, pp. 100–1.
43. E. Táborský, 'Slovakia under Communist Rule: "Democratic Centralism" versus National Autonomy', *Journal of Central European Affairs*, vol. 14 (1954), p. 262.
44. For details of these disputes, see the Foreign Policy Archive of the Russian Federation (AVPRF), IV Evropeiskii otdel, Chekhoslovakiia, op. 26, d. 8, ll. 2, 4, 7, 17, 19. I thank Professor Alfred Rieber, who kindly gave me access to his notes on these archival sources.
45. For example, in 1948 there were over 15,000 private retail outlets in Prague, but by 1951 only 3,200 survived. See M. Franc, 'A Shop Window of the Regime: The Position of Prague as the Capital in the Preferential Supply System of Selected Czechoslovakian Cities, 1950–1970', in P. J. Atkins et al. (eds), *Food and the City in Europe since 1800* (London, 2007), p. 156.

214 NOTES

46. R. K. Evanson, 'Regime and Working Class in Czechoslovakia, 1948–1968', *Soviet Studies*, vol. 37, no. 2 (1985), p. 249.
47. A. Heitlinger, *Women and State Socialism: Sex Inequality in the Soviet Union and Czechoslovakia* (London, 1979), pp. 155, 158, 168. See also D. Nečasová, 'Women's Organizations in the Czech Lands, 1948–89: An Historical Perspective', in H. Havelková and L. Oates-Indruchová (eds), *The Politics of Gender Culture under State Socialism: An Expropriated Voice* (London, 2014), pp. 57–81.
48. Evanson, 'Regime and Working Class', p. 256; M. Pittaway, *Eastern Europe, 1939–2000* (London, 2004), pp. 87, 92.
49. P. Heumos, 'State Socialism, Egalitarianism, Collectivism: On the Social Context of Socialist Work Movements in Czechoslovak Industrial and Mining Enterprises, 1945–1965', *International Labor and Working-Class History*, no. 68 (2005), pp. 47–74; P. Heumos, *'Vyhrňme si rukávy, než se kola zastaví!' Dělníci a státní socialismus v Československu 1945–1968* (Prague, 2006), p. 142.
50. Evanson, 'Regime and Working Class', p. 257.
51. NA, f. 014/12, sv. 10, a.j. 103, l. 2; NA, f. 014/12, sv. 10, a.j. 104, l. 2; NA, f. 014/12, sv. 11, a.j. 168, l. 19.
52. Heumos, *'Vyhrňme si rukávy'*, p. 64.
53. ABS, f. A2/1, a.j. 1861.
54. ABS, f. 310-70-11, ll. 5, 41–3, 46–8.
55. P. Heumos, 'Dělnické stavky v Československu v padesátých letech', *Pohled*, vol. 8, no. 6 (2000), p. 20.
56. Heumos, 'State Socialism, Egalitarianism, Collectivism', p. 47.
57. For details, see K. McDermott, 'Popular Resistance in Communist Czechoslovakia: The Plzeň Uprising, June 1953', *Contemporary European History*, vol. 19, no. 4 (2010), pp. 287–307; State Regional Archive in Plzeň (SOAP), inv. č. 812, k. 108.
58. Kalinová, *Společenské proměny*, p. 197; Škoda Archives (ŠA), Plzeň, ZVIL 203, OS 302.
59. NA, f. 018, sv. 15, a.j. 110, ll. 15–18.
60. Heumos, *'Vyhrňme si rukávy'*, p. 64.
61. Cited in D. C. Engerman, 'The Romance of Economic Development and New Histories of the Cold War', *Diplomatic History*, vol. 28, no. 1 (2004), p. 41.
62. NA, 02/1, sv. 37, a.j. 341, ll. 6, 93; M. Blaive, *Promarněná příležitost: Československo a rok 1956* (Prague, 2001), pp. 302–4.
63. K. Kaplan, *The Overcoming of the Regime Crisis after Stalin's Death in Czechoslovakia, Poland and Hungary* (Cologne, 1986), pp. 25–6. The *aktiv* was composed of full-time party officials and engaged voluntary workers.
64. P. Kenney, 'Peripheral Vision: Social Science and the History of Communist Eastern Europe', *Contemporary European History*, vol. 10, no. 1 (2001), p. 177.
65. F. Eidlin, 'Introduction', in K. Kaplan, *The Communist Party in Power: A Profile of Party Politics in Czechoslovakia* (Boulder, 1987), p. 3.
66. Spurný, 'Political authority', p. 467.
67. Kalinová, *Společenské proměny*, p. 94; see also J. Rákosník, *Sovětizace sociálního státu: lidově demokratický režim a sociální práva občanů v Československu 1945–1960* (Prague, 2010).

Chapter 4: Social Crisis and the Limits of Reform, 1953–67

1. The term is from J. Pernes, 'Ohlas maď'arské revoluce roku 1956 v
   československé veřejnosti. Z interních hlášení krajských správ minister-
   stva vnitra', *Soudobé dějiny*, no. 4 (1996), p. 525.
2. K.-M. Mallmann and G. Paul, 'Resistenz oder loyale Widerwilligkeit?
   Anmerkungen zu einem umstrittenen Begriff', *Zeitschrift für
   Geschichtswissenschaft*, no. 2 (1993), pp. 99–116; A. Port, *Conflict and
   Stability in the German Democratic Republic* (Cambridge, 2007), p. 275;
   T. Lindenberger, 'Tacit Minimal Consensus: The Always Precarious East
   German Dictatorship', in P. Corner (ed.), *Popular Opinion in Totalitarian
   Regimes: Fascism, Nazism, Communism* (Oxford, 2009), pp. 208–22; and
   S. Fitzpatrick and A. Lüdtke, 'Energizing the Everyday: On the Breaking
   and Making of Social Bonds in Nazism and Stalinism', in Geyer and
   Fitzpatrick (eds), *Beyond Totalitarianism*, pp. 266–301.
3. M. Blaive, *Promarněná příležitost*, p. 227.
4. On Czechoslovakia in 1956, see Blaive, *Promarněná příležitost*; and
   K. McDermott and V. Sommer, 'The "Club of Politically Engaged
   Conformists"? The Communist Party of Czechoslovakia, Popular Opinion
   and the Crisis of Communism, 1956', Cold War International History
   Project, Working Paper No. 66 (Washington DC, 2013).
5. Heimann, *Czechoslovakia*, p. 206.
6. E. Goldstücker, *Vzpomínky 1945–1968* (Prague, 2005), p. 114; M. Hájek,
   Paměť' české levice (Prague, 2011), p. 164.
7. NA, f. 02/2, sv. 90, a.j. 108, ll. 4-8, 14.
8. NA, f. 05/1, sv. 391, a.j. 2331, ll. 29, 31, 35; ABS, f. B2, inv. jedn. 5, sv. 2,
   ll. 33, 49, 70, 117, 131, 219, 262b.
9. NA, f. 05/1, sv. 391, a.j. 2331, l. 36; NA, f. ÚV KSČ, Antonín Novotný -
   tajné, k. 4 (unpaginated).
10. M. Shore, 'Engineering in the Age of Innocence: A Genealogy of
    Discourse Inside the Czechoslovak Writers' Union, 1949–67', *East
    European Politics and Societies*, vol. 12, no. 3 (1998), pp. 411–19.
11. Hungarian National Archive (MOL), XXXII-16-a, box 2, file 4, p. 42.
12. J. P. C. Matthews, 'Majales: The Abortive Student Revolt in Czechoslovakia
    in 1956', Cold War International History Project, Working Paper No. 24
    (Washington DC, 1998), pp. 16, 36.
13. NA, f. 05/1, sv. 369, a.j. 2235, l. 10.
14. H. G. Skilling, 'Stalinism and Czechoslovak Political Culture', in
    R. C. Tucker (ed.), *Stalinism: Essays in Historical Interpretation* (New York,
    1977), p. 279.
15. NA, f. 05/1, sv. 375, a.j. 2270, l. 8; NA, f. ÚV KSČ, kancelář 1. tajemníka A.
    Novotného, inv. jedn. 166, k. 117; Slovak National Archive (SNA), f. ÚV
    KSS David, a.j. 73, l. 18.
16. ABS, f. B2, inv. jedn. 15, sv. 2, ll. 286, 428.
17. SNA, f. ÚV KSS David, a.j. 73, l. 3.
18. NA, f. 014/12, sv. 26, a.j. 994, l. 54; NA, f. ÚV KSČ, kancelář 1. tajemníka
    A. Novotného, inv. jedn. 166, k. 117.
19. ABS, H1-4, inv. jedn. 316, l. 57.
20. OSA, 300-30-2 Czechoslovak Unit, microfilms 139 and 140 (unpaginated).

21. The National Archive (TNA), Foreign Office 371/122142, 'Internal Political Situation in Czechoslovakia, 1956'.
22. ABS, f. H-669-2, reports from 2 and 9 November 1956.
23. ABS, f. B2, inv. jedn. 15, l. 86.
24. MOL, XXXII-16-a, box 3, file 5, p. 19.
25. NA, f. 014/12, sv. 25, a.j. 923, l. 10.
26. ABS, f. N2/1, inv. jedn. 5, l. 76.
27. OSA, 300-30-2 Czechoslovak Unit, microfilm 139.
28. ABS, f. B2, inv. jedn. 15, sv. 1, l. 31; MOL, XXXII-16-a, box 2, file 4, pp. 137, 220; SNA, f. ÚV KSS David, a.j. 73, ll. 32, 33.
29. NA, f. 014/12, sv. 25, a.j. 950, l. 22.
30. ABS, f. H-669-2, report from 9 November 1956.
31. M. Hauner, 'The Prague Spring: Twenty Years After', in Stone and Strouhal (eds), *Czechoslovakia* p. 214.
32. For examples of citizens' petitions, see the Archive of the President's Office (AKPR), sign. 01533/68: 'Rehabilitace'.
33. H. G. Skilling, *Czechoslovakia's Interrupted Revolution* (Princeton, 1976), p. 401.
34. NA, f. 014/12, sv. 21, a.j. 732, ll. 6, 10; NA, f. 014/12, sv. 22, a.j. 754, l. 4.
35. NA, f. 014/12, sv. 21, a.j. 733, ll. 4, 6.
36. NA, f. Předsednictvo 1962–1966, sv. 17, a.j. 18, ll. 7, 11, 15.
37. ABS, f. A34, inv. jedn. 2487 (non-paginated). For details on political developments in Slovakia in the late 1950s and early 1960s, see J. Pešek, *Slovensko na prelome 50. a 60. rokov. Politicko-mocenské aspekty vývoja* (Brno, 2005).
38. For details, see S. Brown, 'Prelude to a Divorce? The Prague Spring as Dress Rehearsal for Czechoslovakia's "Velvet Divorce"', *Europe-Asia Studies*, vol. 60, no. 10 (2008), p. 1788.
39. ABS, f. A34, inv. jedn. 1840, report from 28 June 1963 (non-paginated).
40. ABS, f. A34, inv. jedn. 1807, l. 1; ABS, f. A5-81 microfiche 2 (non-paginated).
41. J. Cuhra, 'In the Shadow of Liberalization: Repressions in Czechoslovakia in the 1960s', *Cahiers du monde Russe*, vol. 47, no. 1–2 (2006), p. 423.
42. One amnestant, František Klápště, was assiduously followed for over four years after his release, even though his attitude to the regime was 'indifferent and absolutely passive'. See his file in ABS, f. B4_4, inv. jedn. 23, ll. 1-23.
43. ABS, f. A 34, inv. jedn. 1807, ll. 1-4; ABS, f. H-186, ll. 90, 106; ABS, f. H-186/2 'Amnestie 1960', ll. 35, 52, 134-5; ABS, f. H-186/3, ll. 228, 254, 294, 400.
44. ABS, f. H-186/3, l. 2.
45. ABS, f. H-186/2, l. 47.
46. ABS, f. H-186/2, ll. 46, 51; ABS, f. H-186/3, ll. 1, 14, 69, 204; NA, f. 014/12, sv. 35, a.j. 1378, l. 6.
47. ABS, f. H-186/3, l. 281.
48. ABS, f. A5-81 microfiche 3 (non-paginated).
49. ABS, f. H-186/3, l. 26.
50. ABS, f. H-186/3, ll. 36, 385; ABS, f. H-186/2, ll. 46-7.
51. ABS, f. H-186/2, l. 41.
52. ABS, f. H-186/3, ll. 77, 94.
53. ABS, f. H-186/3, l. 54; ABS, f. H-186/2, l. 47.

54. ABS, f. H-186/3, ll. 26-7.
55. ABS, f. H-186/2, l. 38.
56. ABS, f. H-186/3, ll. 26, 36.
57. ABS, f. H-186/2, l. 46.
58. J. Batt, *Economic Reform and Political Change in Eastern Europe: A Comparison of the Czechoslovak and Hungarian Experiences* (Basingstoke, 1988), p. 91.
59. My summary of the economic reforms is based on Batt, *Economic Reform and Political Change*, pp. 116–25, 140–8, 171–206; and M. Myant, *The Czechoslovak Economy 1948–1988: The Battle for Economic Reform* (Cambridge, 1989), pp. 110–56.
60. Batt, *Economic Reform and Political Change*, p. 187.
61. Batt, *Economic Reform and Political Change*, pp. 173, 185, 189.
62. Skilling, *Czechoslovakia's Interrupted Revolution*, pp. 125–33, quotations at 127, 129.
63. Skilling, *Czechoslovakia's Interrupted Revolution*, pp. 145–52, quotations at 147, 149; V. V. Kusin, *The Intellectual Origins of the Prague Spring: The Development of Reformist Ideas in Czechoslovakia, 1956–1967* (Cambridge, 1971), pp. 109–115.
64. For details, see R. Černý, *Antonín Novotný. Vzpomínky prezidenta* (Prague, 2008), pp. 142–6.
65. Batt, *Economic Reform and Political Change*, pp. 180–2, 194–5.
66. K. Williams, *The Prague Spring and its Aftermath: Czechoslovak Politics 1968–1970* (Cambridge, 1997), pp. 4–6; Myant, *The Czechoslovak Economy 1948–1988*, p. 140.
67. For details, see Inglot, *Welfare States in East Central Europe*, pp. 133, 136–42.
68. On housing, see K. E. Zarecor, *Manufacturing a Socialist Modernity: Housing in Czechoslovakia, 1945–1960* (Pittsburgh, 2011).
69. For details, see K. Hlaváčková, *Czech Fashion 1940–1970: Mirror of the Times* (Prague, 2000).
70. P. Bugge, 'Swinging Sixties Made in Czechoslovakia: The Adaptation of Western Impulses in Czechoslovak Youth Culture', in O. Tůma and M. Devátá (eds), *Pražské jaro 1968: Občanská společnost - média - přenos politických a kulturních procesů* (Prague, 2011), p. 148, fn. 421.
71. For the Soviet perspective, see S. Reid, 'Cold War in the Kitchen: Gender and the De-Stalinization of Consumer Taste in the Soviet Union under Khrushchev', *Slavic Review*, vol. 61, no. 2 (2002), pp. 212–52.
72. For details, see D. Kramerová and V. Skálová (eds), *The Brussels Dream: The Czechoslovak Presence at Expo 58 in Brussels and the Lifestyle of the Early 1960s* (Prague, 2008), pp. 13–60, quotations at 19, 23, 29, 40; and C. M. Giustino, 'Industrial Design and the Czechoslovak Pavilion at EXPO '58: Artistic Autonomy, Party Control and Cold War Common Ground', *Journal of Contemporary History*, vol. 47, no. 1 (2012), pp. 185–212.
73. Kolář, 'Communism in Eastern Europe', p. 207.
74. Kramerová and Skálová (eds), *The Brussels Dream*, p. 29.
75. R. Bell, 'History in the Making: Experiment Invalidovna, Prague 1961', p. 8 (unpublished MS cited with permission of the author).
76. M. Franc, 'Coca-cola je zde! aneb Konzumní společnost v Československu?', in Tůma and Devátá (eds), *Pražské jaro 1968*, p. 141.
77. M. Franc and J. Knapík, *Volný čas v českých zemích, 1957–1967* (Prague, 2013), p. 513.

78. Bugge, 'Swinging Sixties', p. 149.
79. Bugge, 'Swinging Sixties', pp. 146–8, 151.
80. Liehm, *The Politics of Culture*, p. 42. For details on the close relationship between Czech culture and politics, see A. Kusák, *Kultura a politika v Československu 1945–1956* (Prague, 1998).
81. I am indebted to Jan Mervart for these important points of interpretation.
82. M. Holub, 'O zabíjení slov', *Literární listy*, 2 May 1968, p. 1.
83. Skilling, *Czechoslovakia's Interrupted Revolution*, p. 97.
84. P. Hames, *The Czechoslovak New Wave* (Berkeley, 1985), quotations at 279–80.
85. Cited in J. Navrátil et al. (eds), *The Prague Spring 1968: A National Security Archive Documents Reader* (Budapest, 1998), pp. 8, 10. For a detailed analysis of the writers' congress, see J. Mervart, *Naděje a iluze: Čeští a slovenští spisovatelé v reformním hnutí šedesátých let* (Brno, 2010), pp. 182–258.
86. This paragraph is based on Skilling, *Czechoslovakia's Interrupted Revolution*, pp. 72–82, quotation at 73. For details, see J. Pažout, *Mocným navzdory: Studentské hnutí v šedesátých letech 20. století* (Prague, 2008).
87. Skilling, *Czechoslovakia's Interrupted Revolution*, p. 161.
88. Cited in J. Vondrová et al. (eds), *Komunistická strana Československa. Pokus o reformu (říjen 1967 - květen 1968)* (Brno, 1999), pp. 32–9.

Chapter 5: Czechoslovak Spring, 1968–69

1. 'Sasha' is the Russian diminutive form of Alexander.
2. The first quotation is by František Šamalík cited in Skilling, *Czechoslovakia's Interrupted Revolution*, p. 224; the second is from M. Heimann, 'The Scheming *Apparatchik* of the Prague Spring', *Europe-Asia Studies*, vol. 60, no. 10 (2008), pp. 1717–34. On Dubček's broader role in twentieth-century Czechoslovak history, see J. Hoppe and M. Bárta (eds), *Úloha Alexandra Dubčeka v moderních dějinách Československa: Sborník z konference* (Prague, 2002).
3. Cited in M. Kramer, 'The Prague Spring and the Soviet Invasion in Historical Perspective', in G. Bischof et al. (eds), *The Prague Spring and the Warsaw Pact Invasion of Czechoslovakia in 1968* (Cambridge: MA, 2011), p. 53.
4. For the main decisions of the Central Committee in 1968, see *Rok šedesátý osmý v usneseních a dokumentech ÚV KSČ* (Prague, 1969).
5. Cited in Williams, *The Prague Spring and its Aftermath*, p. 101.
6. See Havel's path-breaking article 'On the Subject of Opposition' in R. A. Remington (ed.), *Winter in Prague: Documents on Czechoslovak Communism in Crisis* (Cambridge: MA, 1969), pp. 64–71; for Sviták's writings in 1968, see his *The Czechoslovak Experiment, 1968–1969* (New York, 1971).
7. Williams, *The Prague Spring*, pp. 25–6.
8. English translation in Remington (ed.), *Winter in Prague*, pp. 88–137.
9. Cited in R. G. Pikhoia, 'Czechoslovakia in 1968: A View from Moscow According to Central Committee Documents', *Russian Studies in History*, vol. 44, no. 3 (2005–06), p. 50.

10. From the Action Programme, cited in Remington (ed.), *Winter in Prague*, p. 105.
11. For examples, see S. Brown, *Caricatures of Revolution: Slovak Political Cartoons in the Czechoslovak Spring*, The Carl Beck Papers, no. 2105 (Pittsburgh, 2011).
12. Williams, *The Prague Spring*, pp. 67–9, quotations at 68, 69.
13. For an English translation, see Navrátil et al. (eds), *The Prague Spring 1968*, pp. 177–81.
14. Material on KAN, K-231 and the SDP is drawn from Skilling, *Czechoslovakia's Interrupted Revolution*, pp. 265–8, 547, quotation at 266; for details, see J. Hoppe, *Opozice '68. Sociální demokracie, KAN a K 231 v období pražského jara* (Prague, 2009).
15. For documents on all these organisations, see J. Pecka et al. (eds), *Občanská společnost 1967–1970: Sociální organismy a hnutí pražského jara*, vol. 2 (Brno, 1998), pp. 73–302.
16. V. Prečan, 'Seven Great Days: The People and Civil Society during the "Prague Spring" of 1968–1969', in F. M. Cataluccio and F. Gori (eds), *La Primavera di Praga* (Milan, 1990), p. 166.
17. For details, see R. Gildea et al. (eds), *Europe's 1968: Voices of Revolt* (Oxford, 2013), pp. 38–9, 114–16, 121–3.
18. Bugge, 'Swinging Sixties', p. 151.
19. Statistics from J. Rychlík, *Cestování do ciziny v habsburské monarchii a v Československu. Pasová, vízová a vystěhovalecká politika 1848–1989* (Prague, 2007), pp. 61, 73, 83; and Bugge, 'Swinging Sixties', pp. 149–50.
20. Cited in Navrátil et al. (eds), *The Prague Spring 1968*, pp. 118, 122.
21. R. Applebaum, 'A Test of Friendship: Soviet–Czechoslovak Tourism and the Prague Spring', in A. E. Gorsuch and D. P. Koenker (eds), *The Socialist Sixties: Crossing Borders in the Second World* (Bloomington, 2013), pp. 220–5.
22. For details, see Oxley et al. (eds), *Czechoslovakia*, pp. 151–9; Skilling, *Czechoslovakia's Interrupted Revolution*, pp. 433–43, 579–85.
23. This paragraph is based on J. True, *Gender, Globalization, and Postsocialism: The Czech Republic after Communism* (New York, 2003), pp. 6–7, 39–49.
24. Skilling, *Czechoslovakia's Interrupted Revolution*, pp. 529–31, 560.
25. J. Piekalkiewicz, 'Public Political Opinion in Czechoslovakia during the Dubcek Era', in E. J. Czerwinski and J. Piekalkiewicz (eds), *The Soviet Invasion of Czechoslovakia: Its Effects on Eastern Europe* (New York, 1972), pp. 3–42. For extracts from citizens' letters and many other sources on popular sentiment, see B. Vlčková (ed.), *Ohlas událostí roku 1968. I část* (Prague, 2012).
26. P. Pithart, 'Towards a Shared Freedom, 1968–89', in J. Musil (ed.), *The End of Czechoslovakia* (Budapest, 1995), p. 203.
27. Leff, *National Conflict in Czechoslovakia*, p. 122. For recent Slovak interpretations of developments in 1968, including federalisation, see M. Londák, S. Sikora and coll., *Rok 1968 a jeho miesta v našich dejinách* (Bratislava, 2009), pp. 82–102, 127–39, 210–26.
28. Cited in R. W. Dean, *Nationalism and Political Change in Eastern Europe: The Slovak Question and the Czechoslovak Reform Movement* (Denver, 1972–73), p. 31.

29. Cited in S. Brown, 'Socialism with a Slovak Face: Federalization, Democratization, and the Prague Spring', *East European Politics and Societies*, vol. 22, no. 3 (2008), p. 480.
30. Skilling, *Czechoslovakia's Interrupted Revolution*, p. 453.
31. The material and quotations in this paragraph are from M. Kramer, 'The Czechoslovak Crisis and the Brezhnev Doctrine', in C. Fink et al. (eds), *1968: The World Transformed* (Cambridge, 1998), pp. 122, 127–9.
32. Cited in Pikhoia, 'Czechoslovakia in 1968', p. 45.
33. Kramer, 'The Czechoslovak Crisis', pp. 124–5.
34. Skilling, *Czechoslovakia's Interrupted Revolution*, pp. 406–9, quotation at 407; Williams, *The Prague Spring*, pp. 215–21.
35. Skilling, *Czechoslovakia's Interrupted Revolution*, pp. 637–41.
36. Kramer, 'The Czechoslovak Crisis', pp. 138, 141.
37. Skilling, *Czechoslovakia's Interrupted Revolution*, pp. 617–34, 647–58, quotations at 621, 623, 647.
38. M. J. Ouimet, 'Reconsidering the Soviet Role in the Invasion of Czechoslovakia: A Commentary', in M. M. Stolarik (ed.), *The Prague Spring and the Warsaw Pact Invasion of Czechoslovakia, 1968: Forty Years Later* (Mundelein, 2010), p. 28.
39. Cited in Navrátil et al. (eds), *The Prague Spring 1968*, pp. 253–4.
40. For post-invasion Soviet propaganda attacks on the Czechoslovaks' 'revision of basic Marxist–Leninist principles', see Press Group of Soviet Journalists, *On Events in Czechoslovakia* (Moscow, 1968), pp. 33–52, quotation at 33.
41. Cited in Kramer, 'The Czechoslovak Crisis', pp. 142–4, quotations at 143.
42. Z. Mlynář, *Night Frost in Prague: The End of Humane Socialism* (London, 1980), p. 152.
43. Cited in Kramer, 'The Czechoslovak Crisis', p. 134.
44. Cited in G. Bischof, S. Karner and P. Ruggenthaler, 'Introduction', in Bischof et al. (eds), *The Prague Spring*, p. 8.
45. All citations are from Navrátil et al. (eds), *The Prague Spring 1968*, pp. 64–72.
46. Cited in Navrátil et al. (eds), *The Prague Spring 1968*, pp. 121–2, 124.
47. Cited in Williams, *The Prague Spring*, p. 80.
48. For details, see Pikhoia, 'Czechoslovakia in 1968', p. 56.
49. Throughout 1968 the Romanian leader, Nicolae Ceaușescu, did not take part in multilateral meetings and he did not commit troops to the invasion of Czechoslovakia.
50. For the text of the letter, see Remington (ed.), *Winter in Prague*, pp. 225–31.
51. Kramer, 'The Czechoslovak Crisis', p. 148.
52. Williams, *The Prague Spring*, pp. 100, 102; M. Kun, *Prague Spring – Prague Fall: Blank Spots of 1968* (Budapest, 1999), pp. 85–6.
53. Williams, *The Prague Spring*, p. 102.
54. Cited in Remington (ed.), *Winter in Prague*, p. 258.
55. For the text of the letter, see Navrátil et al. (eds), *The Prague Spring 1968*, pp. 324–5; also M. Kramer, 'The Prague Spring and the Soviet Invasion of Czechoslovakia: New Interpretations', Part II, *Cold War International History Project Bulletin*, no. 3 (1993), p. 3.
56. Kramer, 'The Czechoslovak Crisis', p. 150.
57. Williams, *The Prague Spring*, p. 104.
58. For transcripts of both conversations, see Navrátil et al. (eds), *The Prague Spring 1968*, pp. 336–8, 345–56.

59. O. Tůma, 'Reforms in the Communist Party: The Prague Spring and Apprehension about a Soviet Invasion', in Bischof et al. (eds), *The Prague Spring*, p. 69.
60. N. G. Tomilina et al. (eds), *'Prazhskaia vesna' i mezhdunarodnyi krizis 1968 goda: Dokumenty* (Moscow, 2010), p. 214.
61. Williams, *The Prague Spring*, p. 112.
62. For details, see J. Pelikán (ed.), *The Secret Vysočany Congress: Proceedings and Documents of the Extraordinary Fourteenth Congress of the Communist Party of Czechoslovakia, 22 August 1968* (London, 1971).
63. M. V. Latysh, 'The Czechoslovak Crisis of 1968 in the Context of Soviet Geopolitics', in Stolarik (ed.), *The Prague Spring*, p. 12.
64. See M. Bárta et al., *Victims of the Occupation. The Warsaw Pact Invasion of Czechoslovakia: 21 August–31 December 1968* (Prague, 2008).
65. Kramer, 'The Czechoslovak Crisis', p. 157.
66. For a participant's account, see Mlynář, *Night Frost in Prague*, pp. 209–47.
67. Williams, *The Prague Spring*, pp. 141–2.
68. Skilling, *Czechoslovakia's Interrupted Revolution*, pp. 726–30, 839.
69. Williams, *The Prague Spring*, pp. 35–8, 111.
70. This paragraph is based on K. Williams, 'Civil Resistance in Czechoslovakia: From Soviet Invasion to "Velvet Revolution", 1968–89', in A. Roberts and T. Garton Ash (eds), *Civil Resistance and Power Politics: The Experience of Non-violent Action from Gandhi to the Present* (Oxford, 2009), pp. 112, 121–2, quotation at 112. For details of the nationwide resistance, see J. Pecka (ed.), *Spontánní projevy pražského jara 1968–1969* (Brno, 1993).
71. Cited in G. Golan, *Reform Rule in Czechoslovakia: The Dubček Era, 1968–1969* (Cambridge, 1973), p. 244, fn. 1.
72. Cited in Skilling, *Czechoslovakia's Interrupted Revolution*, p. 801.
73. Dubček was bold enough to ask Brezhnev on 20 November to prohibit the pro-Soviet radio station in Czechoslovakia, 'Vltava', and the neo-Stalinist newspaper *Zprávy*. See Tomilina et al. (eds), *'Prazhskaia vesna'*, pp. 400–2.
74. Latysh, 'The Czechoslovak Crisis', p. 12.
75. Public Opinion Research Centre (CVVM), Prague, 68-171, 'Veřejné mínění o některých politických problémech', p. 23.
76. For details, see P. Blažek and coll., *Jan Palach '69* (Prague, 2009).
77. Williams, *The Prague Spring*, p. 190.
78. This paragraph is based on Williams, *The Prague Spring*, pp. 198–209, quotations at 201, 207.
79. On Husák's takeover, see Z. Doskočil, *Duben 1969: anatomie jednoho mocenského zvratu* (Brno, 2006).

Chapter 6: Everyday Normalisation, 1969–88

1. Cited in B. Wheaton and Z. Kavan, *The Velvet Revolution: Czechoslovakia, 1988–1991* (Boulder, 1992), p. 10.
2. O. Tůma, 'Conspicuous Connections, 1968 and 1989', in Kramer and Smetana (eds), *Imposing, Maintaining, and Tearing Down the Iron Curtain*, p. 502.
3. Cited in Williams, *The Prague Spring*, p. 40, fn. 5.

4. For details, see T. Dickins, 'The Impact Factor of the Language of Czechoslovak Normalization: A Study of the Seminal Work *Poučení z krizového vývoje ve straně a společnosti po XIII. sjezdu KSČ*', *Slavonic and East European Review*, vol. 93, no. 2 (2015), pp. 213-50.
5. M. Kundera, *The Book of Laughter and Forgetting* (Harmondsworth, 1981); T. Garton Ash, 'Czechoslovakia Under Ice', in T. Garton Ash, *The Uses of Adversity: Essays on the Fate of Central Europe* (Cambridge, 1989), pp. 55–63.
6. Williams, *The Prague Spring*, p. 47; K. Williams, 'The Prague Spring: From Elite Liberalisation to Mass Movement', in K. McDermott and M. Stibbe (eds), *Revolution and Resistance in Eastern Europe: Challenges to Communist Rule* (Oxford, 2006), pp. 103–4.
7. See V. Prečan, 'Lid, veřejnost, občanská společnost jako aktér Pražského jara 1968', in J. Pecka and V. Prečan (eds), *Proměny Pražského jara 1968–1969. Sborník studií a dokumentů o nekapitulantských postojích v československé společnosti* (Brno, 1993), pp. 13–36; Williams, *The Prague Spring*, pp. 45–6.
8. Figures from Williams, *The Prague Spring*, pp. 230, 232.
9. V. V. Kusin, *From Dubček to Charter 77: A Study of 'Normalisation' in Czechoslovakia 1968–1978* (Edinburgh, 1978), p. 81.
10. Statistics from J. Maňák, *Čistky v Komunistické straně Československa 1969–70* (Prague, 1997), p. 118; and Williams, *The Prague Spring*, p. 234.
11. See J. Šiklová, 'The "Gray Zone" and the Future of Dissent in Czechoslovakia', *Social Research*, vol. 57, no. 2 (1990), pp. 347–8.
12. Williams, *The Prague Spring*, p. 235.
13. V. Sobell, 'Czechoslovakia: The Legacy of Normalization', *East European Politics and Societies*, vol. 2, no. 1 (1987), p. 37, note 2.
14. H. Renner, *A History of Czechoslovakia since 1945* (London, 1989), p. 99.
15. Kusin, *From Dubček to Charter 77*, pp. 92–4, 98.
16. Such a fate befell the historian Pavel Seifter, who worked as a window cleaner for almost 20 years under normalisation before becoming the Czech Republic's ambassador to the UK in 1997. Both Kohout and Mlynář ended up in Vienna.
17. Williams, *The Prague Spring*, pp. 249–53, quotation at 249.
18. For details, see J. Cuhra, *Trestní represe odpůrců režimu v letech 1969–1972* (Prague, 1997), pp. 11, 115–17, 131–6.
19. Kusin, *From Dubček to Charter 77*, pp. 244–6.
20. S. Wolchik, 'The Status of Women in a Socialist Order: Czechoslovakia, 1948–1978', *Slavic Review*, vol. 38, no. 4 (1979), pp. 587–90.
21. On increasing alcoholism and drug abuse, see Kusin, *From Dubček to Charter 77*, pp. 249–53; on sexual morality, see C. Brennerová, 'Líné dívky, lehké dívky? Příživnictví a disciplinace mladých žen v době normalizace', *Dějiny a současnost*, no. 7 (2013), pp. 19–22.
22. See A. J. Liehm, 'The New Social Contract and the Parallel Polity', in J. L. Curry (ed.), *Dissent in Eastern Europe* (New York, 1983), pp. 173–81.
23. For details, see CVVM, 70-13, 'Názory na některé otázky životní úrovně'; 72-03, 'O nákupech a cenách'; 74-3, 'Aktuální otázky života občanů'; and 77-1, 'Názory na vnitřní trh a zásobování'.
24. H. G. Skilling, *Charter 77 and Human Rights in Czechoslovakia* (London, 1981), p. 178.

25. P. Bren, *The Greengrocer and His TV: The Culture of Communism After the 1968 Prague Spring* (Ithaca, 2010), pp. 159–208 quotations at 164, 207. See also P. Bren, 'Mirror, Mirror, on the Wall ... Is the West the Fairest of Them All? Czechoslovak Normalization and Its (Dis)contents', *Kritika*, vol. 9, no. 4 (2008), pp. 831–54.

26. I am indebted to Vítězslav Sommer for these points.

27. S. Lehr, '"Pište nám!": Dopisy diváků a posluchačů Československé televizi a rozhlasu', *Marginalia Historica*, no. 2 (2012), pp. 71–82.

28. M. Blaive, 'Multiple Identities and Europeanness at the Czech–Austrian and Slovak–Hungarian Borders', *Eruditio - Educatio*, no. 4 (2009), pp. 5–15.

29. Leff, *National Conflict in Czechoslovakia*, pp. 249–50.

30. Kolář, 'Communism in Eastern Europe', p. 207.

31. Leff, *National Conflict in Czechoslovakia*, p. 268.

32. Skilling, *Czechoslovakia's Interrupted Revolution*, p. 874.

33. Pithart, 'Towards a Shared Freedom', pp. 204–5, 208.

34. J. Marušiak, 'The Normalisation Regime and its Impact on Slovak Domestic Policy after 1970', *Europe-Asia Studies*, vol. 60, no. 10 (2008), pp. 1815, 1822.

35. A revealing portrait of StB undercover operations can be found in *Praha objektivem tajné policie – Prague Through the Lens of the Secret Police* (Prague, 2008).

36. Šiklová, 'The "Gray Zone"', p. 356.

37. P. Bren, 'Looking West: Popular Culture and the Generation Gap in Communist Czechoslovakia, 1969–1989', in L. Passerini (ed.), *Across the Atlantic: Cultural Exchanges between Europe and the United States* (Brussels, 2000), p. 320.

38. Private correspondence, 22 July 2014.

39. See the enlightening discussion of 'fear' in Bren, *The Greengrocer and His TV*, pp. 203–8.

40. Private correspondence, 15 June 2014.

41. M. Šimečka, *The Restoration of Order: The Normalization of Czechoslovakia, 1969–1976* (London, 1984), pp. 72–9.

42. See L. Vaculík, *A Cup of Coffee with My Interrogator* (London, 1987).

43. Bren, 'Looking West', pp. 299–300.

44. D. Altshuler, 'Departures from Home: Czech Perspectives on Difference', *The Anthropology of Eastern Europe Review*, vol. 21, no. 2 (2003), p. 9.

45. V. V. Kusin, 'Husak's Czechoslovakia and Economic Stagnation', *Problems of Communism*, vol. 31, no. 3 (1982), p. 28.

46. P. Bren, 'Weekend Getaways: The *Chata*, the *Tramp* and the Politics of Private Life in Post-1968 Czechoslovakia', in D. Crowley and S. E. Reid (eds), *Socialist Spaces: Sites of Everyday Life in the Eastern Bloc* (Oxford, 2002), pp. 123–7, 134–6.

47. On bribery, see V. Zimmermann, '"Deformace právního vědomí"? Úplatkářství jako masový fenomén v ČSSR v sedmdesátých a osmdesátých letech', *Marginalia Historica*, no. 2 (2012), pp. 159–65.

48. P. Bren, 'Tuzex and the Hustler: Living It Up in Czechoslovakia', in P. Bren and M. Neuburger (eds), *Communism Unwrapped: Consumption in Cold War Eastern Europe* (New York, 2012), pp. 27–48.

49. Private correspondence, 14 June 2014.

50. M. Nevrlý, *Karpatské hry* (Prague, 1981; reprinted 2006). I am grateful to Professor Wendy Bracewell for bringing this source to my attention.
51. Bren, 'Looking West', pp. 319–20; see also Kolář, 'Communism in Eastern Europe', p. 213.
52. This section is based on P. Bugge, 'Normalization and the Limits of the Law: The Case of the Czech Jazz Section', *East European Politics and Societies*, vol. 22, no. 2 (2008), pp. 282–318, quotations at 282, 283, 305; see also J. Skvorecký, 'The Unfinished End of the Jazz Section of the Czech Musicians' Union', in A. Heneka et al. (eds), *A Besieged Culture: Czechoslovakia Ten Years after Helsinki* (Stockholm-Vienna, 1985), pp. 142–8.
53. A. Yurchak, *Everything Was Forever, Until It Was No More: The Last Soviet Generation* (Princeton, 2006), pp. 126–33.
54. J. Fürst, 'Where Did All the Normal People Go?: Another Look at the Soviet 1970s', *Kritika*, vol. 14, no. 3 (2013), p. 636.
55. J. Jareš, M. Spurný, K. Volná and coll., *Náměstí krasnoarmějců 2. Učitelé a studenti Filozofické fakulty UK v období normalizace* (Prague, 2012), pp. 392–5.
56. This paragraph is based on Šiklová, 'The "Gray Zone"', pp. 350–5, quotation at 351.
57. This and the next paragraph are drawn from V. Havel et al., *The Power of the Powerless: Citizens Against the State in East-Central Europe* (London, 1985), pp. 23–96, quotations at 28, 36, 37, 39. A critique of Havel's and other dissidents' ideas can be found in B. J. Falk, *The Dilemmas of Dissidence in East-Central Europe: Citizen Intellectuals and Philosopher Kings* (Budapest, 2003), pp. 199–256.
58. J. Bolton, *Worlds of Dissent: Charter 77, the Plastic People of the Universe, and Czech Culture under Communism* (Cambridge: MA, 2012), p. 224. Leading Czech dissidents describe their experiences in M. Long, *Making History: Czech Voices of Dissent and the Revolution of 1989* (Lanham, 2005).
59. Skilling, *Charter 77*, pp. 209–12; for fascinating details on the immediate origins of Charter 77, see Bolton, *Worlds of Dissent*, pp. 139–51.
60. In the 1980s, I would occasionally see people on public transport stealthily reading what I assumed to be banned *samizdat* material carefully covered by *Rudé právo* or some other official publication. Not everyone, evidently, was intimidated by the StB.
61. Skilling, *Charter 77*, p. 179, citing two leading Chartists, Jiří Hájek and Miroslav Kusý.
62. For details, see Bolton, *Worlds of Dissent*, pp. 48, 85–8, 172–82, 244–5, quotations at 87–8, 172, 175.
63. For details, see J. Cuhra, 'Nezávislé aktivity v Československu a Charta 77 – meze protnutí', in M. Dévatá et al. (eds), *Charta 77: Od obhajoby lidských práv k demokratické revoluci, 1977–1989* (Prague, n.d.), pp. 95–104.
64. See the demythologising account in Bolton, *Worlds of Dissent*, pp. 115–43. It is quite likely that nonconformist bands such as the Plastics did not inspire socially conservative members of society. One ditty that was doing the rounds in the 1970s and 1980s went: '*Máš-li dlouhý vlas, nechod' mezi nás!*' (literally, 'If you've got long hair, don't go around with us!').
65. For an in-depth discussion of Benda's ideas, see A. Tucker, *The Philosophy and Politics of Czech Dissidence from Patočka to Havel* (Pittsburgh, 2000), pp. 127–34, quotation at 128; see also Bolton, *Worlds of Dissent*, pp. 30–2.

66. Arguably, the scholar most associated with this line of argument is T. Garton Ash, *We the People: The Revolution of '89 Witnessed in Warsaw, Budapest, Berlin and Prague* (Cambridge, 1990).
67. Bolton, *Worlds of Dissent*, pp. 274–5; a less positive assessment can be found in M. Otáhal, *Opoziční proudy v české společnosti 1969–1989* (Prague, 2011), pp. 166–72, 628–9.
68. J. Krapfl, *Revolution with a Human Face: Politics, Culture, and Community in Czechoslovakia, 1989–1992* (Ithaca, 2013), p. 110.

Chapter 7: 1989 – The Demise of Communism

1. E. Hobsbawm, *The Age of Extremes: The Short Twentieth Century* (London, 1995).
2. Garton Ash, *We the People*, p. 14.
3. One of Gorbachev's aides, when asked what was the difference between *perestroika* and the Prague Spring, quipped 'twenty years'.
4. For details, see S. L. Wolchik, 'Czechoslovakia on the Eve of 1989', *Communist and Post-Communist Studies*, vol. 32, no. 4 (1999), pp. 446–8.
5. P. Kenney, *A Carnival of Revolution: Central Europe 1989* (Princeton, 2002), p. 150.
6. For details on these and other independent groupings and activities, see Otáhal, *Opoziční proudy*, pp. 328–510, 549–56; Wolchik, 'Czechoslovakia on the Eve', pp. 442–4.
7. Kenney, *A Carnival of Revolution*, pp. 82–4, 266–7, quotation at 83.
8. Wolchik, 'Czechoslovakia on the Eve', p. 445.
9. T. Judt, *Postwar: A History of Europe since 1945* (London, 2007), p. 630.
10. M. Pullmann, 'The Demise of the Communist Regime in Czechoslovakia, 1987–89: A Socio-Economic Perspective', in K. McDermott and M. Stibbe (eds), *The 1989 Revolutions in Central and Eastern Europe: From Communism to Pluralism* (Manchester, 2013), pp. 162–3.
11. For details, see Wheaton and Kavan, *The Velvet Revolution*, pp. 23–9, 196–7 (English translation of 'Several Sentences'); J. Vladislav and V. Prečan, *Horký leden 1989 v Československu* (Prague, 1990).
12. Details of the march can be found in Wheaton and Kavan, *The Velvet Revolution*, pp. 39–48.
13. Both Havel's and Dubček's elections involved various intrigues and behind-the-scenes chicanery. For details, see J. Suk, *Labyrintem revoluce: Aktéři, zápletky a křížovatky jedné politické krize (od listopadu 1989 do června 1990)* (Prague, 2003), pp. 225–7.
14. By far the most comprehensive book on the revolution 'from below' is Krapfl, *Revolution with a Human Face*. For an elite perspective, the best source is Suk, *Labyrintem revoluce*. See also J. F. N. Bradley, *Czechoslovakia's Velvet Revolution: A Political Analysis* (Boulder, 1992) and the documentary collection M. Otáhal and Z. Sládek (eds), *Deset pražských dnů (17.-27. listopad 1989). Dokumentace* (Prague, 1990). On Slovakia, see I. Antalová (ed.), *Verejnosť proti násiliu 1989–1991: Svedectvá a dokumenty* (Bratislava, 1998).
15. An extract of an important, but totally confused, speech by Jakeš can be found in Pullmann, 'The Demise', p. 167.

16. See Jakeš's comments in P. Molloy, *The Lost World of Communism: An Oral History of Daily Life Behind the Iron Curtain* (London, 2009), pp. 296–7.
17. For details, see M. Pullmann, *Konec experimentu. Přestavba a pád komunismu v Československu* (Prague 2011), pp. 95–114, 217–27, 237–8, quotations at 224, 238; Pullmann, 'The Demise', pp. 154–60, 164–7.
18. D. A. Green, *The Czechoslovak Communist Party's Revolution, 1986–1990*, PhD thesis, University of Strathclyde (2014), pp. 220, 224–5. I am indebted to the author for sending me a copy of his dissertation and for giving me permission to cite his work.
19. Green, *The Czechoslovak Communist Party's Revolution*, pp. 118–65.
20. J. Krapfl, 'The Diffusion of "Dissident" Political Theory in the Czechoslovak Revolution of 1989', *Slovo*, vol. 19, no. 2 (2007), p. 88. For similar developments in the USSR, see M. Lewin, *The Gorbachev Phenomenon: A Historical Interpretation* (London, 1988), pp. 80–2.
21. See Kenney, *A Carnival of Revolution*, p. 246; Wheaton and Kavan, *The Velvet Revolution*, p. 61.
22. According to one of Gorbachev's wittier advisers, the Brezhnev Doctrine was replaced in 1989 by the 'Sinatra Doctrine', a reference to the crooner's classic 'My Way'.
23. R. H. Donaldson and J. L. Nogee cited in M. Buckley, 'The Multifaceted External Soviet Role in Processes Towards Unanticipated Revolutions', in McDermott and Stibbe (eds), *The 1989 Revolutions*, p. 68.
24. Krapfl, *Revolution with a Human Face*, p. 5.
25. See M. Blaive, 'The 1989 Revolution as a Non-Lieu de Mémoire in the Czech Republic', in A. Gjuričová (ed.), *Sborník z konference, 1989–2009: Společnost. Dějiny. Politika'* (Prague: Heinrich Böll Stiftung), available at www.boell.cz/navigation/19-856.html; and M. Shore, *The Taste of Ashes: The Afterlife of Totalitarianism in Eastern Europe* (London, 2013), pp. 55–7.
26. Krapfl, *Revolution with a Human Face*, p. 111. My material on Slovakia in this sub-section draws heavily on Krapfl's excellent analysis on pp. 111–52, quotations at 130, 142–4, 147–8.
27. F. Fukuyama, *The End of History and the Last Man* (London, 1992).
28. C. S. Leff, *The Czech and Slovak Republics: Nation Versus State* (Boulder, 1997), p. 82.
29. Arnošt Goldflan cited in Wheaton and Kavan, *The Velvet Revolution*, pp. 52–3.
30. Krapfl, *Revolution with a Human Face*, pp. 7, 96.
31. See Tables 4 and 6 in Wheaton and Kavan, *The Velvet Revolution*, pp. 220–1.
32. For more ambivalent survey results, see J. Měchýř, *Velký převrat či snad revoluce sametová?* (Prague, 1999), pp. 43–4.
33. Material in this paragraph is drawn from Krapfl, *Revolution with a Human Face*, pp. 93, 96–101, 105–7, quotations at 96–100, 106–7.
34. Krapfl, *Revolution with a Human Face*, pp. 89–90, 156–70.
35. This section is based on Krapfl, *Revolution with a Human Face*, pp. 74–110, quotations at 87.
36. In a few cases, however, doubts were raised about the participation of Roma in the democratic process. See Krapfl, *Revolution with a Human Face*, p. 93. For wider anti-Roma sentiment, see Wheaton and Kavan, *The Velvet Revolution*, pp. 146–7, 171.
37. Krapfl, *Revolution with a Human Face*, p. 94.
38. Krapfl, *Revolution with a Human Face*, pp. 100–2, 107–8.

Chapter 8: Conclusion – Into the Dustbin of History?

1. 'Law Concerning the Illegitimacy of the Communist Regime', passed by the Czech parliament in July 1993, cited in V. Tismaneanu, *Fantasies of Salvation: Democracy, Nationalism, and Myth in Post-Communist Europe* (Princeton, 1998), pp. 118–19. The ruling was highly contentious, but was finally passed by 129 votes to 34 with three abstentions. The Slovak parliament passed a very similar law in March 1996.
2. I. Klíma, *My Crazy Century: A Memoir* (London, 2014), p. 1.
3. Cited in V. Handl, 'Living with or in the Past? Czech Communists between Canonisation and Coming to Terms with their History', in B. Hofmann et al. (eds), *Diktaturüberwindung in Europa. Neue nationale und transnationale Perspektiven* (Heidelberg, 2010), p. 89.
4. It should be noted, however, that it was only in the 1960s that the 'affluent' west European economies began fully to recover from post-war austerities and rationing, and that the threat of communism entailed a socio-economic dimension, not just a military and politico-ideological one.
5. Renner, *A History of Czechoslovakia*, p. 161. For a hugely controversial condemnation of world-wide communism, see S. Courtois et al. (eds), *The Black Book of Communism: Crimes, Terror, Repression* (Cambridge: MA, 1999).
6. C. Ross, *The East German Dictatorship: Problems and Perspectives in the Interpretation of the GDR* (London, 2002), pp. 50–1. See also Lindenberger, 'Tacit Minimal Consensus', pp. 208–22.
7. The classic 'six-point syndrome' of totalitarianism was elaborated by C. J. Friedrich and Z. Brzezinski. See note 32 in Chapter 1.
8. On internal party implosion, see Pullmann, *Konec experimentu*; Pullmann, 'The Demise'; and Green, *The Czechoslovak Communist Party's Revolution*.
9. M. A. Bracke, '1968', in Smith (ed.), *The Oxford Handbook*, p. 160.
10. On the continuing historical influence of the Prague Spring, see Tůma, 'Conspicuous Connections, 1968 and 1989', pp. 501–14.
11. Milan Kundera cited in Hames, *The Czechoslovak New Wave*, p. 282.
12. Kolář, 'Communism in Eastern Europe', pp. 204, 216.
13. I am indebted to Vítězslav Sommer for many of these points. See also Bren, *The Greengrocer and His TV*; and Blaive, 'The 1989 Revolution as a Non-Lieu de Mémoire in the Czech Republic'.
14. M. Blaive, 'Communism from the Viewpoint of Societies', in M. Blaive (ed.), *La communisme à partir des sociétés / Communism from the Viewpoint of Societies* (Prague, 2006), p. 22.

Bibliography

Archives

National Archive of the Czech Republic (NA), Prague

Archive of the Central Committee of the Communist Party of Czechoslovakia (AÚV KSČ):

Fond 01	Central Committee
Fonds 02/1 and 2	Presidium (Politburo)
Fond 02/3	Organisational Secretariat
Fond 02/5	Political Secretariat
Fond 05/1	Department of Party Organs
Fond 014/12	Party Information Bulletins
Fond	Office of the First Secretary A. Novotný
Fond	Antonín Novotný – tajné (secret)

Slovak National Archive (SNA), Bratislava

Archive of the Central Committee of the Communist Party of Slovakia (AÚV KSS):
Fond David

Security Services Archive (ABS), Prague and Brno-Kanice

Fond 310	Secretariat of the Headquarters of State Security
Fond A2/1 and 2	Secretariat of the Ministry of Interior
Fond H-186	Amnesty, 1960

Fond H-193   Currency Reform, 1953
Fond H-669-2   Ministry of Interior reports on censored
          letters, 1956

Archive of the Institute of Public Memory (AÚPN), Bratislava

Regional police files on popular opinion in 1956

Archive of the President's Office (AKPR), Prague

Fond 0 1533/68   Rehabilitations in the 1960s

All-Trade Union Archive (VOA ČMKOS), Prague

Fond ÚRO – Presidium
Fond ÚRO – Secretariat

Public Opinion Research Centre (CVVM), Prague

Public opinion surveys, 1968–89

State Regional Archive in Plzeň (SOAP)

Materials on the Plzeň uprising, June 1953

Škoda Archives (SA), Plzeň

Materials on the Plzeň uprising, June 1953

Hungarian National Archive (MOL), Budapest

XXX11-16-a, files 2-5, Archive of the Ministry of Interior

Open Society Archive (OSA), Budapest

Czechoslovak Unit, 300-30-2: Microfilms 139 and 140

The National Archive (TNA), London

Diplomatic despatches on Czechoslovakia in the 1950s

Published Documentary Sources: Czech, Slovak and Russian

Antalová, I. (ed.), *Verejnost' proti násiliu 1989–1991: Svedectvá a dokumenty* (Bratislava, 1998).

Gottwald, K., *Spisy*, XII, XIII (Prague, 1955 and 1957).

Jech, K. (ed.), *Vystěhování selských rodin v Akci K ('kulaci') 1951–1953: Seznamy a vybrané dokumenty* (Prague, 1992).

Kaplan, K. and Váchová, J. (eds), *Akce B - vystěhování 'státně nespolehlivých osob' z Prahy, Bratislavy a dalších měst, 1952–1953* (Prague, 1992).

Mervart, J. and Musilová, D., *Dokumenty k dějinám Komunistické strany Československa* (Hradec Králové, 2006).

Ministry of Justice, *Proces s vedením protistátního spikleneckého centra v čele s Rudolfem Slánským* (Prague, 1953).

Murashko, G. P., 'Delo Slanskogo', *Voprosy istorii*, no. 3 (1997), pp. 3–20 and no. 4 (1997), pp. 3–18.

Otáhal, M. and Sládek, Z. (eds), *Deset pražských dnů (17.-27. listopad 1989). Dokumentace* (Prague, 1990).

Pecka, J. (ed.), *Spontánní projevy pražského jara 1968–1969* (Brno, 1993).

Pecka, J., Belda, J. and Hoppe, J. (eds), *Občanská společnost 1967–1970: Sociální organismy a hnutí pražského jara*, 2 vols (Brno, 1998).

Rok šedesátý osmý v usneseních a dokumentech ÚV KSČ (Prague, 1969).

Tomilina, N. G., Karner, S. and Chubarian, A. O. (eds), *'Prazhskaia vesna' i mezhdunarodnyi krizis 1968 goda: Dokumenty* (Moscow, 2010).

Vlčková, B. (ed.), *Ohlas událostí roku 1968. I část* (Prague, 2012).

Volokitina, T. V., Islamov, T. M., Murashko, G. P., Noskova, A. F. and Rogovaia, L. A. (eds), *Vostochnaia Evropa v dokumentakh rossiiskikh arkhivov 1944–1953 gg.*, 2 vols (Moscow, 1997).

Volokitina, T. V., Murashko, G. P., Naumov, O. V., Noskova, A. F. and Tsarevskaia, T. V. (eds), *Sovetskii faktor v vostochnoi Evrope 1944–1953: Dokumenty*, 2 vols (Moscow, 1999).

Vondrová, J. and Navrátil, J. (eds), *Prameny k dějinám Československé krize v letech 1967–1970: Komunistická strana Československa (říjen 1967 - září 1969)*, 4 vols (Brno, 1999–2003).

Published Documentary Sources: English

Fišera, V. (ed.), *Workers' Councils in Czechoslovakia: Documents and Essays, 1968–69* (London, 1978).

Navrátil, J., Benčík, A., Kural, V., Michálková, M. and Vondrová, J. (eds), *The Prague Spring 1968: A National Security Archive Documents Reader* (Budapest, 1998).

Oxley, A., Pravda, A. and Ritchie, A. (eds), *Czechoslovakia: The Party and the People* (London, 1973).

Pelikán, J. (ed.), *The Czechoslovak Political Trials, 1950–1954: The Suppressed Report of the Dubček Government's Commission of Inquiry, 1968* (London, 1971).

Pelikán, J. (ed.), *The Secret Vysočany Congress: Proceedings and Documents of the Extraordinary Fourteenth Congress of the Communist Party of Czechoslovakia, 22 August 1968* (London, 1971).

Press Group of Soviet Journalists, *On Events in Czechoslovakia* (Moscow, 1968).

Procacci, G., Adibekov, G., Di Biagio, A., Gibianskii, L., Gori, F. and Pons, S. (eds), *The Cominform: Minutes of the Three Conferences 1947/1948/1949* (Milan, 1994).

Remington, R. A. (ed.), *Winter in Prague: Documents on Czechoslovak Communism in Crisis* (Cambridge: MA, 1969).

Riese, H.-P. (ed.), *Since the Prague Spring: Charter '77 and the Struggle for Human Rights in Czechoslovakia* (New York, 1979).

Autobiographies, Biographies, Memoirs and Oral Histories: Czech

Bartošek, K., *Zpráva o putování v komunistických archivech: Praha - Paříž (1948–1968)* (Prague, 2000).

Bil'ak, V., *Paměti. Unikátní svědectví ze zákulisí KSČ*, 2 vols (Prague, 1991).

Bouška, T., Pinerová, K. and Louč, M. (eds), *Českoslovenští političtí vězni: Životní příběhy* (Prague, 2009).

Černý, R., *Antonín Novotný. Vzpomínky prezidenta* (Prague, 2008).

Císař, C., *Paměti. Nejen o zákulisí Pražského jara* (Prague, 2005).

Goldstücker, E., *Vzpomínky, 1945–1968* (Prague, 2005).

Hájek, M., *Paměť české levice* (Prague, 2011).

Kaplan, K. and Kosatík, P., *Gottwaldovi muži* (Prague, 2004).

Vaněk, M. and Urbášek, P. (eds), *Vítězové? Poražení? Životopisná interview: Politické elity v období tzv. normalizace* (Prague, 2005).

Autobiographies, Biographies, Memoirs and Oral Histories: English

Bouška, T. and Pinerová, K. (eds), *Czechoslovak Political Prisoners: Life Stories of 5 Male and 5 Female Victims of Stalinism* (Prague, 2009).

Dubcek, A. with A. Sugar, *Dubcek Speaks* (London, 1990).

Dubček, A., *Hope Dies Last: The Autobiography of Alexander Dubček* (New York, 1993).

Gorbachev, M. and Mlynář, Z., *Conversations with Gorbachev: On Perestroika, the Prague Spring, and the Crossroads of Socialism* (New York, 2002).

Kavan, R., *Love and Freedom: My Unexpected Life in Prague* (New York, 1988).
Keane, J., *Václav Havel: A Political Tragedy in Six Acts* (New York, 2000).
Klíma, I., *My Crazy Century: A Memoir* (London, 2014).
Kun, M., *Prague Spring - Prague Fall: Blank Spots of 1968* (Budapest, 1999).
Loebl, E., *Sentenced and Tried: The Stalinist Purges in Czechoslovakia* (London, 1969).
London, A., *On Trial* (London, 1970).
Margolius, I., *Reflections of Prague: Journeys through the 20th Century* (Chichester, 2006).
Margolius Kovaly, H., *Prague Farewell* (London, 1988).
Mlynář, Z., *Night Frost in Prague: The End of Humane Socialism* (London, 1980).
Molloy, P., *The Lost World of Communism: An Oral History of Daily Life Behind the Iron Curtain* (London, 2009).
Sayle, A., *Stalin Ate My Homework* (London, 2010).
Slánská, J., *Report on My Husband* (London, 1969).
Šlingová, M., *Truth Will Prevail* (London, 1968).
Vaculík., L., *A Cup of Coffee with My Interrogator* (London, 1987).

Czech and Slovak Secondary Literature

Blaive, M., *Promarněná příležitost: Československo a rok 1956* (Prague, 2001).
Blažek, P., 'Politická represe v komunistickém Československu 1948–1989', in *Moc verzus občan. Úloha represie a politického násilia v komunizme* (Bratislava, 2005), pp. 8–15.
Brennerová, C., 'Cesta k únoru 1948. Teze k výzkumu soudobých dějin', *Dějiny, theorie, kritika*, no. 2 (2006), pp. 215–30.
Brennerová, C., 'Líné dívky, lehké dívky? Příživnictví a disciplinace mladých žen v době normalizace', *Dějiny a současnost*, no. 7 (2013), pp. 19–22.
Cuhra, J., *Trestní represe odpůrců režimu v letech 1969–1972* (Prague, 1997).
Cuhra, J., 'Nezávislé aktivity v Československu a Charta 77 - meze protnutí', in M. Dévatá, J. Suk and O. Tůma (eds), *Charta 77: Od obhajoby lidských práv k demokratické revoluci, 1977–1989* (Prague, n.d.), pp. 95–104.
Dobeš, J., 'Socialismus v politické teorii a praxi let 1945–1948', in Z. Kokošková, J. Kocian and S. Kokoška (eds), *Československo na rozhraní dvou epoch nesvobody* (Prague, 2005), pp. 276–86.
Doskočil, Z., *Duben 1969: anatomie jednoho mocenského zvratu* (Brno, 2006).
Franc, M., 'Coca-cola je zde! aneb Konzumní společnost v Československu?', in O. Tůma and M. Devátá (eds), *Pražské jaro 1968: Občanská společnost - média - přenos politických a kulturních procesů* (Prague, 2011), pp. 133–42.
Franc, M. and Knapík, J., *Volný čas v českých zemích, 1957–1967* (Prague, 2013).
Heumos, P., 'Dělnické stavky v Československu v padesátých letech', *Pohled*, vol. 8, no. 6 (2000), pp. 20–21.
Heumos, P., *'Vyhrňme si rukávy, než se kola zastaví!' Dělníci a státní socialismus v Československu 1945–1968* (Prague, 2006).

Hoppe, J., *Opozice '68. Sociální demokracie, KAN a K 231 v období pražského jara* (Prague, 2009).

Hoppe, J. and Bárta, M. (eds), *Úloha Alexandra Dubčeka v moderních dějinách Československa: Sborník z konference* (Prague, 2002).

Jareš, J., Spurný, M., Volná, K. and coll., *Náměstí krasnoarmějců 2. Učitelé a studenti Filozofické fakulty UK v období normalizace* (Prague, 2012).

Jech, K. (ed.), *Stránkami soudobých dějin: Sborník statí k pětašedesátinám historika Karla Kaplana* (Prague, 1993).

Kabele, J. and Hájek, M., *Jak vládli? Průvodce hierarchiemi reálného socialismu* (Brno, 2008).

Kalinová, L., *Společenské proměny v čase socialistického experimentu. K sociálním dějinám v letech 1945–1969* (Prague, 2007).

Kaplan, K., *Československo v letech 1945–1948* (Prague, 1991).

Kaplan, K., *Československo v letech 1948–1953* (Prague, 1991).

Kaplan, K., *Nekrvavá revoluce* (Prague, 1993).

Kaplan, K., *Sociální souvislosti krizí komunistického režimu v letech 1953–1957 a 1968–1975* (Prague, 1993).

Kaplan, K., *Sovětští poradci v Československu 1949–1956* (Prague, 1993).

Kaplan, K., *K politickým procesům v Československu 1948–1954: Dokumentace komise ÚV KSČ pro rehabilitaci 1968* (Prague, 1994).

Kaplan, K., *Pět kapitol o únoru* (Brno, 1997).

Kaplan, K., *Nebezpečná bezpečnost: Státní bezpečnost 1948–1956* (Brno, 1999).

Kaplan, K., *Kořeny československé reformy 1968*, 2 vols (Brno, 2000 and 2002).

Kaplan, K., *Kronika komunistického Československa. Doba tání 1953–1956* (Brno, 2005).

Kaplan, K., *Proměny české společnosti 1948–1960. Část první* (Prague, 2007).

Kaplan, K., *Druhý proces. Milada Horáková a spol. - rehabilitační řízení 1968–1990* (Prague, 2008).

Kaplan, K., *Kronika komunistického Československa. Kořeny reformy 1956–1968. Společnost a moc* (Brno, 2008).

Kaplan, K., *Proměny české společnosti 1948–1960. Část druhá. Venkov* (Prague, 2012).

Kaplan, K. and Paleček, P., *Komunistický režim a politické procesy v Československu* (Prague, 2001).

Kaplan, K. and Váchová, J. (eds), *Zemřelí ve věznicích a tresty smrti, 1948–1956* (Prague, 1992).

Knapík, J., *V zajetí moci. Kulturní politika, její systém a aktéři 1948–1956* (Prague, 2006).

Knapík, J., Franc, M. and coll., *Průvodce kulturním děním a životním stylem v českých zemích 1948–1967*, 2 vols (Prague, 2011).

Kocian, J. and Devátá, M. (eds), *Únor 1948 v Československu: Nástup komunistické totality a proměny společnosti* (Prague, 2011).

Křen, J., *Konfliktní společenství. Češi a Němci 1780–1918* (Toronto, 1989).

Kusák, A., *Kultura a politika v Československu 1945–1956* (Prague, 1998).

Lehr, S., '"Pište nám!"': Dopisy diváků a posluchačů Československé televizi a rozhlasu', *Marginalia Historica*, no. 2 (2012), pp. 71–82.

Liška, O. and coll., *Tresty smrti vykonané v Československu v letech 1918–1989* (Prague, 2006).

Londák, M., Sikora, S. and coll., *Rok 1968 a jeho miesta v našich dejinách* (Bratislava, 2009).

Maňák, J., *Čistky v Komunistické straně Československa v letech 1969–1970* (Prague, 1997).

Marjinová, V. V., 'Od důvěry k podezíravosti. Sovětští a českoslovenští komunisté v letech 1945–48', *Soudobé dějiny*, no. 3–4 (1997), pp. 451–67.

Mayer, F., *Češi a jejich komunismus: pamět' a politická identita* (Prague, 2009).

Měchýř, J., *Velký převrat či snad revoluce sametová?* (Prague, 1999).

Mervart, J., *Naděje a iluze: Čeští a slovenští spisovatelé v reformním hnutí šedesátých let* (Brno, 2010).

Murašková, G. P., 'Únorová politická krize roku 1948 v Československu a "sovětský faktor". Z materiálů ruských archivů', *Soudobé dějiny*, no. 3–4 (1997), pp. 468–78.

Musilová, D., 'Ženské hnutí 1945–1948: naděje a zklamání', in Z. Kokošková, J. Kocian and S. Kokoška (eds), *Československo na rozhraní dvou epoch nesvobody* (Prague, 2005), pp. 339–45.

Nečasová, D., *Buduj vlast - posílíš mír! Ženské hnutí v českých zemích 1945–1955* (Brno, 2011).

Nevrlý, M., *Karpatské hry* (Prague, 1981; reprinted 2006).

Otáhal, M., *Opoziční proudy v české společnosti 1969–1989* (Prague, 2011).

Pauer, J., *Praha 1968. Vpád varšavské smlouvy* (Prague, 2004).

Pažout, J., *Mocným navzdory: Studentské hnutí v šedesátých letech 20. století* (Prague, 2008).

Pernes, J., 'Ohlas mad'arské revoluce roku 1956 v československé veřejnosti. Z interních hlášení krajských správ ministerstva vnitra', *Soudobé dějiny*, no. 4 (1996), pp. 512–26.

Pernes, J., *Krize komunistického režimu v Československu v 50. letech 20. století* (Brno, 2008).

Pernes, J. and Foitzik, J. (eds), *Politické procesy v Československu po roce 1945 a 'případ Slánský'* (Brno, 2005).

Pešek, J., *Slovensko v rokoch 1953–1957. Kapitoly z politického vývoja* (Brno, 2001).

Pešek, J., *Slovensko na prelome 50. a 60. rokov. Politicko-mocenské aspekty vývoja* (Brno, 2005).

Praha objektivem tajné policie - Prague Through the Lens of the Secret Police (Prague, 2008).

Prečan, V., 'Lid, veřejnost, občanská společnost jako aktér Pražského jara 1968', in J. Pecka and V. Prečan (eds), *Proměny pražského jara 1968–1969. Sborník studií a dokumentů o nekapitulantských postojích v československé společnosti* (Brno, 1993), pp. 13–36.

Prečan, V., Murashko, G. P., Gibianskij, L. J. and Kaplan, K., 'Zorinova pražská mise v únoru 1948. Nad novými dokumenty', *Soudobé dějiny*, no. 2–3 (1998), pp. 312–20.

Pullmann, M., 'Sociální dějiny a totalitněhistorické vyprávění', *Soudobé dějiny*, no. 3–4 (2008), pp. 703–17.

Pullmann, M., *Konec experimentu. Přestavba a pád komunismu v Československu* (Prague 2011).

Rákosník, J., *Sovětizace sociálního státu: lidově demokratický režim a sociální práva občanů v Československu 1945–1960* (Prague, 2010).

Rataj, J., *Komunistické Československo, 1948–1960* (Plzeň, 1995).

Reiman, P. and coll. , *Dějiny Komunistické strany Československa* (Prague, 1961).

Rychlík, J., *Cestování do ciziny v habsburské monarchii a v Československu. Pasová, vizová a vystěhovalecká politika 1848–1989* (Prague, 2007).

Rychlík, J., *Češi a Slováci ve 20. století. Spolupráce a konflikty 1914–1992* (Prague, 2012).

Rychlík, J., *Devizové přísliby a cestování do zahraničí v období normalizace* (Prague, 2012).

Skála, A., 'Měnová reforma 1. června 1953 v Plzni v hlášení mocenských orgánů', *Minulostí západočeského kraje*, no. 2 (2007), pp. 602–39.

Šlouf, J., *KSČ na Plzeňsku v letech 1945–1948*, MA thesis, Charles University, Prague (2008).

Sommer, V., *Angažované dějepisectví. Stranická historiografie mezi stalinismem a reformním komunismem (1950–1970)* (Prague, 2011).

Spurný, M., *Nejsou jako my. Česká společnost a menšiny v pohraničí (1945–1960)* (Prague, 2012).

Staněk, T., *Odsun Němců z Československa 1945–1948* (Prague, 1991).

Státník, D., 'Závodní rady - iluze a skutečnost', in Z. Kokošková, J. Kocian and S. Kokoška (eds), *Československo na rozhraní dvou epoch nesvobody* (Prague, 2005), pp. 374–86.

Státník, D., 'Socialně politická situace v Československu 1956–1962. Jak Československo vypadalo, jak žilo a co si myslelo', *Česko-slovenská historická ročenka 2006*, pp. 261–79.

Suk, J., *Labyrintem revoluce: Aktéři, zápletky a křížovatky jedné politické krize (od listopadu 1989 do června 1990)* (Prague, 2003).

Tůma O. and Devátá, M. (eds), *Pražské jaro 1968: Občanská společnost - média - přenos politických a kulturních procesů* (Prague, 2011).

Tůma O. and Vilímek, T. (eds), *Pět studií k dějinám české společnosti po roce 1945* (Prague, 2008).

Vladislav, J. and Prečan, V., *Horký leden 1989 v Československu* (Prague, 1990).

Vojtěchovský, O., *Z Prahy proti Titovi! Jugoslávská prosovětská emigrace v Československu* (Prague, 2012).

Zimmermann, V., '"Deformace právního vědomí"? Úplatkářství jako masový fenomén v ČSSR v sedmdesátých a osmdesátých letech', *Marginalia Historica*, no. 2 (2012), pp. 159–65.

English Secondary Literature

Abrams, B. F., *The Struggle for the Soul of the Nation: Czech Culture and the Rise of Communism* (Lanham, 2004).

Abrams, B., 'Hope Died Last: The Czechoslovak Road to Stalinism', in V. Tismaneanu (ed.), *Stalinism Revisited: The Establishment of Communist Regimes in East-Central Europe* (Budapest, 2010), pp. 345–65.

Adamec, Č., Pospíšil, B. and Tesař, M., *What's Your Opinion? A Year's Survey of Public Opinion in Czechoslovakia* (Prague, 1947).

Altshuler, D., 'Departures from Home: Czech Perspectives on Difference', *The Anthropology of Eastern Europe Review*, vol. 21, no. 2 (2003), pp. 7–12.

Applebaum, R., 'A Test of Friendship: Soviet-Czechoslovak Tourism and the Prague Spring', in A. E. Gorsuch and D. P. Koenker (eds), *The Socialist Sixties: Crossing Borders in the Second World* (Bloomington, 2013), pp. 213–32.

Bárta, M., Cvrček, L., Košický, P. and Sommer, V. , *Victims of the Occupation. The Warsaw Pact Invasion of Czechoslovakia: 21 August–31 December 1968* (Prague, 2008).

Bartošek, K., 'Could We Have Fought? The "Munich Complex" in Czech Policies and Thinking', in N. Stone and E. Strouhal (eds), *Czechoslovakia: Crossroads and Crises* (London, 1989), pp. 101–19.

Batt, J., *Economic Reform and Political Change in Eastern Europe: A Comparison of the Czechoslovak and Hungarian Experiences* (Basingstoke, 1988).

Belda, J., 'Some Problems Regarding the Czechoslovak Road to Socialism', *History of Socialism Yearbook 1968* (Prague, 1969), pp. 113–54.

Bell, R., 'History in the Making: Experiment Invalidovna, Prague 1961', unpublished manuscript.

Bischof, G., Karner, S. and Ruggenthaler, P. (eds), *The Prague Spring and the Warsaw Pact Invasion of Czechoslovakia in 1968* (Cambridge: MA, 2011).

Blaive, M., 'The Czechs and their Communism, Past and Present', in D. Gard, I. Main, M. Oliver and J. Wood (eds), *Inquiries into Past and Present* (Vienna, 2005), available at www.iwm.at/index.php?option=com_content&task=view&id=259&Itemid=286

Blaive, M., 'Communism from the Viewpoint of Societies', in M. Blaive (ed.), *Le communisme à partir des sociétés / Communism from the Viewpoint of Societies* (Prague, 2006), pp. 13–22.

Blaive, M., 'Internationalism, Patriotism, Dictatorship and Democracy: The Czechoslovak Communist Party and the Exercise of Power, 1945–1968', *Journal of European Integration History*, vol. 13, no. 2 (2007), pp. 55–68.

Blaive, M., 'Multiple Identities and Europeanness at the Czech-Austrian and Slovak-Hungarian Borders', *Euriditio - Educatio*, no. 4 (2009), pp. 5–15.

Blaive, M., 'The 1989 Revolution as a Non-Lieu de Mémoire in the Czech Republic', in A. Gjuričová (ed.), *Sborník z konference '1989–2009: Společnost. Dějiny. Politika'*, Heinrich Böll Stiftung Praha, available at www.boell.cz/navigation/19-856.html

Bloomfield, J., *Passive Revolution: Politics and the Czechoslovak Working Class, 1945–1948* (London, 1979).

Bolton, J., *Worlds of Dissent: Charter 77, the Plastic People of the Universe, and Czech Culture under Communism* (Cambridge: MA, 2012).

Bracke, M. A., '1968', in S. A. Smith (ed.), *The Oxford Handbook of the History of Communism* (Oxford, 2014), pp. 156–70.

Bradley, J. F. N., *Czechoslovakia's Velvet Revolution: A Political Analysis* (Boulder, 1992).

Bren, P., 'Looking West: Popular Culture and the Generation Gap in Communist Czechoslovakia, 1969–1989', in L. Passerini (ed.), *Across the Atlantic: Cultural Exchanges between Europe and the United States* (Brussels, 2000), pp. 295–322.

Bren, P., 'Weekend Getaways: The *Chata*, the *Tramp* and the Politics of Private Life in Post-1968 Czechoslovakia', in D. Crowley and S. E. Reid (eds), *Socialist Spaces: Sites of Everyday Life in the Eastern Bloc* (Oxford, 2002), pp. 123–40.

Bren, P., 'Mirror, Mirror, on the Wall … Is the West the Fairest of Them All? Czechoslovak Normalization and Its (Dis)contents', *Kritika*, vol. 9, no. 4 (2008), pp. 831–54.

Bren, P., *The Greengrocer and His TV: The Culture of Communism After the 1968 Prague Spring* (Ithaca, 2010).

Bren, P., 'Tuzex and the Hustler: Living It Up in Czechoslovakia', in P. Bren and M. Neuberger (eds), *Communism Unwrapped: Consumption in Cold War Eastern Europe* (New York, 2012), pp. 27–48.

Brown, A. and Wightman, G., 'Czechoslovakia: Revival and Retreat', in A. Brown and J. Gray (eds), *Political Culture and Political Change in Communist States* (London, 1977), pp. 159–96.

Brown, S., 'Socialism with a Slovak Face: Federalization, Democratization, and the Prague Spring', *East European Politics and Societies*, vol. 22, no. 3 (2008), pp. 467–95.

Brown, S., *Caricatures of Revolution: Slovak Political Cartoons in the Czechoslovak Spring*, The Carl Beck Papers, no. 2105 (Pittsburgh, 2011).

Bryant, C., *Prague in Black: Nazi Rule and Czech Nationalism* (Cambridge: MA, 2007).

Bugge, P., 'Czech Democracy 1918–1938: Paragon or Parody?', *Bohemia*, vol. 47, no. 1 (2006–07), pp. 3–28.

Bugge, P., 'Normalization and the Limits of the Law: The Case of the Czech Jazz Section', *East European Politics and Societies*, vol. 22, no. 2 (2008), pp. 282–318.

Bugge, P., 'Swinging Sixties made in Czechoslovakia: The Adaption of Western Impulses in Czechoslovak Youth Culture', in O. Tůma and M. Devátá (eds), *Pražské jaro 1968: Občanská společnost - média - přenos politických a kulturních procesů* (Prague, 2011), pp. 143–55.

Capek, A. and Sazama, G. W., 'Czech and Slovak Economic Relations', *Europe-Asia Studies*, vol. 45, no. 2 (1993), pp. 211–35.

Capoccia, G., 'Legislative Responses against Extremism: The "Protection of Democracy" in the First Czechoslovak Republic (1920–1938)', *East European Politics and Societies*, vol. 16, no. 3 (2002), pp. 691–738.

Clybor, S., 'Laughter and Hatred are Neighbors: Adolf Hoffmeister and E. F. Burian in Stalinist Czechoslovakia, 1948–1956', *East European Politics and Societies*, vol. 26, no. 3 (2012), pp. 589–615.

Connelly, J., 'Students, Workers, and Social Change: The Limits of Czech Stalinism', *Slavic Review*, vol. 56, no. 2 (1997), pp. 307–35.

Connelly, J., *Captive University: The Sovietization of East German, Czech, and Polish Higher Education, 1945–1956* (Chapel Hill, 2000).

Courtois, S,, Werth, N., Panné, J-L., Paczkowski, A., Bartošek, K. and Margolin, J-L (eds), *The Black Book of Communism: Crimes, Terror, Repression* (Cambridge: MA, 1999).

Cuhra, J., 'In the Shadow of Liberalization: Repressions in Czechoslovakia in the 1960s', *Cahiers du Monde russe*, vol. 47, no. 1–2 (2006), pp. 409–26.

Dawisha, K., *The Kremlin and the Prague Spring* (Berkeley, 1984).

Dean, R. W., *Nationalism and Political Change in Eastern Europe: The Slovak Question and the Czechoslovak Reform Movement* (Denver, 1972–73).

Dickins, T., 'The Impact Factor of the Language of Czechoslovak Normalization: A Study of the Seminal Work *Poučení z krizového vývoje ve straně a společnosti po XIII. sjezdu KSČ*', *Slavonic and East European Review*, vol. 93, no. 2 (2015), pp. 213–50.

Douglas, R. M., *Orderly and Humane: The Expulsion of the Germans after the Second World War* (New Haven, 2012).

Dowling, M., *Czechoslovakia* (London, 2002).

Drápala, M., 'A Life of Illusion: The Politics of Vítězslav Nezval', in *The Prague Yearbook of Contemporary History 1998* (Prague, 1999), pp. 177–225.

Eidlin, F., *The Logic of 'Normalization'* (Boulder, 1980).

Evanson, R. K., 'Regime and Working Class in Czechoslovakia, 1948–1968', *Soviet Studies*, vol. 37, no. 2 (1985), pp. 248–68.

Evanson, R. K., 'The Czechoslovak Road to Socialism in 1948', *East European Quarterly*, vol. 19, no. 4 (1985), pp. 469–92.

Evanson, R. K., 'Political Repression in Czechoslovakia, 1948–1984', *Canadian Slavonic Papers*, vol. 28, no. 1 (1986), pp. 1–21.

Falk, B. J., *The Dilemmas of Dissidence in East-Central Europe: Citizen Intellectuals and Philosopher Kings* (Budapest, 2003).

Feinberg, M., *Elusive Equality: Gender, Citizenship, and the Limits of Democracy in Czechoslovakia, 1918–1950* (Pittsburgh, 2006).

Felak, J. R., *After Hitler, Before Stalin: Catholics, Communists, and Democrats in Slovakia, 1945–1948* (Pittsburgh, 2009).

Franc, M., 'A Shop Window of the Regime: The Position of Prague as the Capital in the Preferential Supply System of Selected Czechoslovakian Cities, 1950–1970', in P. J. Atkins, P. Lummel and D. J. Oddy (eds), *Food and the City in Europe since 1800* (London, 2007), pp. 155–64.

Franc, M. and Knapík, J., '"Getting Around to the Human Being in the Next Quarter": Leisure Time in the Czech Lands, 1948–1956', *Czech Journal of Contemporary History*, vol. 1 (2013), pp. 77–100.

French, A., *Czech Writers and Politics, 1945–1969* (Boulder, 1982).

Frommer, B., 'Expulsion or Integration: Unmixing Interethnic Marriage in Postwar Czechoslovakia', *East European Politics and Societies*, vol. 14, no. 2 (2000), pp. 381–410.

Frommer, B., *National Cleansing: Retribution against Nazi Collaborators in Postwar Czechoslovakia* (Cambridge, 2004).

Garton Ash, T., 'Czechoslovakia Under Ice', in T. Garton Ash, *The Uses of Adversity: Essays on the Fate of Central Europe* (Cambridge, 1989), pp. 55–63.

Garton Ash, T., *We the People: The Revolution of '89 Witnessed in Warsaw, Budapest, Berlin and Prague* (Cambridge, 1990).

Gerlach, D., 'Beyond Expulsion: The Emergence of "Unwanted Elements" in the Postwar Czech Borderlands, 1945–1950', *East European Politics and Societies*, vol. 24, no. 2 (2010), pp. 269–93.

Gildea, R., Mark, J. and Warring, A. (eds), *Europe's 1968: Voices of Revolt* (Oxford, 2013).

Giustino, C. M., 'Industrial Design and the Czechoslovak Pavilion at EXPO '58: Artistic Autonomy, Party Control and Cold War Common Ground', *Journal of Contemporary History*, vol. 47, no. 1 (2012), pp. 185–212.

Glassheim, E., 'The Mechanics of Ethnic Cleansing: The Expulsion of Germans from Czechoslovakia, 1945–1947', in P. Ther and A. Siljak (eds), *Redrawing Nations: Ethnic Cleansing in East-Central Europe, 1944–1948* (Lanham, 2001), pp. 197–219.

Glassheim, E., 'Ethnic Cleansing, Communism, and Environmental Devastation in Czechoslovakia's Borderlands, 1945–1989', *Journal of Modern History*, vol. 78, no. 1 (2006), pp. 65–92.

Golan, G., *The Czechoslovak Reform Movement: Communism in Crisis, 1962–1968* (Cambridge, 1971).

Golan, G., *Reform Rule in Czechoslovakia: The Dubček Era, 1968–1969* (Cambridge, 1973).

Green, D. A., *The Czechoslovak Communist Party's Revolution, 1986–1990*, PhD thesis, University of Strathclyde (2014).

Gross, J. T., 'Themes for a Social History of War Experience and Collaboration', in I. Deák, J. T. Gross and T. Judt (eds), *The Politics of Retribution in Europe: World War II and Its Aftermath* (Princeton, 2000), pp. 15–35.

Hames, P., *The Czechoslovak New Wave* (Berkeley, 1985).

Handl, V., 'Living with or in the Past? Czech Communists between Canonisation and Coming to Terms with their History', in B. Hofmann, K. Wezel, K. Hammerstein, R. Fritz and J. Trappe (eds), *Diktaturüberwindung in Europa. Neue nationale und transnationale Perspektiven* (Heidelberg, 2010), pp. 84–100.

Hauner, M., 'The Prague Spring: Twenty Years After', in N. Stone and E. Strouhal (eds), *Czechoslovakia: Crossroads and Crises, 1918–1988* (Basingstoke, 1989), pp. 207–30.

Hauner, M., 'Crime and Punishment in Communist Czechoslovakia: The Case of General Heliodor Píka and his Prosecutor Karel Vaš', *Totalitarian Movements and Political Religions*, vol. 9, no. 2–3 (2008), pp. 335–54.

Havel, V., 'The Power of the Powerless', in V. Havel et al., *The Power of the Powerless: Citizens Against the State in Central-Eastern Europe*, edited by J. Keane (London, 1985), pp. 23–96.

Heimann, M., 'The Scheming *Apparatchik* of the Prague Spring', *Europe-Asia Studies*, vol. 60, no. 10 (2008), pp. 1717–34.

Heimann, M., *Czechoslovakia: The State That Failed* (New Haven, 2009).

Heitlinger, A., *Women and State Socialism: Sex Inequality in the Soviet Union and Czechoslovakia* (London, 1979).

Heumos, P., 'State Socialism, Egalitarianism, Collectivism: On the Social Context of Socialist Work Movements in Czechoslovak Industrial and Mining Enterprises, 1945–1965', *International Labor and Working-Class History*, no. 68 (2005), pp. 47–74.

Hlaváčková, K., *Czech Fashion 1940–1970: Mirror of the Times* (Prague, 2000).

Holy, L., *The Little Czech and the Great Czech Nation* (Cambridge, 1996).

Hruby, P., *Fools and Heroes: The Changing Role of Communist Intellectuals in Czechoslovakia* (Oxford, 1980).

Inglot, T., *Welfare States in East Central Europe, 1919–2004* (Cambridge, 2008).

Jancar, B. W., *Czechoslovakia and the Absolute Monopoly of Power: A Study of Political Power in a Communist System* (New York, 1971).

Judt, T., *Postwar: A History of Europe since 1945* (London, 2007).

Kaplan, K., *Dans les Archives du Comité Central: 30 ans de secrets du Bloc soviétique* (Paris, 1978).

Kaplan, K., *Political Persecution in Czechoslovakia, 1948–72* (Cologne, 1983).

Kaplan, K., *The Overcoming of the Regime Crisis after Stalin's Death in Czechoslovakia, Poland and Hungary* (Cologne, 1986).

Kaplan, K., *The Communist Party in Power: A Profile of Party Politics in Czechoslovakia* (Boulder, 1987).

Kaplan, K., *The Short March: The Communist Takeover in Czechoslovakia, 1945–1948* (London, 1987).

Kaplan, K., *Report on the Murder of the General Secretary* (London, 1990).

Kenney, P., *A Carnival of Revolution: Central Europe 1989* (Princeton, 2002).

Kieval, H. J., *Languages of Community: The Jewish Experience in the Czech Lands* (Berkeley, 2000).

King, J., *Budweisers into Czechs and Germans: A Local History of Bohemian Politics, 1848–1948* (Princeton, 2002).

Kirschbaum, S. J., *A History of Slovakia: The Struggle for Survival*, 2nd edn (Basingstoke, 2005).

Kolář, P., 'Communism in Eastern Europe', in S. A. Smith (ed.), *The Oxford Handbook of the History of Communism* (Oxford, 2014), pp. 203–19.

Korbel, J., *The Communist Subversion of Czechoslovakia, 1938–1948: The Failure of Coexistence* (Princeton, 1959).

Kovanda, K., 'Works Councils in Czechoslovakia, 1945–47', *Soviet Studies*, vol. 29, no. 2 (1977), pp. 255–69.

Kramer, M., 'New Sources on the 1968 Soviet Invasion of Czechoslovakia', Part I, *Cold War International History Project Bulletin*, no. 2 (1992), pp. 1, 4–13.

Kramer, M., 'The Prague Spring and the Soviet Invasion of Czechoslovakia: New Interpretations', Part II, *Cold War International History Project Bulletin*, no. 3 (1993), pp. 2–13, 54–5.

Kramer, M., 'The Czechoslovak Crisis and the Brezhnev Doctrine', in C. Fink, P. Gassert and D. Junker (eds), *1968: The World Transformed* (Cambridge, 1998), pp. 111–71.

Kramer, M., 'The Prague Spring and the Soviet Invasion in Historical Perspective', in G. Bischof, S. Karner and P. Ruggenthaler (eds), *The Prague Spring and the Warsaw Pact Invasion of Czechoslovakia in 1968* (Cambridge: MA, 2011), pp. 35–58.

Kramerová, D. and Skálová, V. (eds), *The Brussels Dream: The Czechoslovak Presence at Expo 58 in Brussels and the Lifestyle of the Early 1960s* (Prague, 2008).

Krapfl, J., 'The Diffusion of "Dissident" Political Theory in the Czechoslovak Revolution of 1989', *Slovo*, vol. 19, no. 2 (2007), pp. 83–101.

Krapfl, J., *Revolution with a Human Face: Politics, Culture, and Community in Czechoslovakia, 1989–1992* (Ithaca, 2013).

Krátký, K., 'Czechoslovakia, the Soviet Union and the Marshall Plan', in O. A. Westad, S. Holtsmark and I. A. Neumann (eds), *The Soviet Union in Eastern Europe, 1945–89* (Basingstoke, 1994), pp. 9–25.

Krejčí, J. and Machonin, P., *Czechoslovakia, 1918–1992: A Laboratory for Social Change* (Basingstoke, 1996).

Kundera, M., 'The Tragedy of Central Europe', in G. Stokes (ed.), *From Stalinism to Pluralism: A Documentary History of Eastern Europe since 1945* (Oxford, 1991), pp. 217–23.

Kusin, V. V., *The Intellectual Origins of the Prague Spring: The Development of Reformist Ideas in Czechoslovakia, 1956–1967* (Cambridge, 1971).

Kusin, V. V., *Political Grouping in the Czechoslovak Reform Movement* (London, 1972).

Kusin, V. V., *From Dubček to Charter 77: A Study of 'Normalisation' in Czechoslovakia 1968–1978* (Edinburgh, 1978).

Kusin, V. V., 'Husak's Czechoslovakia and Economic Stagnation', *Problems of Communism*, vol. 31, no. 3 (1982), pp. 24–37.

Leff, C. S., *National Conflict in Czechoslovakia: The Making and Remaking of a State, 1918–1987* (Princeton, 1988).

Leff, C. S., *The Czech and Slovak Republics: Nation Versus State* (Boulder, 1997).

Liehm, A. J., *The Politics of Culture* (New York, 1973).

Liehm, A. J., 'The New Social Contract and the Parallel Polity', in J. L. Curry (ed.), *Dissent in Eastern Europe* (New York, 1983), pp. 173–81.

Lindenberger, T., 'Tacit Minimal Consensus: The Always Precarious East German Dictatorship', in P. Corner (ed,), *Popular Opinion in Totalitarian Regimes: Fascism, Nazism, Communism* (Oxford, 2009), pp. 208–22.

Long, M., *Making History: Czech Voices of Dissent and the Revolution of 1989* (Lanham, 2005).

Lukes, I., 'Rudolf Slansky: His Trials and Trial', Cold War International History Project, Working Paper No. 50 (Washington DC, 2006).

Lukes, I., *On the Edge of the Cold War: American Diplomats and Spies in Postwar Prague* (New York, 2012).

Mace Ward, J., *Priest, Politician, Collaborator: Jozef Tiso and the Making of Fascist Slovakia* (Ithaca, 2013).

Mamatey, V. S. and Luža, R. (eds), *A History of the Czechoslovak Republic, 1918– 1948* (Princeton, 1973).

Marušiak, J., 'The Normalisation Regime and its Impact on Slovak Domestic Policy after 1970', *Europe-Asia Studies*, vol. 60, no. 10 (2008), pp. 1805–25.

Matthews, J. P. C., 'Majales: The Abortive Student Revolt in Czechoslovakia in 1956', Cold War International History Project, Working Paper No. 24 (Washington DC, 1998).

McDermott, K., 'A "Polyphony of Voices"? Czech Popular Opinion and the Slánský Affair', *Slavic Review*, vol. 67, no. 4 (2008), pp. 840–65.

McDermott, K., 'Stalinist Terror in Czechoslovakia: Origins, Processes, Responses', in K. McDermott and M. Stibbe, (eds), *Stalinist Terror in Eastern Europe: Elite Purges and Mass Repression* (Manchester, 2010), pp. 98–118.

McDermott, K., 'Popular Resistance in Communist Czechoslovakia: The Plzeň Uprising, June 1953', *Contemporary European History*, vol. 19, no. 4 (2010), pp. 287–307.

McDermott, K. and Sommer, V., 'The "Club of Politically Engaged Conformists"? The Communist Party of Czechoslovakia, Popular Opinion and the Crisis of Communism, 1956', Cold War International History Project, Working Paper No. 66 (Washington DC, 2013).

McDermott, K. and Pinerová, K., 'The Rehabilitation Process in Czechoslovakia: Party and Popular Responses', in K. McDermott and M. Stibbe (eds), *De-Stalinising Eastern Europe: The Rehabilitation of Stalin's Victims after 1953* (London, 2015), pp. 109–31.

Myant, M. R., *Socialism and Democracy in Czechoslovakia, 1945–1948* (Cambridge, 1981).

Myant, M. R., *The Czechoslovak Economy 1948–1988: The Battle for Economic Reform* (Cambridge, 1989).

Myant, M. R., 'New Research on February 1948 in Czechoslovakia', *Europe-Asia Studies*, vol. 60, no. 10 (2008), pp. 1697–1715.

Nečasová, D., 'Women's Organizations in the Czech Lands, 1948–89: An Historical Perspective', in H. Havelková and L. Oates-Indruchová (eds), *The Politics of Gender Culture under State Socialism: An Expropriated Voice* (London, 2014), pp. 57–81.

Orzoff, A., *Battle for the Castle: The Myth of Czechoslovakia in Europe, 1914–1948* (New York, 2009).

Paul, D. W., 'Czechoslovakia's Political Culture Reconsidered', in A. Brown (ed.), *Political Culture and Communist Studies* (Basingstoke, 1984), pp. 134–48.

Pešek, J., 'The Establishment of Totalitarianism in Slovakia after the February Coup of 1948 and the Culmination of Mass Persecution, 1948–1953', in M. Teich, D. Kováč and M. D. Brown (eds), *Slovakia in History* (Cambridge, 2011), pp. 284–98.

Piekalkiewicz, J., *Public Opinion Polling in Czechoslovakia, 1968–69* (New York, 1972).

Piekalkiewicz, J., 'Public Political Opinion in Czechoslovakia during the Dubcek Era', in E. J. Czerwinski and J. Piekalkiewicz (eds), *The Soviet Invasion of Czechoslovakia: Its Effects on Eastern Europe* (New York, 1972), pp. 3–42.

Pikhoia, R. G., 'Czechoslovakia in 1968: A View from Moscow According to Central Committee Documents', *Russian Studies in History*, vol. 44, no. 3 (2005–06), pp. 35–80.

Pithart, P., 'Towards a Shared Freedom, 1968–89', in J. Musil (ed.), *The End of Czechoslovakia* (Budapest, 1995), pp. 201–22.

Pittaway, M., *Eastern Europe, 1939–2000* (London, 2004).

Pravda, A., *Reform and Change in the Czechoslovak Political System: January - August 1968* (Beverly Hills, 1975).

Prečan, V., 'Seven Great Days. The People and Civil Society during the "Prague Spring" of 1968–1969', in F. M. Cataluccio and F. Gori (eds), *La Primavera di Praga* (Milan, 1990), pp. 165–75.

Prečan, V., 'The Czech Twentieth Century?', *Czech Journal of Contemporary History*, vol. 1 (2013), pp. 7–19.

Pullmann, M., 'The Demise of the Communist Regime in Czechoslovakia, 1987–89: A Socio-Economic Perspective', in K. McDermott and M. Stibbe (eds), *The 1989 Revolutions in Central and Eastern Europe: From Communism to Pluralism* (Manchester, 2013), pp. 154–71.

Raška, F. D., *Fighting Communism from Afar: The Council of Free Czechoslovakia* (Boulder, 2008).

Renner, H., *A History of Czechoslovakia since 1945* (London, 1989).

Rieber, A. J., 'Popular Democracy: An Illusion?', in V. Tismaneanu (ed.), *Stalinism Revisited: The Establishment of Communist Regimes in East-Central Europe* (Budapest, 2010), pp. 103–28.

Ripka, H., *Czechoslovakia Enslaved* (London, 1950).

Riveles, S., 'Slovakia: Catalyst of Crisis', *Problems of Communism*, vol. 17, no. 3 (1968), pp. 1–9.

Ross, C., *The East German Dictatorship: Problems and Perspectives in the Interpretation of the GDR* (London, 2002).

Rupnik, J., *Histoire du Parti communiste tchécoslovaque: des origines à la prise du pouvoir* (Paris, 1981).

Rupnik, J., 'The Roots of Czech Stalinism', in R. Samuel and G. Stedman Jones (eds), *Culture, Ideology and Politics: Essays for Eric Hobsbawm* (London, 1982), pp. 302–20.

Sayer, D., *The Coasts of Bohemia* (Princeton, 1998).

Schmidt, D. A., *Anatomy of a Satellite* (Boston, 1952).

Shore, M., 'Engineering in the Age of Innocence: A Genealogy of Discourse Inside the Czechoslovak Writers' Union, 1949–67', *East European Politics and Societies*, vol. 12, no. 3 (1998), pp. 397–441.

Shore, M., *The Taste of Ashes: The Afterlife of Totalitarianism in Eastern Europe* (London, 2013).

Šimečka, M., *The Restoration of Order: The Normalization of Czechoslovakia, 1969–1976* (London, 1984).

Skilling, H. G., *Czechoslovakia's Interrupted Revolution* (Princeton, 1976).

Skilling, H. G., 'Stalinism and Czechoslovak Political Culture', in R. C. Tucker (ed.), *Stalinism: Essays in Historical Interpretation* (New York, 1977), pp. 257–80.

Skilling, H. G., *Charter 77 and Human Rights in Czechoslovakia* (London, 1981).

Skilling, H. G., 'Czechoslovak Political Culture: Pluralism in an International Context', in A. Brown (ed.), *Political Culture and Communist Studies* (Basingstoke, 1984), pp. 115–33.

Skilling, H. G., *Samizdat and an Independent Society in Central and Eastern Europe* (Basingstoke, 1989).

Skilling, H. G. (ed.), *Czechoslovakia 1918–1988: Seventy Years from Independence* (London, 1991).

Skvorecký, J., 'The Unfinished End of the Jazz Section of the Czech Musicians' Union', in A. Heneka, F. Janouch, V. Prečan and J. Vladislav (eds), *A Besieged Culture: Czechoslovakia Ten Years after Helsinki* (Stockholm-Vienna, 1985), pp. 142–8.

Smetana, V., 'Concessions or Conviction? Czechoslovakia's Road to the Cold War and the Soviet Bloc', in M. Kramer and V. Smetana (eds), *Imposing, Maintaining, and Tearing Open the Iron Curtain: The Cold War and East-Central Europe, 1945–1989* (Lanham, 2014), pp. 55–85.

Sobell, V., 'Czechoslovakia: The Legacy of Normalization', *East European Politics and Societies*, vol. 2, no. 1 (1987), pp. 35–68.

Spurný, M., 'Political authority and popular opinion: Czechoslovakia's German population 1948–60', *Social History*, vol. 37, no. 4 (2012), pp. 452–76.

Steiner, E., *The Slovak Dilemma* (Cambridge, 1973).

Stolarik, M. M. (ed.), *The Prague Spring and the Warsaw Pact Invasion of Czechoslovakia, 1968: Forty Years Later* (Mundelein, 2010).

Suda, Z., *Zealots and Rebels: A History of the Ruling Communist Party of Czechoslovakia* (Stanford, 1980).

Svášek, M., 'The Politics of Artistic Identity: The Czech Art World in the 1950s and 1960s', *Contemporary European History*, vol. 6, no. 3 (1997), pp. 383–403.

Sviták, I., *The Czechoslovak Experiment, 1968–1969* (New York, 1971).

Szulc, T., *Czechoslovakia since World War II* (New York, 1972).

Táborský, E., 'Slovakia under Communist Rule: "Democratic Centralism" versus National Autonomy', *Journal of Central European Affairs*, vol. 14 (1954), pp. 255–63.

Taborsky, E., *Communism in Czechoslovakia, 1948–1960* (Princeton, 1961).

Teich, M. (ed.), *Bohemia in History* (Cambridge, 1998).

Teich, M., Kováč, D. and Brown, M. D. (eds), *Slovakia in History* (Cambridge, 2011).

Tismaneanu, V., *Fantasies of Salvation: Democracy, Nationalism, and Myth in Post-Communist Europe* (Princeton, 1998).

True, J., *Gender, Globalization, and Postsocialism: The Czech Republic after Communism* (New York, 2003).

Tucker, A., *The Philosophy and Politics of Czech Dissidence from Patočka to Havel* (Pittsburgh, 2000).

Tůma, O., 'Conspicuous Connections, 1968 and 1989', in M. Kramer and V. Smetana (eds), *Imposing, Maintaining, and Tearing Down the Iron Curtain: The Cold War and East-Central Europe, 1945–1989* (Lanham, 2014), pp. 501–14.

Ulč, O., *Politics in Czechoslovakia* (San Francisco, 1974).

Valenta, J., *The Soviet Intervention in Czechoslovakia, 1968: Anatomy of a Decision*, revised edn (Baltimore, 1991).

Wheaton, B. and Kavan, Z., *The Velvet Revolution: Czechoslovakia, 1988–1991* (Boulder, 1992).

Wightman, G. and Brown, A. H., 'Changes in the Levels of Membership and Social Composition of the Communist Party of Czechoslovakia, 1945–73', *Soviet Studies*, vol. 27, no. 3 (1975), pp. 396–417.

Williams, K., *The Prague Spring and its Aftermath: Czechoslovak Politics 1968–1970* (Cambridge, 1997).

Williams, K., 'The Prague Spring: From Elite Liberalisation to Mass Movement', in K. McDermott and M. Stibbe (eds), *Revolution and Resistance in Eastern Europe: Challenges to Communist Rule* (Oxford, 2006), pp. 101–17.

Williams, K., 'Civil Resistance in Czechoslovakia: From Soviet Invasion to "Velvet Revolution", 1968–89', in A. Roberts and T. Garton Ash (eds), *Civil Resistance and Power Politics: The Experience of Non-violent Action from Gandhi to the Present* (Oxford, 2009), pp. 110–26.

Wingfield, N. M., 'The Politics of Memory: Constructing National Identity in the Czech Lands, 1945 to 1948', *East European Politics and Societies*, vol. 14, no. 2 (2000), pp. 246–67.

Wolchik, S., 'The Status of Women in a Socialist Order: Czechoslovakia, 1948–1978', *Slavic Review*, vol. 38, no. 4 (1979), pp. 583–602.

Wolchik, S. L., *Czechoslovakia in Transition: Politics, Economics and Society* (London, 1991).

Wolchik, S. L., 'Czechoslovakia on the Eve of 1989', *Communist and Post-Communist Studies*, vol. 32, no. 4 (1999), pp. 437–51.

Yurchak, A., *Everything Was Forever, Until It Was No More: The Last Soviet Generation* (Princeton, 2006).

Zarecor, K. E., *Manufacturing a Socialist Modernity: Housing in Czechoslovakia, 1945–1960* (Pittsburgh, 2011).

Zeman, Z. A. B., *Prague Spring: A Report on Czechoslovakia 1968* (Harmondsworth, 1969).

Index

248 INDEX

émigrés   38, 62, 74, 81, 85, 98, 99, 160,
   194
environmentalism / ecology   175, 177,
   179, 185, 190, 201
'Euro-communism'   121, 151, 203
Evanson, R. K.   74, 75
expulsion ('transfer'), of German minority
   19, 21, 36, 37, 42, 44–7, 64, 76

F
factory councils   36, 51, 55, 56, 83, 84
fascism   3, 13, 99, 104, 130, 142
Federal Assembly   188, 194
federalisation   19, 48, 102, 103, 116,
   132, 133, 134, 148, 163, 164, 205
Federation of Railway Engine Crews   129
Fierlinger, Z.   xiv, 37, 44
First Republic, 1918–38   2–13, 17, 25
flats   *see paneláky*
food   24, 55, 83, 85, 88, 148
foreign travel and tourism   113, 118,
   126, 129, 130, 158, 166, 169
Fučík, J.   25
Fukuyama, F.   195

G
Garton Ash, T.   155, 182
General Strikes
   1920   6
   1948   57
   1968   148
   1989   188, 198
'Geneva spirit'   88
glasnost   121, 184, 186, 189, 192, 203
Glassheim, E.   47
Gomułka, W.   99, 135, 141, 163
Gorbachev, M. S.   xiv, 17, 121, 151, 152,
   184, 185, 186, 188, 191, 192, 195, 203
Gosiorovský, M.   102
Gottwald, K.   xiv, xv, xvi, 13, 14, 31, 34,
   37, 38, 39, 48, 49, 54–8, 61, 66, 67,
   70–5, 86, 88, 203
'Government of National
   Understanding'   188
Grand Alliance   29, 39
Great Depression   8, 10
Grechko, A.   137, 145
Greek Civil War   31
Green, D.   189, 190
'grey zone'   162, 171, 172, 189, 190
Grospič, J.   134
Gross, J.   24

H
Habsburg Empire   2, 3, 4
Hájek, J.   138, 175
Hamšík, D.   64

'happenings'   175, 179, 184
Hauner, M.   100
Havel, V.   xiv, xv, 117, 125, 158, 172–9,
   187, 188, 194, 197
Heimann, M.   74
Helsinki Final Act   174
Hendrych, J.   107, 117
Henlein, K.   10
Heumos, P.   84, 85
Heydrich, R.   23
Hitler, A.   25, 71
Hlinka Guard   11, 103, 104
Holocaust   9, 22, 23, 73
Holub, M.   116
Honecker, E.   195
Horáková, M.   53, 54, 65
housing   46, 82, 88, 105, 107, 111, 160
Hrabal, B.   170
Hrad   7
Hübl, M.   134, 159
human rights   *see* civil and human rights
humour   112, 116, 127, 147, 198
Hungarian (Magyar) minority   6, 9,
   19, 37, 42, 45, 46, 47, 98, 129, 159,
   185, 192
Hungarian Revolution, 1956   93, 97, 98,
   99, 106, 127, 141
Hus, J.   40
Husák, G.   xiv, xv, xvi, 81, 102, 133, 134,
   148–53, 155–64, 166, 173, 180, 183,
   184, 188, 195, 203
'hustlers'   167, 168
'hyphen debate'   194

I
Independent Peace Association   185
'indigenous Stalinism'   15, 60, 97, 105,
   120
Indra, A.   124, 145, 157
Institute for the Study of Totalitarian
   Regimes   200
intellectuals   4, 7, 9, 23, 38–41, 58, 96,
   97, 101, 102, 103, 106, 107, 110,
   114–7, 119, 120, 124, 125, 128, 129,
   130, 139, 150, 153, 159, 160, 162,
   166, 171, 174, 175, 177, 178, 182,
   186, 192, 195, 199
Iron Curtain   3, 199

J
Jáchymov labour camp   65
Jakeš, M.   xiv, xvi, 157, 184, 188
Jazz Section   170
Jehovah's Witnesses   103
Jičínský, Z.   134
Jirous, I.   178, 179
John Lennon Peace Club   185